PEOPLE, PROTEST

AND POLITICS

Case Studies in Twentieth Century Wales

GOMER PRESS
1987

CONTENTS

Welsh History Teaching Materials (14-16)

A project funded by the Welsh Office Education Department and based at University College, Swansea

Director: Dr. Gareth Elwyn Jones
Research Officer: David Egan

Steering Committee:

O. E. Jones, HMI (Chairman)
Alun Morgan, HMI

Ian Green
Mrs. Mary-Lynne Perren
Miss Elaine Thomas
Mrs. Peggy George

Secretary: Brian Duddridge
Secretarial Assistant: Mrs. A. M. White

Printed by Gomer Press, Llandysul, Dyfed

First Impression - January 1987

ISBN 0 86383 345 4

The author wishes to acknowledge with gratitude
the invaluable assistance of the following staff at
University College, Swansea:

Mrs. Campbell, South Wales Miners' Library;
Mr. Guy Lewis, Department of Geography;
Miss Frances Wood and the Staff of the Education Library.

Time Line

1858—Revival of National Eisteddfod marks growing popularity of Eisteddfod movement.

1865—Attempt to start Quarrymen's Union, Penrhyn.

1874—North Wales Quarrymen's Union founded.

1881—Welsh Sunday Closing Act—public houses closed on Sundays.

Welsh Rugby Union founded.

1885—William Abraham (Mabon), miners' leader, elected to Parliament for new Rhondda seat.

Dispute at Dinorwic quarry.

1887—First branch of *Cymru Fydd* founded.

1889—Welsh Intermediate Education Act sees start of spread of secondary school education in Wales.

Welsh County Councils set up.

1890—Lloyd George becomes M.P. for Caernarfon Boroughs.

1893—Foundation of University of Wales.

1896-7—Dispute at Penrhyn.

1896—Effective end of *Cymru Fydd*.

1898—Following defeat of miners in six months lock-out, South Wales Miners Federation formed.

1899—Death of Tom Ellis.

1900-3—Penrhyn Lockout.

1900—Keir Hardie elected to Parliament for Merthyr Tydfil. First 'Labour' M.P. from Wales.

1904-5—Religious Revival sweeps Wales.

1905—Wales defeats New Zealand 'All Blacks' in rugby international in Cardiff.

1909—National Library of Wales founded.

1910-11—Cambrian Combine Dispute and riots at Tonypandy.

1912—*Miners' Next Step* published.

1913—Peak production of South Wales coalfield.

439 men killed at Universal Colliery, Senghenydd.

1914-1918—The Great War.

1916—South Wales coalfield taken over by the Government.

1919—Royal Commission on Coal Industry recommends nationalisation of the industry.

1920—Disestablishment of Church in Wales.

1921—Coal industry handed back to coalowners. Followed by miners' defeat in lock-out and reduced wages.

1922—*Urdd Gobaith Cymru* founded.

1925—*Plaid Genedlaethol Cymru* founded.

1926—General Strike and Miners' Lock-out ends in defeat for miners, reduced wages and longer hours.

Creation of South Wales Miners' Industrial Union.

1927—First hunger march against unemployment leaves South Wales.

1930—Height of mass unemployment in South Wales and emigration from the area.

1934—Struggle between S.W.M.F. and Company Unionism at height.

1935—Stay-down strikes at South Wales collieries.

1936-8—Spanish Civil War.

1936—Symbolic burning of bombing school at Penyberth, Llŷn.

1939-45—World War II.

1939—First Welsh language primary school.

1948—Advisory Council for Wales.

1951—Ministry for Welsh Affairs.

1955—Cardiff official capital of Wales.

1957—Drowning of Tryweryn valley.

1962—Lecture, *Tynged yr Iaith*, by Saunders Lewis.

Cymdeithas yr Iaith Gymraeg founded.

1964—Secretary of State appointed for Wales.

1966—Gwynfor Evans wins Carmarthen by-election. First *Plaid Cymru* M.P.

1967—Welsh Language Act passed.

1969—Royal Commission on Constitution.

1973—Kilbrandon Commission Report.

Wales T.U.C. founded.

1974—New Welsh county boundaries.

1979—Referendum on Devolution.

1982—S4C starts transmission of programmes.

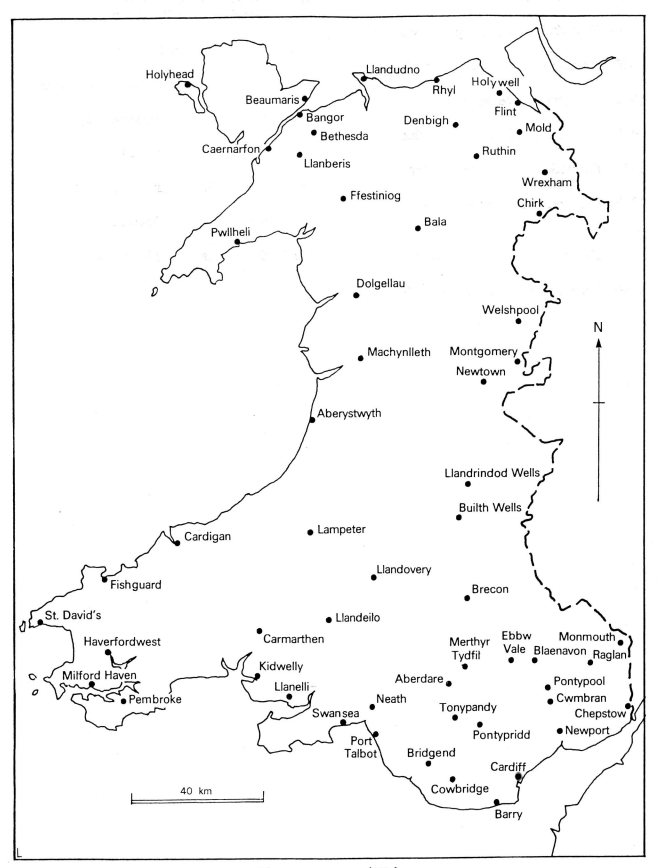

Place-name map of Wales

Historical Evidence

In this book we shall study aspects of the history of Wales in the twentieth century. The author will tell part of the story. The sources will tell the rest of the story. These sources are mainly documentary, although there are also many visual and oral sources.

Documents

Documents are those written records of any period in history which survive. Everything which is written down or, more recently, typed, is a document and may be of some use to the historian. Any notes which you might write to each other are historical documents. They might, sometime in the future, be of use to a historian—if they survive. It is highly unlikely, of course, that they will survive. More important documents than those, affecting the lives of hundreds of people—or millions of people, have not survived. These papers have been eaten by rats, destroyed in floods, burned or torn up or just decayed. Out of what has survived we try to find out what has happened in the past.

Other sources

We do not only have documents, or written sources, to help us build up a picture of twentieth century Wales. Buildings tell us a great deal about wealth, living conditions, lifestyle, and religious habits for example. The photographs of such buildings, and the photographs of people and events included in this book are important sources of information. Any clothes, or furniture, or weapons, or musical instruments, or pots and pans help to build up the picture. For a period as recent as this we are very fortunate in that we can ask people who were involved in events to recall them for us, usually on to a tape so that we have a record of what they say.

Evidence

The documents, buildings, artefacts (the name given to man-made and woman-made articles) and recollections together make up our *evidence*. This is all that remains of the past. We cannot know anything about the past if there is no evidence. It is only from what survives that we can build up a picture of the past. This is what makes *primary* evidence so important and why it is important to understand the difference between *primary* and *secondary* evidence.

Primary evidence

People studying history divide their sources of information into primary sources and secondary sources. The topic of our study is episodes in the history of twentieth century Wales. Let us take the history of the events in Tonypandy, 1910-11 as an example. All those documents, artefacts or recollections which actually came into existence during those years of 1910-11 are primary sources of evidence. Where people who were involved in these events and have recorded their memories of them later we usually class these as primary evidence as well.

Not all primary evidence is equally valuable. Some of it is very important indeed. For example the Home Office papers which tell us exactly what decisions were taken by the Home Secretary of the time are vital clues about the role of the Government. They are also reliable evidence about decisions which were taken. A man named David Evans wrote a book about the dispute while it was going on. There are extracts from his book in our chapter on Tonypandy. David Evans's book is a primary source. It is *literary* evidence. The information provided by literary evidence may not be as reliable as, say, records of the Home Office. It is still very important because it will at least tell us something about the person who wrote it even if it does not tell us a great deal about the topic.

Secondary evidence

To continue with the example of the Tonypandy riots, ever since they occurred people studying history have looked back at the events of 1910-11 and tried to explain what happened. Welsh historians regard events in Tonypandy as of great importance, not only in the history of Glamorgan and Wales but in British history of the twentieth century generally. Such historians build up their picture, like us, by using primary sources. When they write down their ideas in articles and books these books become sources of information themselves. The books and articles which students of history write are called *secondary* sources. In other words secondary sources are those accounts of the Tonypandy riots which have come into existence *after* the years in which they occurred.

In all the chapters of this book, the parts of the story which the author has written are secondary sources. The rest of the story is told by other people. Most of the extracts are primary sources; some of them are secondary sources.

*   *   *

Many people who go on to study history as adults have the idea that primary sources are true and secondary sources are merely opinions. This is not so. Let us suppose that you write a diary of everything which has happened to you today and that it survives for a hundred years. Let us suppose, too, that in a hundred years time a historian is trying to reconstruct life in your school. Is the class register likely to be accurate? Yes, probably, within narrow limits. But the historian may want to get an idea of what people thought of their schools in the twentieth century, so he or she will use your diary. It is a primary source for the period, like the register. But now the historian has got to be very careful. He is dealing with a literary source. How truthful a picture do you think your diary would give, and how complete will the information be? It is just the same for us looking at twentieth century Wales. There are many useful primary sources but we have got to be very careful with them. Before we reach the end of the book we will find that historical sources, primary and secondary, can all too easily mislead us.

The Quarrymen of North Wales

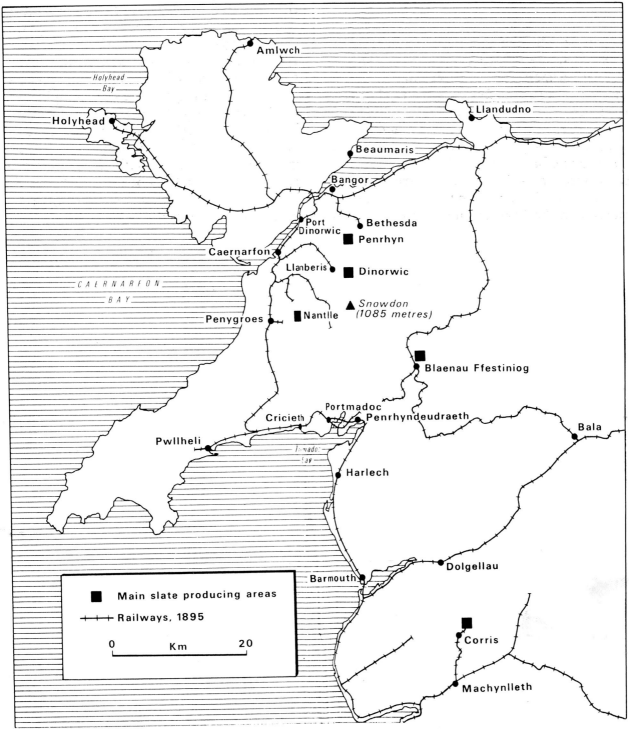

Source: R. Merfyn Jones, *The North Wales Quarrymen, 1874-1922* (Cardiff, 1981).

Introduction

The photograph (Source 2) was taken in 1907 in Penrhyn slate quarry in north Wales. Can you guess what became of the great blocks of slate on the trolley? They were transported to London. There they were cut to shape, thick wooden table legs were attached to support the considerable weight and the slate was covered with green cloth. King Edward VII had a new billiard table.

I am writing this sentence with a ball-point pen, or 'biro', on paper. You will be reading the sentence as black print on paper. You, too, will be using some kind of pencil or pen to write on the paper of your exercise books. It is very difficult to imagine a world in which pens and paper were not available whenever they were wanted.

A hundred years ago you would almost certainly have left school before the age of 15.

Source 2

Source: Gwynedd Archive Service

But if you *had* been at elementary school you would not be using pen and paper for your writing. You would almost certainly have been writing with a soft slate pencil on a piece of slate. One of slate's properties is that you can mark it clearly with another piece of slate. It is very convenient that you can easily rub out what you have written and the same piece of slate can be used over and over again. It is a bit less convenient if you want to check something you wrote some days ago.

Do you think more slate from north Wales was used for billiard tables or for making school slates in the late 19th century? Neither of these uses would have made the slate-quarrying industry of Gwynedd world-famous at this time. So what did?

If you live in a fairly new house it is highly likely that the roof is made of concrete tiles. If you live in a house which is about sixty or seventy years old it is probably roofed with slates. Although the nails fastening the slates might have rusted, the slates themselves will be in good condition. During the nineteenth century and the early years of the twentieth century, slate was used as roofing material for the new houses being built in Britain. Virtually all that slate was mined, quarried, split and dressed in north-west Wales.

Why should the use of slate for roofs have resulted in the dramatic increase in demand for it? Sources 3 and 4 provide the answer.

In 1801 Wales had a population of not much more than half a million. By 1901 it was just over two million. The roofs of the winding rows of south Wales miners' houses you see in source 3 were built from the slate quarried by the skilled and hard labour of north-west Wales. And it was not only in Wales and England that new houses were being built. What does source 5 tell us about the slate industry?

Source 3

Source: Cyril Batstone. Printed in Dai Smith, *Wales! Wales!* London, 1984.

Source 4

THE CHANGING POPULATION OF SOME WELSH TOWNS

	1801	1851	1901	1939
Merthyr Tydfil	7705	46378	69228	61852
Swansea	6099	21533	94537	162852
Carmarthen	5548	10171	10025	11574
Amlwch	4977	5813	2994	2471
Wrexham	4039	6660	14966	27486
Neath	2502	5778	13720	32197
Cardigan	1911	2981	3510	3275
Cardiff	1870	18351	164333	227689
Aberystwyth	1758	5189	8014	10704
Llandovery	1395	1927	1809	2015
Newport	1135	19323	67270	96699
Newtown	990	3784	6500	5239
Ffestiniog	732	3460	11670	8498
Builth Wells	677	1158	1805	1679
Llandrindod Wells	192	217	1827	3541

Source: D. Evans: *Wales in Modern Times,* Arnold, 1979, p.93.

Source 5

Source: D. Morgan Rees, *Historic Industrial Scenes, Wales.* Moorland Publishing.

On the left of the picture are the slates stacked and ready for loading on to the ships at the quayside of Port Penrhyn. This was the dock of one of the two greatest of the north Wales slate quarries, the Penrhyn quarry. How had the slates got to the quayside? Source 6 shows a similar type of scene in the most prosperous period of the slate industry. This time the scene is Port Dinorwic, linked by a seven-mile-long tramway to the other great slate quarry of Dinorwic.

Source 6

Source: Rees, *Historic Industrial Scenes.*

Slate

Once slate was mud. The layers of mud, squeezed together over millions of years with a force which we cannot imagine, became, eventually, layers of slate rock. A large area of north-west Wales is composed of slate rock. It is not all suitable for quarrying or mining but there are areas of Gwynedd in which it is possible to quarry or mine slate which can, with great skill, be fairly easily split into thin 'slices' of rock which can then be cut to size. The inhabitants of north Wales had quarried some slate for their own local use since the days of the Romans. Then, in the 19th century, the industry expanded at an amazing rate. We have seen that expansion was due to a great increase in demand for slate.

So, the slate rock was available and the demand was there. What was necessary now?

Owners and their Capital

Up to the end of the 18th century slate was being produced on a small scale for local needs mainly. Ownership was on a small scale, too, so that many independent owners produced small quantities of slate. From the end of the 18th century all this changed. The small-scale quarriers were bought out by a few owners. Of these the two most important families, by far, were the Pennant family, one of whom eventually became Lord Penrhyn; and the Assheton-Smith family. From 1782 Richard Pennant took over the Penrhyn estate. This included all the small quarries on the estate which he made into one great quarrying enterprise. The quarriers who were taken over became his labourers. He was able to do this because he had money—money he had made as a merchant dealing in the West Indies slave trade. In 1809 the Assheton-Smith family took control of the second of the large quarries—Dinorwic. This family also invested their money in slate, though their money had come from the profits of their local estate. Penrhyn and Dinorwic were not the only quarries in north Wales. There were nearly a hundred at one time. The other areas of slate production were around Corris, Blaenau Ffestiniog and Nantlle. But Penrhyn and Dinorwic were by far the biggest quarries. In fact, at the end of the 19th century they were the biggest slate quarries in the world.

The money which merchants and landowners invested in the quarries paid off and made the Penrhyn family and the Assheton-Smith family enormously rich, even richer than they were already as landowners. The Penrhyn family estate was the biggest in Caernarfonshire. The Assheton-Smith estate was the third biggest. To the income which they got from their tenants on their estates was now added income from the sale of slate. In 1898 Lord Penrhyn's quarries made a profit of £133,000. It enabled him to live in this house and enjoy the standard of living which went with it.

Source 7

Source: Jean Lindsay, *A History of the North Wales Slate Industry*, Newton Abbot, 1974.

Quarrymen and Their Skills

Producing roofing slate from a slate mountain was an art as well as a craft, and many men were involved. In 1881 there were 14,000 men working in the industry and nearly 3,000 of them worked in the Penrhyn quarry alone.

The men teamed up in the following way.

ROCKMEN   SPLITTER   DRESSER
(2)   (1)   (1)

(Formed a team to get the slate out and produce finished slate. About half quarrymen worked in such teams. Negotiated with quarry management as to how much they would be paid for producing slates from a particular area of rock over a period of a month. Agreement known as the 'bargain'.)

'BAD ROCK' MEN
(3)

(Most of rock not suitable for making slates. The 'bad' rock had to be removed to vast slate rubbish tips nearby—see Source 8).

ASSISTANTS

(Boys over twelve years of age, learning skills of quarrying and looking for work where any quarrymen needed assistance).

Slate quarries were of two kinds—mountains and mines, but we will concentrate here on the vast mountain quarries of Penrhyn and Dinorwic. When the quarrymen faced these mountains of slate on cold, wet winter mornings or on hot summer days they faced a hard, unpleasant, sometimes impossible, incredibly skilful job. Look at sources 9, 10 and 11 carefully. They are open quarries. In a few numbered points *compare* and *contrast* what you see.

Source 8

Source: M. J. T. Lewis, *Slate* (Gwynedd Archives Service, 1976).

Source 9

Source: M. J. T. Lewis, *Slate* (Gwynedd Archives Service, 1976).

You may, first of all, have noticed that Source 9 and Source 10 are photographs, while source 11 is a painting. You will probably also have noticed the clues as to how slate was transported. You will certainly have noticed that both quarries (Sources 9 and 11 are of Penrhyn and Source 10 of Dinorwic) are

stepped or terraced. This was the main feature of the open quarries. In Dinorwic there were 22 terraces, each of them about 50 to 80 feet high. A team of quarrymen worked a section of a terrace. The first problem was for a rockman, dangling over the rock face and held only by a rope or a chain, to bore a hole and set an explosive charge. If the charge was set in exactly the right place it would loosen pillars of rock of the right size. You can get an idea of the width of the 'pillars' of slate slabs from Sources 12 and 17.

Knowing where to place the explosive to loosen blocks of slate in exactly the right place was one of the great arts of the quarryman. It was accepted that to learn this art, to be able to

Source 10

Source: Lewis, *Slate.*

Source 11

The Penrhyn Quarry by Henry Hawkins, 1832.
Source: Penrhyn Castle guide.

Source 12

Source: Lewis, *Slate.*

'read' the rock, he had to start very young because it was only experience and instinct that guided him. In the words of a quarry manager in 1865:

Source 13

'I have read the best of German, American, English authors on geology and I have not seen one single passage in any one of their works that can help, assist or enlighten a quarryman in any one of his operations. It is all very well to talk of things and compile large volumes, but bring these great authorities face to face with Nature or to a slate quarry and I will be bold enough to affirm that I can point to more than one hard working Welshman that will shame the best of them!
Source: The Main Journal, 1865. Quoted in R. Merfyn Jones, *The North Wales Quarrymen 1874-1922* (Cardiff, 1981).

Drilling into the rock was a long process if, as in this photograph taken about 1905, there was no mechanical drill.

Source 14

Source: Lewis, *Slate.*

By this time drills driven by steam or compressed air did exist but they were not used in Penrhyn quarry until after 1912.

Then came the gunpowder. It had to be rammed firmly down the drilled hole. Since this was virtually the same process as loading an old gun it is not surprising that there could be very nasty accidents, as this report from Penrhyn in 1810 shows.

Source 15

Shocking Accident at the Slate Quarries, Nant Francon.—In blasting the slates, an instrument called a stamper, which is 30 inches long and 2½ in circumference, is used to ram down the charge of gunpowder; it is supposed the friction of working out the stamper, produced a spark, which communicated and caused a sudden explosion, driving this thick iron rod up the muscles of the workman's arm, entered through to the neck, advancing nearly eight inches beyond! His death was instantaneous—With laudable and humane attention, we understand, that a trial is to be immediately made with *copper* stampers, which will, perhaps, obviate the danger of explosion.

Source: Lewis, *Slate.*

Later on in the century there were detailed regulations to try to ensure that accidents did not happen.

Source 16

Rules for Blasting.

1. Blasting is allowed hourly, at the end of every hour.
2. **SIGNALS:**
   A **RED FLAG** will be hoisted upon a conspicuous spot for Seven Minutes during the blasting operations.

   Also a **STEAM WHISTLE** will be blown thus:—

   ONE WHISTLE means that the men must retire to a place of safety; after the lapse of two minutes, **TWO WHISTLES** in rapid succession mean that the **FUSE** must be lighted; and after the lapse of five minutes more, **THREE WHISTLES** in rapid succession, and the lowering of the **RED FLAG**, mean that all **BLASTING** has ceased, and that the men can return to their working places.
3. When Blasting takes place during the Dinner hour, or immediately after working hours are over, the above signals (Flag and Whistles) must be strictly observed. Five minutes, however, must be allowed from the time the whistle to cease work has been blown before the first of the above signals are given.
4. When the Whistle to cease work is blown before 5.30 p.m. no blasting can take place after 4 p.m.

Source: Lewis, *Slate.* Relates to Penrhyn, 1810.

Blocks of good slate which had broken off after explosions were put on sleds to be taken off to the splitting sheds. Blocks which had been loosened were broken off.

Source 17

Source: Lewis, *Slate.*

Source 18

Source: D. Morgan Rees, *Historic Industrial Scenes.*

The good slate on its way to be dressed (split and shaped into roofing slates) or the bad rock, on its way to the slate rubbish heaps, went on tramways in trucks which were usually pushed by hand. Obviously with the high terraces of the quarries, trams had to be raised and lowered. At one quarry, Penrhyn, there were water-balance hoists. As you can see from source 18 trucks went up and down on two sides of the hoist. From the visual evidence, and the name, how do you think the hoists worked?

Another method of getting trucks up and down from working levels is demonstrated in the next source. Loaded trucks coming down by gravity are pulling empty trucks to the top.

Source 19

Source: Lewis, *Slate.*

The good slate, in large blocks often weighing many tons, was now available for producing the finished slate. At one time this work went on out-of-doors but later was done in small shelters like the ones you can see on the right of the next photograph.

Source 20

Source: Lewis, *Slate.*

Producing roofing slates from blocks was a highly skilled job, with just this range of tools available.

Source 21

Source: Lewis, *Slate.*

What do you think the big mallet and the wedges were used for? You can see most of the tools being used in the next source (22)

With high-quality rock a block of 20 to 30 tons, prised off the side of the mountain, could end up in dressed slate one thirty-second of an inch thick. The finished slates could now be carefully stacked in trucks which would take them to the quayside for export or for loading into railway trucks. But for all the beautifully-stacked finished slate there was almost 30 times more waste rock from an open quarry.

Source 22

Source: Lewis, *Slate.*

The Quarryman's Life

Most quarrymen and their families lived in villages and towns which had been created out of the slate industry: Blaenau Ffestiniog, Llanberis, Bethesda and Nantlle, for example.

Source 24

Source: Dewi Tomos, *Llechi Lleu*, Caernarfon, 1980, p. 79.

This is a photograph of Nantlle taken before 1900. You can see one building standing out

Source 23

Source: Lewis, *Slate.*

above the line of the houses. The chapel was the main centre of village and town life.

Source 25

Wel, i ddechrau 'roedd pawb bron yn mynd i'r capel yr amser hynny ac 'roedd llawer mwy o bobl yn byw yn y pentrefi. 'Roedd teuluoedd mawr yn beth cyffredin, 6, 8, neu 10 o blant. Allwch chi ddychmygu'r tad a'r fam a'r plant yn un rhes hir y tu ôl iddynt yn cerdded i'r capel; teuluoedd eraill yn dod o'u cartrefi ac ymuno â hwy nes bod y ffordd yn llawn o bobl yn mynd y naill ffordd neu'r llall i'r gwahanol gapeli.

Source: Tomos, *Llechi Lleu*, p. 78.

Compare the photograph of Nantlle with the picture of Tonypandy in the next section (source 70). How would you describe the differences?

Tonypandy, a south Wales coalmining town, was a very busy centre, full of shops. There were many public houses, and tramcars in the main street. The quarrying towns of north Wales were set in hill and mountain country. They were in areas in which, for centuries, farmers had tried to make a living from poor land in a cold and wet climate.

The expanding quarrying industry was set in an area of small hill farms. The quarrymen worked in a great industry but they did not lose contact with the land on which their ancestors had worked for centuries. Many quarrymen continued to be farmers on a small scale. They rented a few acres of land for crops and a few animals which they hoped would give them some food and income. Far more quarrymen helped out with the harvest in summer on land owned by relatives or friends. The life of the quarryman/farmer was especially hard.

One of Wales's greatest novelists in the 20th century was Kate Roberts. Her father was a quarryman who also owned a smallholding. Kate Roberts wrote many stories about the area in which she was brought up. *Feet in Chains* is the title of a novel originally written in Welsh but translated into English. It is the story of Jane and Ifan Gruffydd.

Source 26

'She (Jane) had been very happy during her courting days, but she had the sense to know that life would not go on at such a pitch of emotion. Ifan was everything she had hoped for but he was much more tired-looking now than when she saw him first time he came to Lleyn with Guto the Drover. In her own mind she knew well that working in the quarry and running the smallholding was too much for him. But what was to be done? She had heard enough about the quarries to know how uncertain were the wages: and it was a wonderful thing to have plenty of milk and butter'.

Source: Kate Roberts, *Feet in Chains*, Corgi Books, 1977, p. 22.

The exhaustion of the quarrymen, even those who did not also have smallholdings, is easy to understand.

The journey to work could be exhausting before the day's work started because even when the quarryman arrived at the quarry he would not be ready to start work. He and his team had to make their way to terraces high up the mountain and perhaps a mile or so away. In the more remote quarries the men had to live in barracks during the week so as to be near their work. Living conditions in the barracks were extremely primitive. The barracks were not much more than shelters. In wet conditions men remained soaked to the skin for hours on end. The cold was numbing. The heat was not much better because slate changes in temperature very quickly and soon becomes uncomfortably hot to work.

Source 27

PENRHYN QUARRIES.

WORKING HOURS.

1900		FROM	TO
January	1st to January 6th,	7 50 a.m.	4 30 p.m.
January	8th to January 13th,	7 50 a.m.	4 40 p.m.
January	15th to January 20th,	7 45 a.m.	4 50 p.m.
January	22nd to January 27th,	7 45 a.m.	5 0 p.m.
January	29th to February 3rd,	7 35 a.m.	5 10 p.m.
February	5th to February 10th,	7 20 a.m.	5 30 p.m.
February	12th to February 17th,	7 10 a.m.	5 30 p.m.
February	19th to October 13th,	7 0 a.m.	5 30 p.m.
October	15th to October 20th,	7 0 a.m.	5 20 p.m.
October	22nd to October 27th,	7 0 a.m.	5 10 p.m.
October	29th to November 3rd,	7 10 a.m.	5 0 p.m.
November	5th to November 10th,	7 20 a.m.	4 45 p.m.
November	12th to November 17th,	7 25 a.m.	4 30 p.m.
November	19th to November 24th,	7 30 a.m.	4 25 p.m.
November	26th to December 1st,	7 35 a.m.	4 20 p.m.
December	3rd to December 8th,	7 40 a.m.	4 20 p.m.
December	10th to December 15th,	7 50 a.m.	4 20 p.m.
December	17th to December 22nd,	7 50 a.m.	4 20 p.m.
December	24th to December 29th,	7 50 a.m.	4 20 p.m.

NO WORK AFTER NOON ON SATURDAYS.

MEAL HOUR 12 NOON TO 1 P.M.
(BOYS UNDER 18, 11 TO 12 O'CLOCK).

Blasting Hours.
ON AND AFTER MONDAY, JANUARY 1st 1900
9 a.m., 11 a.m., 12 noon, 12.55 p.m., 3.0 p.m.
When the BELL for ceasing work sounds at 5.0 p.m. or later, blasting is allowed at 4.0 p.m.

PAY DAYS DURING THE YEAR 1900.

January	27th	August	11th
February	24th	September	8th
March	24th	October	6th
April	21st	November	3rd
May	19th	December	1st
June	16th	December	29th
July	14th		

HOLIDAYS.

Good Friday	April 13th	Whit-Monday	June 4th
Saturday	April 14th	Harvest Thanksgiving	
Easter Monday	April 16th	Christmas Day	Dec. 25th
Ascension-day	May 24th		

PENRHYN QUARRIES,
December 1st, 1899.   E. A. YOUNG.

Source: Lewis, *Slate*.

What is the length of the average working week in this country now? Using source 27 compare it with a quarryman's working week. How much annual holiday might some-one working in industry get now? How does it compare with a quarryman's holidays at the end of the 19th century? Again the information you need is in source 27.

There were dangers at work. We have already seen that accidents could occur when the rock was being blasted. It is easy to imagine the possible accidents which could occur to men working on the steep terraces, tied only by ropes, or down in the underground quarries. Pushing tramfuls of slate was not the safest of work either. Why? Those quarrymen who worked in the sheds where slates were dressed breathed in slate dust which gave them the terrible chest disease of silicosis—though doctors did not always realise this in the nineteenth century and perhaps later did not want to realise it.

Source 28

Penrhyn Quarry Hospital,
Bethesda, N. Wales.
6/1/22

We have no case of Silicosis in this quarry of which I am aware, and I became convinced after four years' experience here that Slate dust is not merely harmless, but beneficial. The record of the men who have worked in the dusty shed at the mill since 1870 is available, and they were mostly alive prior to the war. I can send you a copy of the list. The light that recent research work has shed on the influence of dust inhalation upon the incidence of Phthisis all goes to support my view, and I would challenge anyone to prove otherwise.

J. Bradley Hughes
Medical officer
4th January, 1922.

During my experience it is remarkable to say that no quarryman has ever complained of cough or choking sensation due to inhalation of Slate dust, taking for granted they do inhale dust which is doubtful, as Slate dust is heavy and mostly seen in machinery sheds which are well ventilated.

I have not examined Slate dust microscopically, but am of opinion that the particles are soft and none irritant, also it contains very little silicate and a good deal of iron and sulphur, the latter is regarded as a germicide, neither have I performed a post mortem upon a tubercular quarryman.

The facts already stated and my experience convinces me, that Slate dust is neither an irritant exciting or a predisposing cause of Tuberculosis.

(Signed) John Roberts, L.R.C.P., &c.

January 16, 1922

Source: Gwynedd Archive Service.

When there were accidents at work the help immediately available was primitive.

Source 29

Source: Lewis, *Slate.*

If there was a serious accident the quarry hooter sounded, filling all who heard it with dread. The quarrymen then went home early.

There were hospitals. Source 30 is a macabre reminder of quarrying accidents. It is a photo of the wooden leg kept at the quarrying hospital. It was lent to any quarryman who had lost a leg in an accident.

Source 30

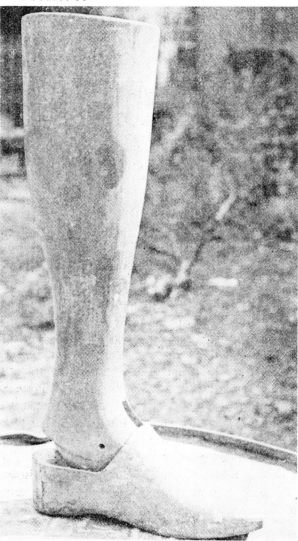

Source: Emyr Jones, *Canrif y Chwarelwyr*, Gee, 1963.

The men paid a subscription for the hospital. They paid about a shilling a week. This bought them medical care and a small allowance if they were away from work through ill-health.

Generally, then, the quarryman's life was not a healthy one and at the end of the 19th century he could expect to be dead, on average, before he reached his fiftieth birthday.

Illnesses

Source 31

The most common ailments that I have encountered are those of the respiratory organs, the digestive system, rheumatism in its various forms, such as lumbago, sciatica, and rheumatic fever. I have examined this week the counterfoils of my death certificates for the last 10 years, and I find that in that period there were 157 males who died above the age of 16 years, the average age at death being 50-75. Of that 157, the deaths from diseases of the respiratory organs numbered 78, being nearly half the total number of deaths. The number of deaths from consumption *(phthisis)* was 38, the average age of those dying from that disease being 40.5. The deaths from consumption represent a percentage of 24.1 of the total deaths amongst males. The number of deaths from pneumonia was 20, which is equal to 12.8 per cent. of the total. There were also 20 deaths from other affections of the lungs. During the same period the deaths amongst females numbered 129, the average age being 47.8. Diseases of the respiratory organs accounted for 31 of these deaths. Phthisis was the cause of 15 deaths or 12 per cent. of the total, and the deaths from pneumonia were 6, equal to 3.5 per cent. of the total.

Source: Merionethshire Slate Mines Inquiry, 1893.

Accidents

Source 32

The most common accidents I have met with are simple fractures and injuries to the head. The fractures in most cases are produced by rock slipping, and the head injuries from small pieces of rock falling from the roofs of the chambers or from the sides of pillars, and also from being struck with the handles of the crances. Blasting accidents are also of frequent occurrence. The injuries amongst the slate-makers are mostly injuries to the hands.

Source: Merionethshire Slate Mines Inquiry, 1893.

It was not only the quarrymen who had a hard life. The wives of quarrymen had to try to keep a house and feed a family on low wages. Household chores took much more time and effort then than they do now.

Source 33

At the time, Jane was busy scouring the quarryman's clothes on an old table outside by the spring. She was scrubbing the corduroy trousers after the first washing; the water squeezed out was thick and grey. With the back of the hand holding the brush she wiped the sweat off her face and pushed back a lock of hair. The working-jacket was boiling on the fire in the house.

Taking the trousers from the table and rinsing them in a bucket of clean water from the spring, she carried them into the house.

"Washing working-clothes is a tiring old job," said Sioned.

"Yes, but I'll get used to it," said Jane.

"I don't know. You mark my words, washing a quarryman's clothes will be something you'll never get used to."

Source: Kate Roberts, *Feet in Chains*, pp.11-12.

Then there was the problem of damp in the houses in that damp part of the world. The houses themselves were stone-built and the roofs made of slate so they were very strong. That did not keep out the moisture. This is how Jane Gruffydd, in Kate Roberts's novel, felt about her house.

Source 34

One thing troubled her greatly—that was the condition of the house. The kitchen was the only comfortable room. The bedrooms, especially the back one, were damp and quite unhealthy for anyone to sleep in. The dampness ran down the walls, spoiling the paper, and water dripped on to the bed from the wooden ceiling during frosty weather. She would like to have a new part built alongside the old house so that she would at least have a good parlour and two bedrooms. There were enough stones on Ffridd Felen to build such an extension, and getting rid of the stones would improve the land. But Ifan would have to blast the stones and that would be more work for him. So what was the use of day-dreaming?

Source: Feet in Chains, p. 22.

Probably the worst ordeal for the quarryman's wife, as it was for the coalminer's wife, was the anxiety. We can only imagine the fear which must have gripped the hearts of quarrymen's families when they heard the hooter which meant that there had been a serious accident. A novelist or poet might be best at communicating this. Why?

Source 35

Cân Gwraig y Creigiwr

Dedwydd, dedwydd yw fy mhlentyn
Yn ei ddwfn brydnawnol gyntun.
Gwelai lygad mam wrth huno,
Ond ni welai'r cwmwl ynddo;
Ac ni chlywai ar ei dwyfron
Swn yr ofnau a'r pryderon.

Tawel, tawel yw yr hafddydd,
Pobpeth sydd yn hyfryd lonydd;
Ysgafn cerdd y chwäon tyner,
Fel yn ofni deffro pryder:
Bychan wyddant am y cynnwr'
Sydd yng nghalon gwraig y creigiwr.

Chwi, awelon sydd yn hedeg
Heibio'm bwthyn yn eich adeg,
Peidiwch cludo sŵn ergydion,
Peidiwch sibrwd am beryglon:
Ni raid i chwi chwyddo'r dwndwr
Sydd yng nghalon gwraig y creigiwr.

Pa'm mae dynion adre'n dyfod
Cyn yr awr ar derfyn diwrnod?
Pa'm mae'r merched yn y drysau?
Beth yw'r holi yn y conglau?
Gallai nad oes fraw yn teithio—
Gwell nag ofni yw gobeithio.

Pa'm y rhaid i mi ddyfalu
Pan y clywaf graig yn chwalu?
Pa'm y gwelaf mewn breuddwydion
Elor ar ysgwyddau llwydion?
Nid yw'n gofyn moeth na seigiau—
Dim ond nawdd i wŷr y creigiau.

Alafon
(t. 48 Cathlau Bore a Nawn)

Source: Printed in Dewi Tomos, *Llechi Lleu*, Caernarfon, 1980, p.79.

For the quarrymen at work there were some compensations. One of the most important during the working day was the all-important lunch-hour with fellow-workers. The lunch itself was not a marvellous one—tea and bread and butter. But there was often a chance to have word competitions, singing, general knowledge competitions, and to compose poetry—all in Welsh. Is this one reason why this part of north Wales should have produced so many fine poets and novelists? The hut, or *caban*, where the men gathered at lunch-hour, was also a centre for discussing trade union affairs when the quarrymen's union was set up.

The North Wales Quarrymen's Union

Why do you think that the quarrymen wanted to organise themselves into a union? We have seen that quarrymen's jobs were highly skilled but extremely hard. Yet they were not well paid and they were well aware that the owners were making vast profits. In 1899 Lord Penrhyn made £133,000 profit from the Penrhyn quarries.

Wages were not at the centre of all disputes. Because of the kind of job they did, because of the high degree of skill they had, quarrymen were very independent people. The way their work was organised made them even more independent. They knew, better than the quarry managers, how good sections of rock were for producing slates. Men and managers negotiated by completing a 'bargain'—an agreement as to how much the men should be paid for quarrying a particular section of rock. Every time there was discussion over the monthly 'bargain' there was a chance of disagreement. Quarries were very large places in which to work and there were few managers. Therefore the men worked largely unsupervised. Gradually the owners tried to increase the amount of supervision and appointed tougher managers. When these managers had much less knowledge of slate than the quarrymen they were resentful.

There were many reasons, therefore, why the quarrymen should see advantages in combining together in some sort of organisation to negotiate wages and conditions of work. The quarrymen would obviously have more influence and power united than divided. The owners, particularly people like Lord Penrhyn, did not want the men united. The owners were used to a different kind of relationship with the men who worked for them. The owners felt that they provided the jobs—but more than this.

They helped set up hospitals and sick-clubs, for example. They believed that because it was their money which set up the quarry it was their right to do as they wished in running the quarries. There were other clashes of interest. The skilled quarrymen, with their interest in the language and culture around them were wholly Welsh. Owners like the Penrhyn family had much more in common with the English aristocracy—in education, life-style and language. The quarrymen supported the Liberal party; the owners supported the Tory party. The quarrymen, like most of the workers in Wales, attended chapels—they were Nonconformist in religion. The important quarry owners, like most of the wealthiest landowners in Wales, supported the Church of England. All these differences were at the centre of political struggles in Wales especially in the last thirty years of the 19th century. But, at the bottom of everything, there was one fact which could not be disputed. Lord Penrhyn, the owner of the Penrhyn quarries, was one of the wealthiest men in Wales. The Assheton-Smith family who owned the Dinorwic quarry, were not too far behind. These people thought that power should go with their wealth, power to control

Source 36

their quarries, power to play an important part in the government of the community and country in which they lived. They were not going to accept any real threat to that power if they could possibly help it. They were not likely to negotiate as equals with the men. Singly, the men had no chance of forcing the owners to negotiate. That is why the owners always wanted to deal with their employees singly. Together, in combination, the quarrymen could have some share in power. Their skill, their labour, was just as essential as Lord Penrhyn's money. This is how the quarrymen summed up the relationship between master and men:

Source 37

'There were some who denied the rights of the workmen to have a voice in the management of the works, and that that was the privilege of the master, who had invested his money, his capital in the quarries . . . this was partly true, but when the master was not careful in his selection of proper agents, the workmen under such circumstances had a right to raise their voices and object because the appointment of incompetent managers endangered their lives. If the argument was that the master, because he invested his capital, had the right to appoint the managers, was logic, then for the very same reason, the workmen ought to have a voice in their appointment. What were the workmen's labour and their lives, but their capital?'

Source: Caernarvon and Denbigh Herald, 2 January, 1886. Quoted in Merfyn Jones, *The North Wales Quarrymen.*

You are now in a position to understand the significance of the complex banner of the North Wales Quarrymen's Union (Source 36).

In 1865 there was an attempt to start a union in the Penrhyn quarry. It followed disputes between the quarrymen and the managers. There was a fourteen-day strike. Colonel Pennant, the owner who the following year became Lord Penrhyn, promised to do something about the men's complaints but the leaders of the men's committee at Penrhyn decided to set up a Union, just for this quarry. It started in September, 1865, and about 1800 men joined. The owner's reaction could not have been more direct in this notice read out to the committee and distributed to the quarrymen:

Source 38

Penrhyn Castle, December 2nd, 1865.

"In re-setting the quarry, Colonel Pennant is anxious to make a few remarks on the attempt that has recently been made by certain self-sufficient individuals, calling themselves a Committee, to form a species of Trade Union among the quarrymen. The attempt signally failed, owing, Colonel Pennant hopes, to the good sense of the majority; and the effective measures he was on the point of taking to repress the evil are now no longer necessary; at the same time he is desirous of giving a few words of advice, as well as a few words of caution, to his workmen. His advice is that they should not listen to this so-called Committee, the effect of whose proceedings (whatever may be their pretences or designs) would be to estrange him from his quarrymen, towards whom he has always hitherto endeavoured to act as a friend, and to establish an ill-feeling between himself and his workmen which both parties would soon regret. One of the pretended objects of the Committee is the elevation of the labourer; but Colonel Pennant calls upon the older to point out to the younger quarrymen the difference of the state of this country now from what it was 25 years ago as regards cottages, gardens, clubs, schools, hospitals, etc., and to say if these improvements have not already tended to that end which the Committee pretend to be their object. Improvements on his part must at once cease as soon as that confidence which has hitherto existed between the employer and the employed is broken down. He would advise the men, therefore, to consider well before they listen to agitators. Colonel Pennant's word of caution is to avoid having anything to do with such a movement as a Trade Union in future, as on the very first rumour of such a state of feeling, he will immediately close the quarry, and only re-open it and his cottages to those men who declare themselves averse to any such scheme as a Trade Union."

Source: Gwynedd Archives Service.

Why do you think the threat was effective? What do you think the men did?

Source 39

"To Colonel the Hon. E. G. D. Pennant, M.P.—We, the undersigned do hereby in the most explicit manner protest against a portion of the circular read and distributed on the 2nd inst., at Brynderwen, in the presence of Colonel the Hon. Mr. Pennant; Captain Iremonger; Messrs. W. and J. Francis, and a number of the quarrymen. We refer to that part of the circular which sets forth the character of the Committee as agitators. They were only delegates appointed by us, the great majority of the quarrymen, and acting merely as our representatives. And we are sorry to find that any of the said Committee have to suffer on our behalf. We also beg to state that we have entirely renounced the idea of a Trade Union, trusting that Colonel Pennant will act according to his promise—that there will be no

more 'severity or avenge.' December 22nd, 1865.''
Source: Gwynedd Archives Service.

The 1874 Dispute

It was another nine years before there was another attempt to set up a union but then, on 27 April 1874, the North Wales Quarrymen's Union came into existence.

Source 40

Source: Lewis, *Slate.*

Immediately the owners and managers of the quarries tried to destroy the Union. The battle of will was most fierce at the two biggest quarries, Dinorwic and Penrhyn. At Dinorwic, when the time came for the monthly deals or 'bargains' between men and management, the owner, Assheton-Smith, gave the men no option. They could join the Union, or they could work. Virtually all the Dinorwic quarrymen refused to give in. They walked out of the quarry and eventually the owner had to give in to them. The quarrymen at Penrhyn, Lord Penrhyn's quarry, collected money for the Dinorwic men. Lord Penrhyn objected to this. But none of these disputes had just a single cause. The existence of the Union was certainly something which Penrhyn objected to. It was against his whole idea of the relationship between owner and workers. As the owner he regarded himself as the person who should decide, through managers, how the quarry should be run. In return, he would provide the work which enabled the men and their families to live. He could probably not even *understand* why anyone should think he would be *forced* to do anything he did not want to do in his own quarry. So, the Union was basically a fight for rights. One of those rights was a decent wage and the 1874 dispute was also about wages. The men at Penrhyn wanted a basic wage—of 30 shillings a week for quarrymen, for example— even if the bargain they struck over the amount of rock which they could work in a month gave them less than this. The dispute lasted from July until September, 1874. As always in a long strike, there was great hardship. There was also a sense of injustice. The men wanted to debate the case with the owner. This letter, an appeal for help for the quarrymen in their plight, shows that. It comes from the general secretary of the N.W.Q.U. Here is a transcript. The letter itself is on p. 19. Try reading the original first.

THE STRIKE AT PENRHYN QUARRIES

4 Williams Court
Bethesda
September 1874

Dear Sir

The men have been now out for weeks, and there appears to be no prospects of an early settlement. Over 2200 quarrymen are out on strike and above 300 old men have been 'turned out' by Lord Penrhyn for whom some provision must be made to keep them from the Union house. Some of these old men have been working at Lord Penrhyn's quarries for 40, 50 and 60 years and some of them even more than this, and simply because the bulk of the quarrymen ventured to ask for an increase of wages, these poor innocent old men were cruelly punished by being thrown upon the parish for any provision Lord Penrhyn was ready to make for them. This certainly is not charity!

The men have now only to face all lovers of liberty justice and fair play for assistance to help them or to sustain themselves. They are determined not to give in if they are out for a twelve months if they can anyhow get sufficient to support for the most needy until they get employment elswhere. This is clearly a question of might against right.

W. J. Parry, the leader of the N.W.Q.U., headed the strike committee. The committee is seen (Source 42) with Parry second from left and Lord Penrhyn on the right.

Source 41

The Strike at Penrhyn Quarries No 1

4 Williams Court
Bethesda   September 1874

Dear Sir

These men have been now out for   weeks, &
there appears to be no prospect of an early settlement. Thr 2200
Quarrymen are out on strike and above 300 Old men have been
"turned out" by Lord Penrhyn, for whom some provision must
be made to keep them from the Union house. Some of these
Old men have been working at Lord Penrhyn's Quarries
for 40, 50 & 60 years, and some of them even more than this,
And simply because the bulk of the Quarrymen ventured to
ask for an increase of wages, these poor innocent old men
were cruelly punished by being thrown upon the parish for
any provision Lord Penrhyn was ready to make for them.
This certainly is not Charity!

The men have now only to face all lovers of
liberty justice and fair play for assistance to help
them on to sustain themselves. They are determined
not to give in if they are out for a twelve months, if
they can anyhow get sufficient support for the most
needy until they get employment elsewhere. This
is clearly a question of might against right.

Source: Gwynedd Archives.

Source 42

Source: Lewis, *Slate.*

The vast majority of the quarrymen supported the strike. Source 43 shows that some did not. They protested to Lord Penrhyn that the committee should be done away with.

Eventually, strikers and management came to an agreed set of terms for the men to return to work.

There was still more trouble to come, because management did not put the agreement into practice when the men returned to work. The men just walked out again. This time the men, through their Union, did win a victory. The managers who had refused to put the agreement into practice were sacked, the agreement was honoured and the men returned to work.

Why do you think the men had won? Does it seem at all remarkable to you that they should have won? If so, why?

We know that the Union became much more popular after this dispute. Why? Most of the workers at the two biggest quarries, Dinorwic and Penrhyn, joined and there were branches, or lodges, in all the main quarrying areas. Membership grew to over 8,000 by 1878. At the same time there were difficulties in making the N.W.Q.U. a powerful, united union. The owners were far more powerful—and far richer. Quarrymen were very independent people and, as we saw in source 39, some objected to having a union at all. Part of the quarrymen's independence came from the fact that they were individual craftsmen, working often in wide-open spaces. Individual quarries were spread over a large area of north Wales. This was very different from organising a union in a factory. Why?

Source 43

Now, since the committee is composed of extreme characters, and are to persisting in bringing forward groundless and unfair charges, and the same being heard, the workmen are kept in suspense from day to day, so as to render the strike to be far more prolonged than it should really be. But our constant expectation is for your lordship putting an end to the reception of the committee, because we know and are certain that nothing but harm is to be expected from them both to the master as well as to the men.

And if it please your lordship to put an end to the committee, we assure you that hundreds of us will find our way cleared to go to our work, because the feeling is strengthening here among hundreds daily.

On behalf of ourselves and fellow-workmen,
Robert Rd. Jones, Rhiwlas.
John Williams, Rhiwlas.

Source: Gwynedd Archives Service.

The men had come out on top in 1874. The outcome of any future struggle might not be so clearcut. And a new struggle was always likely. The demand for slate was always going up and down, and so were profits. Lord Penrhyn was not likely to be content with having been defeated in 1874.

The Dinorwic Dispute of 1885-6

The next major dispute did not, in fact, occur in Penrhyn but in Dinorwic. After Penrhyn, this was the biggest slate-quarry in the world with 2,700 men employed. The immediate cause of the dispute was that the men were locked out on October 23, 1885:

Source 44

'Notice to all Men and Boys employed at the Dinorwic Quarries. In as much as a mass meeting was held during working hours on Monday afternoon, the 12th October instant in defiance of an order made in July last when you were cautioned that such a meeting, if held during working hours, would not be tolerated.

   Notice is hereby given,
that your service will not be required after Saturday, the 31st October instant, and that all barrack furniture, tools, velocipedes, materials, and other effects, belonging to you must be removed before twelve o'clock at noon on Saturday the 31st October instant.

Source: Notice put up by management. Quoted in Merfyn Jones, *The North Wales Quarrymen*, pp. 149, 150.

There was terrible distress.

Source 45

Y GÂN

O ddyngarwyr Cymru anwyl
   Rhowch eich help i weithwyr tlawd;
Sydd yn ymladd dros eu rhyddid
   Mewn sefyllfa ddrwg eu ffawd:
Gan ddialedd y gorthymydd,
   Ein "Cloi allan" oll a wnaed;
Am na phlygem ni i roddi'n
   Hegwyddorion o dan draed.

Dioddefasom flwyddi meithion
   Dan wasgfeuon fwy na mwy,
Gan fflangellau trais a gormes
   Ganwaith cawsom erchyll glwy';
Ofer ydoedd ini ymbil
   Am gyfiawnder yn y gwaith,
Diystyrid ein holl gwynion—
   Gwawd a wneid o'n gruddiau llaith.

Mathrwyd ar ein holl iawnderau—
   Cosbwyd ni heb brawf na rhaith;
Ac am ini feiddio sefyll
   Dros ein hawliau,—cloed y gwaith—

Cloi y gwaith yn nhrymder gauaf,
   Taflu'r gweithwyr mewn sarhâd,
Allan o bob modd i ennill
   Bara i'w teuluoedd mâd.

Mae'n cartrefi dan y trallod
   Yn griddfanu nos a dydd,
A ffurfafen ein cysuron
   Dan erch yn chwyrn ymdeithio
   Megis hen gadridog du,
Gan osgorddio ei fyddinoedd
   I'n dinystrio ar bob tu.

O, bob dydd mae yn gwaethygu
   Trymach, duach yw o hyd,
A gwyllt lifa ffrydiau adfyd,
   Mwyfwy i'n haelwydydd clyd;
Tristwch sydd yn toi'n heolydd,
   Galar trwy drigfanau'n gwlad,
Ac mae newyn du echrydus

O! mae edrych ar ein teulu
   Sydd mor llwm a'u gwedd yn llwyd
Yn trwm wylo ar ein gliniau
   Am gael tamaid bach o fwyd,
Dyna letha ein hysbrydoedd,
   Nes y mae ein dagrau glân
Yn ymsuddo yn ein mynwes,
   Megis diferynau tân.

A all calon gwraig ymatal
   Heb roi ffordd i ddagrau'n lli,
Gwel'd y tad yn rhannu'r crystyn—
   Crystyn olaf yn y tŷ,
Wrth y bwrdd trwy len o ddagrau
   Sylla'r fam ar wedd ei phlant,
Gwel'd y crystyn wedi darfod
   Heb ddim mwy i dori'u chwant.

Wrth ei bron mae baban bychan
   Yn dyrchafu aml ysgrech,
Sugna'n awchus, ond O! siomiant,
   Y mae bron y fam yn sech,
Rhwygir calon y tad tyner
   Dan y ddu olygfa hon,
Gwel'd ei blant a'i anwyl briod
   Yn dihoeni ger ei fron.

Oer anneddau, gwag gypbyrddau,
   Prudd aelwydydd sydd trwy'n bro,
Odlau cân a phob llawenydd
   Cilio wnaethant oll ar ffo,
Ocheneidiau a dioddefaint
   Leinw'n pebyll fore a hwyr,
O pa bryd daw'n gwaredigaeth?
   Nid oes ond y nef a wyr.

O tosturwch wrth ein cwynfan,
   Rhowch gynorthwy ini 'nawr
Er gwaredu ein teuluoedd
   Heddyw sydd mewn cyni mawr,
Lleddfwch ein gofidiau trymion—
   Llonwch ein helbulus rawd,
Hoff ddyngarwyr, O! tosturwch
   Heddyw wrth chwarelwyr tlawd.

Source 46

THE LOCK-OUT
AT
THE DINORWIC QUARRIES,
LLANBERIS.

Dear Friends,

"Succour the needy, and defend the oppressed,"—

2,700 industrious and honest workmen have, in bad times, and in the teeth of a severe winter, been suddenly thrown out of employment; our hearths are overshadowed with gloom, and our homes are in danger of being broken up and ruined. Having been thrown upon the world by the cruel treatment of unfeeling men. We deeply regret the necessity of coming in this manner before the public for support; but however degrading this may be to us, yet, we prefer it rather than to be lead to slavery. We reckon it more honourable to be poor and the recipients of charity than degraded servile vassals.

We appeal for help to all mankind to assist us, and prevent a class of Welsh workmen being trodden upon as mere slaves. We are not a band of agitators; we seek nothing more from our employer than to be ruled and treated as *men*, and as **MEN**—as subjects of the British Empire in the 19th century.

"God is our guide, no sword we draw,
We seek to light no battle fh es,
By union, reason, justice, law,
We claim the birthright of our sires."

Source: Gwynedd Archives Service.

In the end the Dinorwic men were defeated. They had to go back on the management's terms.

The Penrhyn Disputes

Penrhyn 1896-7

In the year of the Dinorwic lockout in 1885 the relations between quarrymen and owner became very much worse in Penrhyn also. The situation was building up slowly which would eventually lead to one of the biggest and most important, and most tragic labour disputes in Welsh history.

What had happened in Penrhyn in 1874?

In 1885 George Douglas Pennant who, when his father died the following year became the new Lord Penrhyn, decided, without any consultation with the men, to withdraw from the agreement which had settled the 1874 dispute. Pennant did this in a notice to the quarrymen (Source 47, page 23). What evidence is there in this notice that the 1874 dispute still had not really been settled?

Not surprisingly the quarrymen protested. The protest came from Union and non-Union men alike. The protest was rejected by G. D. Pennant. His reply could leave no doubt of his position.

Source 48

Dealing first with that part of the subject, I must point out that in accordance with the notice dated May the 4th, that so called agreement terminated at the end of last quarry month, and I may now add that under no circumstances will I consent to the restoration of it. The excessive cost of production during the last ten years which has been the direct consequence of that arrangement, has brought about a disastrous state of affairs which cannot continue, and unless put at once upon a different footing, would inevitably result in such serious distress to all deriving their living from the Penrhyn Quarries, that it is my duty in the interest of all concerned, to resist all attempts at the restoration of the cause of the evil.

Date: 20 May 1885.

Source: Gwynedd Archives Service.

For five years the demand for slate was not very strong and the quarrymen in Penrhyn and the Union were in no position to bargain with management or with Lord Penrhyn. Then, from 1890, the slate market improved and the Union revived. Relations with the Penrhyn manager, E. A. Young, and Lord Penrhyn, were not good. Lord Penrhyn met demands for increased wages by saying that if the demand for, and price of, slate were sufficient he would award the men a pay rise without being asked. Why do you think this did not satisfy the men?

In 1896 matters came to a head. Once more it was the existence of a Union to represent the men's demands which was one of the basic matters at issue. In July the quarrymen's committee put in applications for wage increases. First E. A. Young, the manager, then Lord Penrhyn, turned the demand down, flat. On 28 September, 1896, the quarrymen's committee proposed a strike, though not immediately:

Source 49

'We believe that it is our duty as workmen to announce that it is our intention to strike in March next if we don't see in the meantime that the principal points in our demands and complaints as different classes in the works have been granted.'

Source: Merfyn Jones, *North Wales Quarrymen*, p. 185.

Source 47

PENRHYN CASTLE,

BANGOR,

May 4th, 1885.

Circumstances have come to my knowledge which give me reason to doubt whether some of the principal points in the approaching alterations in Quarry affairs (recently announced by MR. ARTHUR WYATT) have been clearly understood by the whole body of Penrhyn Quarrymen, and I, therefore, now (to avoid misapprehension) state them in writing.

The basis for setting the bargains at the Penrhyn Quarry will be more in accordance with the rate of wages paid at other quarries in the county.

All settings to be dealt with and carried out according to the general principles of contracting.

The bargains to be re-set at the beginning of every quarry month, unless a contract has been entered into for a longer period.

Wages to be calculated on the actual working days.

Termination at the end of the present quarry month of what was called "MR. PENNANT LLOYD's agreement."

Wishing to act with the strictest impartiality, I feel bound to state that I am well aware that there are two parties in the quarry, which may be described as Union and non-Union men; and as it is only fair that the views and complaints of the latter body should be as freely expressed as those of the former, I now announce that all complaints of a serious character, whether individual or collective, are to be made direct to the Chief Manager (MR. ARTHUR WYATT), by whom they will be submitted to myself. I decline altogether to sanction the interference of anybody (corporate or individual) between employer and employed in the working of the Quarry, and in order to ensure fairness for all parties, no deputation or memorial professing to speak for the general body of quarrymen will be received or considered, unless it *equitably* represents the views of both non-Union as well as Union men; but in the event of questions arising which may lead to discussion between employer and employed, I should always be ready to treat with a deputation composed of quarrymen, equally in number representing the non-Union as well as the Union Men.

As attempts will probably be made by interested parties to give a political tone and colouring to some of these changes, it may be necessary for me to point out that (notwithstanding any representations of that nature which may be made) these changes will be made and carried out in a spirit of fair-play to all concerned.

Whilst deploring the present stagnation of trade, I must congratulate the men generally upon the good feeling which has so far characterized their receipt of the news of the proposed alteration in wages; and although it must be borne in mind that I do not by this settlement pledge myself indefinitely to this or any other rate of wages, I hope that the new scale and the arrangements in connection therewith, will enable the men generally to feel that their trade interests are likely to stand upon a sounder footing than of late.

Source: Gwynedd Archive Service.

G. DOUGLAS PENNANT.

That same day 74 quarrymen, most of them members of the committee, were handed a note from quarry manager E. A. Young. Jeremiah Thomas was one who received the note.

Source 50

Source: Gwynedd Archives Service.

The Penrhyn quarrymen came out on strike. There was, as always, great hardship. The North Wales Quarrymen's Union had still not recovered financially from the Dinorwic dispute ten years earlier. However, the support from other Trade Unions in Britain was first-class and the very large sum of £7,500 came from a fund started by the *Daily Chronicle* newspaper.

Attempts by Lord Penrhyn and his manager to re-open the quarry without agreement failed. There was no response to such notices as the one in Source 51 *(See page 25).*

Lord Penrhyn was determined not to give up what he believed to be his right to control his property—the quarry—in whatever way he liked. He was not even prepared to allow a government department—the Board of Trade—to interfere with this.

Source 52

'The Board of Trade made an endeavour to promote a friendly conference between yourself and your workmen . . . the conditions, however, upon which you insist make it useless for them to continue the endeavour.'
Letter from Board of Trade, December 1896.

Source: Merfyn Jones, *North Wales Quarrymen*, p. 192.

The strike went on until August, 1897. The men went back on Lord Penrhyn's terms. But that was not the end of the story.

The Penrhyn Lockout, 1900-1903

For the next three years management drove home the victory, controlling the Penrhyn quarry very firmly. Membership of the quarrymen's Union fell. In April 1900 E. A. Young, the Penrhyn manager, even stopped the Union collecting Union subscriptions in the quarry. What was the purpose of this?

This move went wrong. The quarrymen actually rallied to the Union as a result. The men were now even more resentful of the high-handed way in which they had been treated since the defeat of 1897. Trouble could not be far away. It came in November 1900.

There were *long-term* causes and *short-term* causes of the dispute. Before you read on try to think of what the long-term causes might be.

We have seen that the quarrymen of north Wales had a highly-skilled job which took years of experience to master. Indeed, some never mastered the art of splitting the rock away from the mountainside. Because of this high degree of skill the quarrymen were extremely proud of their ability. This ability was much greater than that of the managers or foremen to whom they were responsible. Therefore, the quarrymen had a lot of independence and some control over how and when they worked. This independence was encouraged by the system of payment which, we have seen, resulted from a 'bargain' struck between the men and the management. No-one could take away the quarrymen's skill, but increasingly owners and management objected to the independence which went with it. Steadily the owners tried to bring the quarrymen more and more under their control. It was this that the quarrymen resented most of all because when it came to working the slate the quarrymen knew they knew best.

Matters of pride and independence were bound to get caught up in disputes which involved the quarrymen's union. The union was concerned to look after the pay and

Source 51

To the late Employés at the Penrhyn Quarries.

I am again instructed by Lord Penrhyn to make you the accompanying offer of work on the same condition as before, viz.:

That there shall in future be no attempt on the part of any Committee to interfere with the management of the Quarry, or to prevent Employés from obeying the orders of the Managers.

Upon the above distinct understanding, all applications (including those of the 71 men who were suspended on 28th Sept., 1896) will be impartially considered, and as many of the late employés as there can be found room for, will be re-engaged, without reference to the events connected with the strike.

As misapprehension appears to exist with regard to the 71 men to whom notice of suspension was given (Sept. 28), I must point out that the suspension of those men (*ipso facto*) ceased immediately the present strike was declared, whereby the men severed their connection with their employer, thus making it obviously necessary for you all to apply individually for re-engagement if you are desirous of obtaining work at the Penrhyn Quarry.

E. A. YOUNG.

NOTICE.

WANTED AT

THE PENRHYN QUARRIES

Blacksmiths, Badrockmen, Boys, Brakesmen, Engine-drivers, Fitters, Foundry-men, Joiners, Journeymen, Loaders, Labourers, Masons, Machiners, Miners, Quarrymen, Rybelwyr, Sawyers, Stokers, Tippers, &c.

Applicants for work can apply on Monday or Tuesday next (February 15th and 16th), between the hours of 10 a.m. and 3 p.m., at the following Offices :

To apply at the Yard Office - - -	Blacksmiths, Fitters, Foundrymen, Joiners, &c.
To apply at the Slab Mill Office - -	Sawyers, &c.
To apply at Tross-y-fordd Office - -	Badrockmen and Journeymen.
To apply at the Pay Office - - -	Quarrymen and Journeymen.
To apply at the Pay Office - - -	Boys.
To apply at the Marker's Office - -	Loaders, Masons, Miners, Machiners, Engine-drivers, Stokers, Brakesmen, Tippers.
To apply to William Parry, Overlooker's Office - - - - - - -	Rybelwyr.

Port Penrhyn, Bangor,
8th February, 1897.

E. A. YOUNG.

Source: Gwynedd Archives Service

conditions of the men and to negotiate when there were disputes. Owners like Lord Penrhyn would not tolerate the idea of negotiation of this sort. From his point of view the men were his employees and therefore he had the right to decide their pay and conditions in the end, although he acknowledged that he had responsibilities towards them as individuals. But doing things for them as a good employer, which he accepted as right, was very different from bargaining with them through the union, as if the union had powers like the owners.

Lord Penrhyn's purpose in running his quarry through his managers was to make as much money as he could. One way in which his managers felt he might be able to do this was to change the old system of dealing with each single small team of men over how much they should be paid for a month's work and how much they should produce in that time. If, instead, the managers were to let out large areas of the quarry to contractors then the whole process, from the managers' point of view, would be simplified. Each contractor would then be responsible for getting the most slate possible from his particular part of the quarry, and the men would be responsible to him rather than the managers.

This system of 'contracting' was very different from the old system of making a 'bargain'. Putting it into practice was at the root of the Penrhyn dispute. Why do you think the quarrymen resented this new system so much?

At any time these *long-term* causes could lead to an actual dispute. Here is how the historian of the quarrymen has described the *short-term* causes of the dispute.

Source 53

'The Penrhyn lock-out had its immediate causes in a series of confusing incidents starting in mid-October 1900. The trouble began with a disagreement between fourteen men working on *Ponc Ffridd* and their overseeing underagent concerning the contract of two of the men. The fourteen refused to work on Saturday and were suspended for three days. A fortnight later the fourteen were told that they were no longer to work on the same gallery but that they were to be scattered through the quarry, and their bargains let in one contract to a 'big contractor'. When that contractor appeared on the *Ponc*, however, he was threatened, assaulted and thrown out of the quarry. A week later a similar incident occurred elsewhere in the quarry and legal proceedings were started

against twenty-six men. Three hundred dragoons (soldiers) entered the area in case more serious trouble should break out.

The twenty-six men were dismissed from the quarry before trial and, as most were thought to be innocent by the rest of the quarrymen, feeling ran very high. When the case came up in Bangor on 5 November the whole body of quarrymen marched to the town in their support. This insubordination earned the whole workforce a fortnight's suspension from work. Of the twenty-six tried, twenty were found not guilty.'

Source: Merfyn Jones, *The North Wales Quarrymen*, p. 211.

The notice which Dr. Jones refers to, suspending the men for a fortnight, is Source 54 *(See page 27).*

After this 14-day suspension the men returned to work. They soon discovered that 800 quarrymen were not being given work immediately. On 22 November 2000 quarrymen said they would not work until the other 800 had been taken on. E. A. Young, the manager, refused. That day 2,800 men left the great Penrhyn quarry. 1000 never returned. 1000 more stayed on strike for three years.

What was one of the first effects on the men and their families?

Source 55

THE PENRHYN DISPUTE.

AN APPEAL ON BEHALF OF THE SUFFERERS.

We, the undersigned, being ministers of Churches in London, desire to appeal to the public generally, but especially to the thousands of Welshmen in the Metropolis, on behalf of our fellow-countrymen and country-women, who are suffering great privations owing to the unfortunate dispute at the Penrhyn Quarries. The men may be right, or they may be wrong in the action they have taken, but it is quite clear that they are convinced that their cause is a just one, and worthy of many sacrifices. Both parties seem determined to carry on the struggle indefinitely. In the meantime, hundreds of old men, women and children are suffering very great hardships, many of them deprived of even the necessaries of life. Our concern is for them; it is their case that we recommend to the sympathetic generosity of those who are able to assist.

Delegates from the Relief Committee are now in London. These men are personally known to us. They are men who are instigated solely by pity for their fellow human-beings. We hope and pray that their visit may result in securing substantial aid for those upon whom this sad dispute has brought such heavy tribulation.

(Signed)

REV. OWEN EVANS, D.D.
,, J. E. DAVIES, M.A.
,, ISHMAEL EVANS.
,, LLEWELYN EDWARDS, M.A.
,, R. E. WILLIAMS.
,, THOS. NICHOLSON.
,, T. EYNON DAVIES.
,, J. OSSIAN DAVIES.
,, W. PEDR WILLIAMS.
,, WM. PIERCE.

Source: Gwynedd Archives Service.

Source 54

PENRHYN QUARRY.

NOTICE.

Inasmuch as a number of the Penrhyn Quarry Employees has during the last fortnight actively participated in certain acts of violence and intimidation against some of their fellow-workmen and officials, and to-day nearly all the Employees have left their work without leave, Notice is hereby given that such Employees are suspended for 14 days.

E. A. YOUNG

PORT PENRHYN,
Bangor, November 6th, 1900.

Chwarel y Penrhyn.

RHYBUDD.

Yn gymaint ag i nifer o weithwyr Chwarel y Penrhyn yn ystod y pythefnos diweddaf gymeryd rhan weithredol mewn ymosodiadau o greulondeb a bygythiadau yn erbyn rhai o'u cyd-weithwyr a swyddogion, ac heddyw i agos yr oll o'r gweithwyr adael eu gwaith heb ganiatad, rhoddir Rhybudd drwy hyn fod y cyfryw weithwyr yn cael eu hatal am bedwar-diwrnod-ar-ddeg.

E. A. YOUNG

PORT PENRHYN,
Bangor, Tachwedd 6ed, 1900

Source: Gwynedd Archives Service.

There was help from Trade Unions all over Britain.

Source 56
DESOLATE BETHESDA.

Fellow Workers,

The old men and women, the wives and children of the Slate Quarrymen of Bethesda are suffering great want and privation ; and support is urgently needed.

To help to provide this support, and to let it be known that the workers of Barnsley and district are not deaf to the cry for help of their fellow workers in Wales, several Trade Union and kindred societies have arranged for the **Bethesda Quarrymen's Prize Choir** to give several **Concerts** in and about Barnsley.

You are perhaps aware that, by his arbitrary action, begot of his hatred to the men's Trade Union, my Lord Penrhyn has made it impossible for employer and employees at the Bethesda Quarries to work in harmony. This has resulted in a dispute that has already lasted more than seven months. It is true that his Lordship is generously allowing the men to return to work, but on the degrading condition that they forsake their Union, which has been their true friend through many bitter years. Remember ! this dispute, which is causing such wholesale suffering and ruin throughout the district, is the outcome of a sustained effort on the part of an obsolete and obstinate feudal relic to smash up Trade Unionism on " his property." By his action, Lord Penrhyn bars the way to **15,000** peoples' means of life!

In asking you for your support at one or more of the Concerts, or by subscription, we feel that every worker ought to support the Quarrymen, because for years a deliberate attempt has been made to smash all combination among these workers. Will you help ? What is your response ?

Any communications addressed to the undersigned will receive prompt attention.

WILL MELLOR, Hon. Sec.,
Ardsley, Barnsley.

Source: Gwynedd Archives Service.

The quarrying communities helped themselves as far as possible.

Source 57 *(See opposite column)*

There was a generous response by people appalled at the hardship being caused to quarrymen's families:

Source 58 *(See opposite column)*

After two years the relief committee which had been trying to help wives and children with gifts of food, was in increasing difficulty. The Bethesda choir tried desperately to provide some money for relief.

Source 59 *(See page 29)*

Source 57

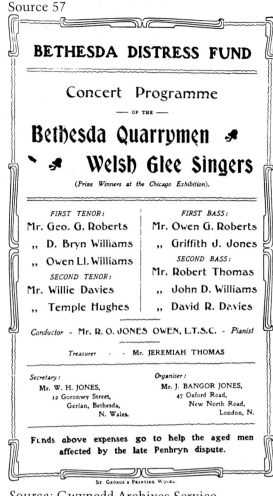

Source: Gwynedd Archives Service.

Source 58

Source: Gwynedd Archives Service.

Source 59

BETHESDA CHOIR IN LINCOLN.

I note with pleasure that, through the spirited action of the Lincoln Trades and Labour Council, on Saturday next, October 4th, the famed Bethesda Welsh Choir is coming to Lincoln again. Those who heard this famous choir on their former visit will doubtless be anxious to hear them again. I need not remind my readers of the object for which these sweet singers are travelling through the country. The dispute between Lord Penrhyn and the quarrymen, at Bethesda, still drags on. The only difference is that the men, and the women and children, too, are now faced, not only with the implacable determination of Lord Penrhyn to force them to accept his terms, but are faced with starvation, too. Let me quote from the special correspondent of the Daily News:—How to live—that, as I write, is the problem pressing on Bethesda. To-day is Black Wednesday, and, for the first time since the strike began, there is something like consternation in the trim slate cottages nestling so daintily against the hill side. The Relief Committee have announced that they can make no distribution of provisions this week, and some seven hundred persons find themselves faced literally with starvation! But, worse than the case of the men, is that of the women and children. It is these, the widows and offspring of the quarrymen, that the Relief Committee have been looking after. For two years the Committee has managed to ensure them, at least, a bare subsistence by distributing provisions, through various tradesmen, to those in the direct need. Now, even that refuge is denied to those poor sufferers in a dispute, which is not their own, and they find themselves with the hand of famine closing on their thrapples.

*Source:
The Lincoln
Leader,* 27 Sept.
1902. Facsimile
from Gwynedd
Archive Service

Both sides in the dispute tried hard to justify their case. Here is a photograph of the strike committee which led the quarrymen.

Source 60

What kind of case would they have put forward to justify their actions? Some of the answers—not all—are mentioned in this appeal by members of the relief committee.

Source 61 *(See page 30)*

Lord Penrhyn and his managers were equally prepared to justify their actions in refusing to negotiate on the men's complaints. What sort of case do you think Lord Penrhyn would make? The general manager of Dinorwic quarry represented the views of employers generally.

Source 62 *(See page 31)*

The Liberal newspaper, the *Cambrian News* had its own ideas of why the strike was a struggle which was significant far outside Caernarfonshire.

Source 63

'Workingmen throughout the country have been more or less persuaded that they create all the wealth and that capitalists are their despoilers. This is not by any means true, but the subject is too large for the present article. We have no objection to the Bethesda quarrymen refusing to work on the terms Lord Penrhyn offers. We have never questioned their right for a moment. What we say is absurd is that our correspondent or anybody else, should claim for the workmen rights

(Continued on p. 31).

Source: Gwynedd Archive Service, *Chwareli a Chwarelwyr,* 1974.

Source 61

The Penrhyn Lock Out.

——————:o: ——————

WE make an appeal on behalf of Old Men, Widows, and Orphans, who are already suffering great hardships in consequence of the Lock Out.

We who are on the spot, and are sufferers ourselves, know full well the justice of the men's cause, and the oppression they have suffered ever since the present Lord Penrhyn came into possession. The good feeling that existed between his late noble father and his workmen was destroyed at a stroke by the present lord within three months of his coming into the property, and all his dealings with them ever since have been tyrannical. He terminated at a month's notice the conditions under which they worked with his noble father. He took away from them virtually the management of their Sick Benefit Club,—compelling them to take as Medical Officer one selected by himself,—they still paying the same amount of monthly subscription towards the club as they did when they had the right to select their own medical man. If they were allowed to select their own they would be more likely to accept his service, while now the bulk of the men go to others, whom they have to pay in addition to their present subscription to the Quarry Club. He did all this without consulting the wishes of the men to whom it was of vital importance. He has by his actions endeavoured to create ill-feeling in the quarry between Unionist and Non-unionist workmen. On one occasion, after a deputation of the men had approached him with a written statement on behalf of the whole quarry, he called the

[2]

three Union Members of the Deputation before him, and without giving them a proper opportunity to defend themselves, he read out to them a previously prepared notice of dismissal, for a supposed offence, for which there was no ground whatever, and was proved afterwards by the written defence of the men. This has been set out in the written defence of the men sent to his lordship in 1885, and never denied.

All his treatment of the men confirms the warning of his noble father to a Deputation that appeared before him in August, 1865, and which was given in the presence of the present lord, and in the presence of one of us, viz., "Beware that you do not offend George, for if you do he will never forgive, he can never forgive." It is generally believed that the results of the elections of 1868 and 1880 has something to do with his treatment of his men.

The circumstances of the Strike of 1896-7 for securing the Right of Combination are so familiar to all that we need not enter into them.

Lord Penrhyn claims that he has provided for the proper representation of grievances; but as the management will only consider complaints that are **personally** made by the aggrieved, it is obvious that complainants become marked men, and trifling faults can afterwards be made the cause of their dismissal.

The fact is clear to us all here, and there is no doubt in the minds of anyone in the district, that 5 men who took an active part in that movement have been dismissed from the quarry **without any reason whatever been given for their dismissal, and the reasons have been refused to those of the men who asked for them.** We all look upon it as a despotic act on the part of Lord Penrhyn, and believe that they have suffered for having done what they considered their duty as the representatives of their fellow-workmen. This has been of a piece with the treatment of his men since he came into the property.

It appears to us that the men are determined now to remain out till these men are reinstated, and their just rights are granted them; and we, with confidence, appeal to the public generally for support to enable them to secure these things.

On behalf of the Relief Committee,

W. J. PARRY, Chairman.

G. ROBERTS, J.P., Vice-Chairman.

DANIEL LLOYD, Treasurer.

Rev. W. W. LLOYD, General Secretary.

February 6, 1901.

Source: Gwynedd Archive Service.

Source 62

FROM THE HON. W. W. VIVIAN, PORT DINORWIC, BANGOR, N. WALES.

SHEET No.

To .... Lord Wemyss, ...

May 22nd 19_1, ————— 18

Dear Lord Wemyss,

I have received your letter of the 21st. inst. with copy of a proposed address to Lord Penrhyn.

Without hesitation I say, the large Employers of England owe Lord Penrhyn a debt of gratitude for the stand he has made "for a principle". This "principle" is surrounded on all sides with entire right & justice, as is well known to all persons possessing a practical knowledge as to facts in connection with this sad affair.

For his own & his childrens' future welfare I wish the Employed of the United Kingdom would each one think & act more for himself & so strive to "scotch" the Agitator & certain of our M.P's who having no stake in this old country's future, take to Parliamentary life as means by which to gain their daily bread; these two classes cannot thrive, except by constant striving (indirectly of course!!) to rouse up ill feelings & strife on the part of the "Employed" toward the Employer.

Source: Gwynedd Archive Service.

which they refuse to the employer. Lord Penrhyn is in our opinion as fully entitled to refuse the men's terms as the men are to refuse his terms.

Date: 19 April, 1910.

Source: Gwynedd Archive Service.

Lord Penrhyn had far more resources than the quarrymen. For one thing, he owned an enormous estate in Caernarfonshire which provided him with enough income to live in the style to which he was accustomed—a style rather different from the quarrymen even when they were working. He also had another card to play. He owned the quarry so he could—and did—try to start it up without the strikers, as this notice of 20 May, 1901, shows. It promised police protection to working men.

Source 64 (See page 32)

By the following month there were 700 men working in the quarry while over 2,000 remained on strike. The strikers did not have a high opinion of those working. They regarded them as 'blacklegs'. In Welsh they were known as 'cynffonwyr'. The word means 'flatterers'—but 'cynffon' also means 'tail'. This was the real insult. To the Penrhyn strikers the strike-breakers were animals:

Source 65

'creatures of a man's shape with tails, yet they were not men. If Prof. Darwin were living in Bethesda now he would not have to go far to find something to prove his point that man is descended from the ape.'

Source: Yr Herald Cymraeg, 6 August, 1901. Quoted in Merfyn Jones, *North Wales Quarrymen,* p. 92.

Source 64

RHYBUDD.

Bydd Chwarel y Penrhyn yn agored ar ddydd Mawrth, Mehefin 11eg, i'r holl weithwyr diweddar sydd wedi apelio am waith ac a dderbyniwyd.

Fel yr hysbyswyd yn Chwefror diweddaf, mae y Rheolau Disgyblaeth wedi eu cyfnewid, ac y mae rheol newydd wedi ei thynu allan a chytuno arni, pa un, yn ymarferol, a rydd haner diwrnod o Wyl ar y dydd olaf o bob mis, yn mhob peth arall y mae Rheolau y Chwarel yn parhau yr un fath ag o'r blaen. (Y mae y Rheolau Newyddion y cyfeirir atynt yn argraffedig isod.)

Yn ystod y pythefnos nesaf (h.y., dim diweddarach na Mehefin 4ydd), yr wyf yn barod i dderbyn ceisiadau pellach oddiwrth weithwyr diweddar (heblaw bechgyn) a ddymunant ddychwelyd i weithio. Rhaid i bob ymgeisydd roddi eu rhif blaenorol yn y Chwarel a'r "Bonc," hefyd enw llawn a chyfeiriad.

Ni ellir ystyried ceisiadau oddiwrth "fechgyn" am ail-ddychwelyd i'r Chwarel hyd o leiaf bythefnos ar ol i'r dynion ail-ddechreu gweithio.

Mewn trefn i gario allan y gyfraith mewn perthynas i fygwth neu boeni trwy ormes neu fodd arall (o dan Ddeddf Cyd-fradwriaeth ac Amddiffyniad), y mae amddiffyniad heddgeidwadol digonol wedi ei addaw gan y Prif Gwnstabl, Colonel Ruck.

E. A. YOUNG.

Port Penrhyn, Bangor,
20 Mai, 1901.

RHEOLAU NEWYDDION.

Disgyblaeth.---Bydd pob ceryddon trwy "ataliad" neu ddiswyddiad. Er engraifft, os bydd gweithiwr yn dyfod yn hwyr (oddieithr drwy afiechyd neu achos sydyn o bwysigrwydd mawr), fe gaiff y tro cyntaf ei rybuddio, yr ail waith atelir ef am chwarter diwrnod, y trydydd droseddiad ataliad am haner diwrnod; ond ceryddir troseddwyr parhaus yn fwy difrifol neu a diswyddiad.

Diwedd y Mis.---Ar y dydd Mawrth diweddaf · yn mhob Mis y Chwarel bydd y gweithwyr ar ol rhoddi eu cerrig a'u cyfrifon i fyny a threfnu eu bargeinion am y Mis dyfodol yn rhydd i adael y Chwarel, os dewisant, am y gweddill o'r dydd.

Source: Gwynedd Archives Service.

The hatred for the 'cynffonwyr' also comes out in this song composed during the strike.

Source 66

PUNT Y GYNFFON

Mesur, *"Y Mochyn Du."*

Glywsoch chwi'r ystori anfwyn—
Stori'r brâd, a stori'r cynllwyn?
Gwaeth na Brad y Cyllill Hirion
Yw ystori Punt y Gynffon.

Cydgan,

O! mor drwm yr ydym ni,
O! mor drwm yr ydym ni;
Y mae arnom alar calon,
Punt y Gynffon,—ach â hi!

Ofer siarad am bersonau,
Baich y testyn yw cynffonau
Os am helynt—"teulu'r gynffon"
Holwch urdd y "crysau gwynion."

Cydgan,—O! mor drwm, &c.

Rhaid cael corph i ysgwyd cynffon,
Pwy yw hwnw'r—corpws gwirion?
Rhyfedd iawn 'does ond cynffonau
Oll yn chware ar y bonciau!

Cydgan,—O! mor drwm, &c.

O! mor werthfawr yw *cymeriad!*
'Does â'i pryn holl aur y cread;
Dei'll yr hollfyd brynu *dynion*—
Fe eill *sofren* brynu cynffon!

Cydgan,—O! mor drwm, &c.

Bydd yn ffyddlon, O Chwarelwr!
Actia'r *dyn* gerbron uchelwr
Nis gall oesoedd tragwyddoldeb
Ddattod dyn o'i *gyfrifoldeb.*

Cydgan,—O! mor drwm, &c.

Weithwyr! Cariwch bawb eich croesau,
Chwi gewch fendith mil o oesau;
'Welir "cynffon" ar fynyddoedd
Yn hollti creigiau'r mil blynyddoedd?

Cydgan,—

O! mor hardd fydd eu gwedd!
O! mor hardd fydd eu gwedd!
Dynion cryfion—bawb yn ffyddlon,
A phob "Cynffon" yn ei fedd!!

"OLL YN CHWAREU AR Y PONCIAU"

The hatred of those who continued to work from the middle of 1901 was shown in other ways.

Source 67

July, 1901.

To His Majesty's Secretary of State for the Home Department.

The humble petition of the workmen now employed at the Penrhyn Slate Quarries. Bethesda, in the County of Carnarvon. sheweth—

That a large number (about 2,000 in number) of the late employees at the Penrhyn Quarry are now out on strike.

That your petitioners have been working at the Penrhyn Slate Quarries since the eleventh day of June last, and that since that date a large force of police has been brought into the neighbourhood for our protection.

That the protection is not sufficient, because we are molested and intimidated by the men who are still on strike, and their sympathisers.

That we and the members of our families are not allowed to walk the streets, for the purpose of transacting business, without being followed and molested.

That there are many instances where we or members of our families, women and children, have been molested in the public streets and compelled by large and disorderly crowds to return to our homes escorted by the crowd, hooting and shouting, and using violence toward us.

That assaults have been committed in the public streets, stones thrown through our windows and at our houses, both in the daytime and at night.

That on several Saturday nights now, large crowds have been congregating in the village of Bethesda for the purpose of watching and molesting us and our wives and children, in going and returning from the village, where we are obliged to go for the purpose of obtaining the necessaries of life.

That actual violence has been committed upon these occasions, and the houses and shops, where we happened to be, have been surrounded and watched by these crowds for several hours.

That these crowds are most threatening and disorderly, and are beyond the control of the force of police now stationed here.

That the police are obstructed and resisted in the execution of their duty, and they are unable to prevent the crowds from molesting and assaulting us.

Source: Gwynedd Archive Service.

Eventually the strike had to come to an end. In the last months of the strike it was clear to the quarrymen and their leaders that they had no hope of winning. Lord Penrhyn, without his quarries, had an income which would not mean any hardship for him. The quarrymen had no answers. Some took the alternative of going to south Wales where the coalfields gave them work. Some quarrymen emigrated to the U.S.A. For those who stayed in north Wales there was hardship which was near starvation. They believed wholeheartedly that they were right and this sense of right stopped them giving in for many months even when it was clear that they could not win. They fought on from a sense of right and pride in themselves and their communities. In the end the suffering became too much. Slowly, surely, a few men went back to work. Eventually the men voted, in small groups, to go back, forced by famine.

The end is recorded in the minutes of the North Wales Quarrymen's Union.

Source 68

Helynt Bethesda. Hysbysodd Henry Jones ganlyniad y bleidlais ddiweddaf. Mwyafrif o 31 ym Methesda dros ddiweddu yr ymdrechfa. Ychydig o daydddordeb wedi cael ei ddangos ynddi gan y rhai sydd yn gweithio oddicartref. Na Sadwrn Iach. 14 1903 penderfynus yn swyddogol fod y frwydr ar ben.

                       Dated 28 November, 1903.

Source: Gwynedd Archive Service.

The importance of the great Penrhyn dispute

Who do you think won in this dispute? How do you think (a) Lord Penrhyn (b) the quarrymen regarded the situation at the end of the dispute? Why was it an important dispute? Before you carry on reading try to think of three or four reasons.

1. It had a great personal importance for the quarrymen and their families. Despite the help that came in from outside they suffered terribly, with very little money even to buy food. It is impossible to know the consequences of this in terms of disease and malnutrition.

2. It was important for the community— particularly the quarrying areas like Bethesda where Penrhyn men lived. There was marvellous community spirit as people helped each other; but there was also hatred between those who kept solid behind the strike and those who went back to work and broke the strike.

3. The dispute was important for Wales. Lord Penrhyn was exactly the kind of person which Welsh radical politicians were most opposed to in the late 19th century. He was English in his speech, in his ways and in his loyalties. He was a Tory whose family had always regarded it as their right to have a local parliamentary seat and represent the area as M.P. The Welsh people at this time were overwhelmingly members of the Liberal party and only since the Reform Act of 1884 had they really been able to have their choice as Member of Parliament. Lord Penrhyn was a member of the Church of England. He represented the established Church which was by law the Church of Wales as well. The great majority of Welsh people were Nonconformists, that is Independents (Congregationalists), Baptists and Methodists. If they worked on the land, as tenants of people like Lord Penrhyn, they had to pay, indirectly, towards the upkeep of the Church of England to which they did not belong. The quarrymen of north Wales were overwhelmingly Welsh-speaking, Nonconformist and voted Liberal in elections. This made them members of a very different world from that of Lord Penrhyn. It was a rural Welsh world in language and life-style. At the same time it had something in common with the industrial world of south Wales as we shall see in the next chapter.

4. It was not the Welshness of the dispute which made it extremely important to the British trade union movement. Lord Penrhyn was not only an old-style landowner. He was an enormously wealthy industrialist. He owned the Penrhyn quarry, one of the biggest in the world. He owned the land on which his workers' houses were built. He built and owned the tram-roads and trams which took the slate away from the quarries. He believed that since all this was his property that he should decide exactly how it should be run. In return he would provide men with jobs and some of the things, like hospitals which were important to them. But he would decide what these were.

The quarrymen did not *basically* dispute Lord Penrhyn's view that he, through his managers, should control the quarry. But without their labour, above all without their great skill, Lord Penrhyn would make no profit. And the men worked in extremely hard conditions. They wanted some say in deciding how much of a share they got of the quarry's profits, not only for the money but because it recognised the skill which made the profit. Perhaps, above all, they wanted recognition of the pride they had in that skill and that meant they wanted to control their own working conditions. They did not want interfering managers who knew much less about the rock than they did telling them how and when to work. They also did not want managers trying to end long-established customs and practices. They did not want interference with the system of 'bargaining' directly with the managers over their work for the coming month.

In many ways, then, a Welsh dispute was a modern industrial dispute, between owners and workers. The owner had enormous power because of his wealth. The quarrymen wanted to combat this power in the only possible way. Individually, they were power-less. In a Union they could fight. No wonder Lord Penrhyn was opposed to the Union.

After the Dispute

The Penrhyn lock-out in the end meant defeat for everybody. At this time, the coal industry in south Wales was still prosperous and expanding. Many people from Gwynedd who would once have gone into the slate industry went south to Glamorgan and Gwent to look for work. The slate industry never recovered. The war of 1914-18 caused a great slump in demand for slate. Can you think why?

Slate is not used on a big scale today. Why is this? In 1918 there was 500 times less slate being produced in Wales than in 1898. In 1973 an industry which once produced 500,000 tons of slate produced only 20,000 tons. Of the two great slate quarries, Dinorwic has closed—in 1969-71. Penrhyn is only a shadow of the quarry which was once the greatest slate quarry in the world. There is another irony. In the area of Wales which once depended so desperately for employment and prosperity on its great slate quarries it is now difficult to find men to work in the quarries which remain. Why should this be?

Work on the Evidence

Source 1: From the evidence in the map what do you think were (a) the advantages (b) the problems in developing an important trade in slate both in Britain and abroad?

Source 5: On the evidence of this photograph what industries, other than slate, would have benefited from the growth in the slate trade?

Source 9: Using just this photograph as evidence, make a list of any difficulties you can think of in producing roofing slates.

Source 16: What does this document tell you about life in a slate quarry—directly and indirectly?

Source 17: Imagine yourself doing this job. On the basis of what you have read so far how would you have liked it?

Source 21: How many tools are there in this photograph? Using source 22 describe what each of them was used for.

Source 23: What does this photograph tell us about quarrymen?

Source 26: This is an extract from a novel. Is it reasonable to use it as a source for a history book? Why? Can you think of any weaknesses it might have as an historical source?

Source 27: Why do you think the hours of work per day varied?

Source 28: What further information would you like about the medical officers to help you decide how much you could rely on their judgement?

Source 35: Why might a poem be good historical evidence?

Source 38: Colonel Pennant obviously does not like the idea of a quarrymen's union. How does he get this dislike across to the men?

Source 41: Can you detect any evidence of bias in this document?

Source 43: What information would it be useful to have about Robert Jones and John Williams before using this document?

Source 45: What evidence is there of bias in this source, if any?

Source 47: On the basis of this document what would you say was the attitude of Pennant to
(a) the quarrymen generally
(b) the quarrymen's union?

Source 51: What specialist words are there in this document which you would need to understand before making full use of it? What does the document tell you about the way information was communicated in 1897?

Source 54: Would you regard the information given in this document as reliable? Why?

Source 56: Why do you think there is a reference here to 'old men' suffering in the dispute? Source 41 should provide you with the answer.

Source 57: What information does this document give about Welsh society around 1900?

Source 59: What would you need to know about
(a) the writer of the article
(b) the owner of the paper
before using this as evidence?

Source 60: Compare this photograph with source 23. What statements could you make about the strike committee as a result of this comparison?

Source 61: Would you expect this source to be biased? Why?

Source 63: On the basis of this document what would you say about the attitude of the *Cambrian News* to the strike?

Source 67: What accusations are being made here? Would you accept these at face value? Why?

Tonypandy 1910-1911

Introduction

Can you think of any similarities or differences which there might be between the slate industry and the coal industry? Some of these similarities and differences will become evident as we go on to look at the coal industry. But make a list at this stage. A list of *any* length will be useful.

Do you remember those rows of terraced houses pictured in source 3? They needed large amounts of slate from north Wales to roof them. In houses like this lived the thousands upon thousands who mined coal from under the barren ground of the south Wales valleys. We have been discussing the two largest slate quarries in the world at the end of the 19th century. If it was slate which made north-west Wales an important part of the world's economic life it was coal which made Wales one of the most important countries in the world at the same time. This is something which we find almost impossible to imagine now. It is as if Wales were now to find that somewhere deep in the rock beneath there was a vast oilfield similar to those in the North Sea. What do you think the consequences would be for the people of Wales if there was such a discovery? Do you think they would all be good ones?

* * *

One fine Sunday afternoon in 1765 James Watt went out for a walk in Glasgow. By the time he came back from that walk he had worked out in his own mind one of the most important inventions of the industrial revolution. There was already a steam engine in existence, but it was a low-pressure engine. This meant that it did not produce much power. If only all the enormous power available as water was converted to steam could be harnessed then engines powerful almost beyond imagination, working at speeds beyond imagination, could replace the slow, ponderous, inefficient low-pressure engines. James Watt designed such an engine.

In doing so, he had as great an influence on the history of Wales as anyone has done. In one sense it was Wales which allowed Watt to produce his engine. In very simple terms a steam engine works by the pressure of steam in a cylinder pushing a piston which fits tightly into that cylinder. Can you think of any *mechanical* problem which would make it difficult to change a low-pressure into a high-pressure engine?

Watt's steam engine needed iron cylinders bored so accurately that the high pressure steam could not escape. He tried various iron-works; none of them had the skill to do the job. For a long time there was a *design* but it could not be made. Then, finally, from Bersham, near Wrexham in north Wales, from ironmasters named Wilkinson, came the answer. They succeeded in making cylinders to Watt's specification. Wales had changed the world. Now the world proceeded to change Wales because the fuel for this steam engine was coal.

Demand for coal was increasing anyway. As the population increased so did demand for coal to heat houses. The iron industries and the other metal industries needed coal to fuel their furnaces. But the high pressure steam engine was a vital breakthrough. Steam engines could work all kinds of machinery. If you built a carriage, of the kind pulled by horses, round a steam-engine and put it on rails you had a railway engine. From the 1840s the transport of goods and people was revolutionised all over Britain, and eventually all over the world. Steam engines moved goods and people at a speed previously undreamed of; it was coal which produced the steam. Steam engines placed in ships which had previously been propelled by sail changed the whole nature of the British shipping fleet—merchant navy and royal navy. It was the biggest fleet of ships in the world, trading with the most widespread empire the world has ever known. It was mainly Welsh coal which fuelled these ships.

The South Wales Coalfield

Most of this coal came from the south Wales coalfield, though there was a smaller coalfield in north-east Wales also. It was in south Wales that the coal ideally suited to fuelling steam engines could be found. The result was that for more than half a century Wales was one of the centres of the world's economy. Underneath the poor soil of the south Wales valleys there was black gold. Wales grew rich as a result. Some, of course, grew richer than others.

By 1874 the south Wales coalfield was producing 16½ million tons of coal. There were pits all over the coalfield but the most famous of the coal valleys was the Rhondda valley. The coal here was deep in the ground and difficult to mine but it was some of the best steam coal in

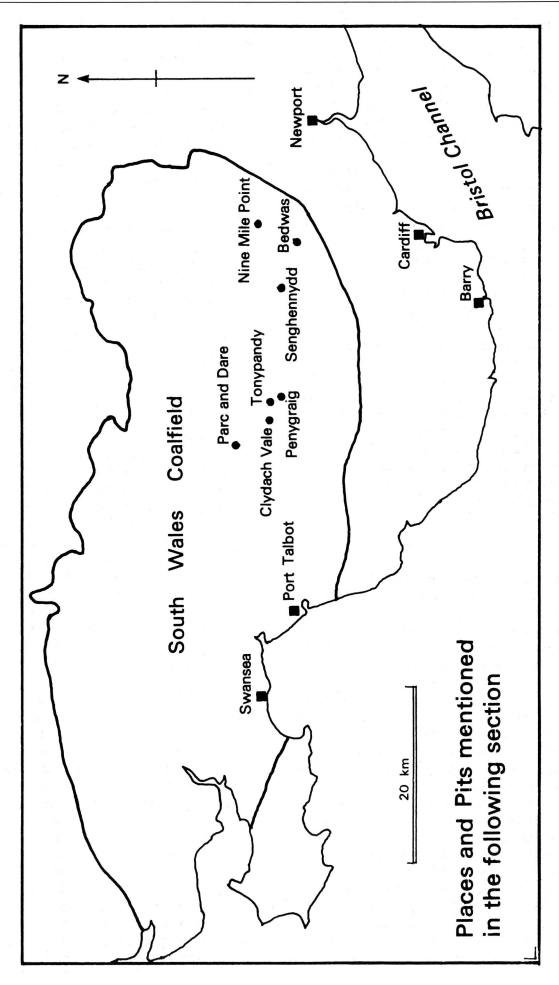

South Wales Coalfield

Newport

Bristol Channel

Cardiff

Barry

Nine Mile Point

Bedwas

Senghennydd

Parc and Dare

Tonypandy

Clydach Vale

Penygraig

Port Talbot

Swansea

20 km

Places and Pits mentioned in the following section

the world. The difficulties of mining and transporting the coal to the expanding port of Cardiff were overcome. By 1913 south Wales produced 20% of British coal. Almost a third of the total world exports in coal came from south Wales. There were 485 collieries in Wales. 323 of these were in Glamorgan. Over a quarter of a million men worked in Welsh collieries. 41,000 worked in the Rhondda mines. In these Rhondda mines coal production went up from 5½ million tons in 1885 to over 9½ million tons in 1913. The population of Rhondda at the time of the Tonypandy troubles was over 150,000 (152,781 in 1911).

The people who owned the coal mines of south Wales made fortunes. Not all the people who had put their money into opening coalmines in the early 19th century had succeeded but some were lucky. One who was lucky was Samuel Thomas, a grocer in Merthyr. His son, D. A. Thomas built up a great coal empire. He controlled the Cambrian collieries in Clydach Vale, the pits of the Glamorgan Coal Company in Llwynypia, four pits in Penygraig and Tonypandy and the Britannic Merthyr Colliery in Gilfach Goch. Together these pits made up the Cambrian Combine. It produced about half Rhondda's coal. About 12,000 men worked in D. A. Thomas's collieries. His Cambrian Combine was important not only to Britain's trade but also to the world's trade.

One of the pits which was part of this Cambrian Combine was the Ely pit in Tonypandy. Eight hundred men were employed here. On 1st September, 1910 they were locked out from their work because of a pay dispute. The troubles in Tonypandy had begun.

*   *   *

Look at these pictures of Tonypandy at the time—sources 70, 71.

What kind of community do these photographs suggest to you? Can you see any evidence which suggests that it was a prosperous community? There was money in coal and some of that money went into places like Tonypandy, its shops and its trams, its chapels and its schools, the houses and the clothes. The coalowners and big shareholders made fortunes. They could build mansions. They had great wealth and enormous power as a result. In this they resembled Lord Penrhyn and the Assheton-Smiths in the north Wales quarrying industry. The miners who actually dug the coal and brought it to the surface did less well.

Source 70

Source: National Museum of Wales.

Source 71

Source: Cyril Batstone, *Old Rhondda in Photographs*, Stewart Williams, 1974.

Dangers of coal-mining

For one thing the miners were the people who faced the dangers of getting coal deep out of the ground—dangers of gas explosions, roof falls, accidents with trams full of coal and easily able to crush people.

Here is a description provided by someone who actually experienced conditions underground.

Source 72

The hewe   own in the mine away from the sunligl   resh air, sometimes in a temperature   90 degrees, every movement of the day in ling coal and shale dust, perspiring so abnorma y (unusually) as few men in other industries can realize; head throbbing with the almost inhuman exertion (effort); the roof, perhaps, eighteen inches low, perhaps, twenty feet high; ears constantly strained for movements in the strata on which his limbs or his life is dependent, breathing   s noxious (harmful) smells due to the ab   of any kind of sanitation, and to gases . . . subject at any moment to the terrible list of mining diseases, most common of which is the dreaded nystagmus (an eye disease), which may, if neglected, lead to insanity; liable always to wounds and death from falls of roof . . . and over and over all the sickening dread of the awful explosion . . .

Source: N. Ablett. *What we wo   and Why*, 1922.
Quoted in D. Egan, *Coal Societ* 1986.

The 'awful explosions' were all too frequent. They devastated families and communities. The horror of these situations comes home to us just a little in these accounts, written and pictorial, of terrible disasters in the late nineteenth century and early twentieth century.

Source 73

TERRIBLE COLLIERY EXPLOSION IN MONMOUTHSHIRE
LOSS OF NEARLY 300 LIVES

GREAT CONSTERNATION IN THE DISTRICT
THE MANAGER AND ENGINEER BAFFLED
RETURN OF THE EXPLORING PARTY
270 COLLIERS ENTOMBED IN THE WORKINGS

Abercarne, Wednesday night, Nine o'clock . . . It was about five minutes to twelve when the inhabitants of the valley were startled by the reverberation of three distinct explosions, which were heard for a long distance off . . . A dense volume of smoke issued from the mouth of the shaft and fierce flames were clearly distinguishable . . . In a remarkably short space of time the roads leading to the pit were crowded with men, women, and children—wives, mothers, brothers and sisters who were hastening forward to ascertain what had really happened . . .

Searching parties were without delay then formed . . . These gentlemen entered the cage, and were carefully let down to the bottom. But what a picture was there presented to their gaze! . . . Dead bodies lay in heaps on the roadways, dark, shapeless, charred masses, which a short time ago were moving about, animated with life. Here and there could be clearly seen the terrible results of the explosion. The brattices, of course, had been blown to pieces; overturned trams were strewed about, and by the faint light of the safety lamps could be seen, intermingled with the dead human bodies, those of the horses, who, along with the colliers, had met a fearful death . . . The first exploring party remained down a long time, and I am happy to say that in the interval a portion of the miners were enabled to make their escape. Eighty-two of the poor fellows were crowded together at the bottom of the shaft struggling with each other to get up first. Some of them were severely burned, and the fearful look which hung about their faces as they were drawn up the shaft to the open air again will perhaps never be forgotten by those who were ready and willing to help them as they left the cage . . . But the rejoicing on the part of some of those on the bank proved to be short-lived, for, alas, several of the 82 colliers, though brought up from the fiery tomb had received a shock to the system, and the after-damp had so effectively done its work, that shortly after death released them from their sufferings . . . It will thus be seen that 373 men entered the pit in the morning; 23 afterwards left work, and after the explosion seven bodies were found, while 82 colliers were rescued. The number left in the pit, upon this calculation, is, therefore, 262, and no hope whatever is entertained that they are alive. The disaster is, perhaps, the most terrible one that has happened in South Wales and Monmouthshire.''

Source: South Wales Daily News, 13 September, 1878.

Source 74 *(See page 41)*

Source 76

Eight from one house

"Eight from one house": husband, four sons, two brothers, and one brother-in-law!
Can words paint or imagination depict the desolation of the woman bereft in one stroke of her whole household. Eight coffins in one home!
The hills around were dotted with groups here and there, and in the roadways along the valley there was movement and life and colour against a background of verdant-clad mountains, bathed in sunshine; but near the colliery, and especially the mortuary, the crowd was tense, voiceless, almost motionless. The numerous lady members of the Red Cross brigade . . . busied themselves amongst the women who were waiting for news of husband, brother, father, etc., helping and comforting, and trying to console those to whom the certainty of bereavement had come.

Source: Western Mail, 16 October 1913. Printed in *Topics in Welsh History*.

Source 75

Source: National Museum of Wales.

Source 74

THE COLLIERY DISASTER AT ABERKENFIG, SOUTH WALES.

FROM SKETCHES BY OUR SPECIAL ARTIST.

GENERAL VIEW OF NORTH'S NAVIGATION COMPANY'S COLLIERIES, INCLUDING THE PARK SLIP COLLIERY.

THE HOME SECRETARY VISITING THE HOUSE OF HENRY WHITE.

CARRYING AWAY THE DEAD.

ENTRANCE TO THE PARK SLIP COLLIERY: BRINGING UP THE LAST MAN ALIVE.

Problems of Pay and Conditions

Inevitably, with such a large workforce working in such different conditions from pit to pit and with the dangers so great there were disputes over pay.

The south Wales coalfield has superb quality coal in it but it is difficult to get out. There are 'faults' or 'fractures' in the seams which make working conditions difficult and dangerous. Some of the best coal is very deep in the ground.

The coal industry was very labour intensive, especially in the difficult conditions in south Wales. About 70% of costs went on paying employees. Therefore owners and managers were very concerned to keep wages low, since this would keep overall costs low. This became even more important when there was increasing foreign competition in coal and more difficulty in selling Welsh coal. Another problem was the big differences in wages paid in different pits. Do you remember how wage rates were agreed in the quarries of north-west Wales? A similar kind of system existed in the coal industry of south Wales except for the job of actually cutting the coal. For that job miners were paid on a sliding scale. When the price of coal was high wages were high; when the price of coal fell, wages fell. Are there any jobs which are paid in this way today? What are the advantages and disadvantages? For other miners, like those employed to move and stack waste stone or those who put up the pit props, there was a bargaining system with the foreman. It is no coincidence that the Tonypandy troubles started in Ely pit in which there was a lot of waste stone. With a system like this there was bound to be trouble when men in different pits were paid such different wages.

Disputes were by no means always due to men wanting increases in pay. In 1875 the employers insisted on reducing wages. They were prepared to lock their workers out for five months in order to get their way. The miners had to go back on the owners' terms. This was when the sliding scale came in and here is an example of how it worked.

Source 77 *(See opposite column)*

(The table on p. 128 gives some idea of how much the price of coal might be in present-day money. What other information do we need before being able to judge just how much a miner's standard of living might be affected?)

Source 77

The Sliding Scale introduced in the Ocean collieries of David Davies, Llandinam, December, 1875.

When Average Price Realised per ton shall be		Wages shall be
not less than	and under	
8s 6d	9s 3d	10 per cent below the standard
9s 6d	10s 6d	5 per cent below the standard
10s 0d	10s 9d	The standard
10s 9d	11s 6d	2½ per cent above the standard
11s 6d	12s 3d	5 per cent above the standard
12s 3d	13s 0d	7½ per cent above the standard
13s 0d	13s 6d	10 per cent above the standard
13s 6d	14s 0d	13 per cent above the standard
14s 0d	14s 6d	16 per cent above the standard
14s 6d	15s 0d	19 per cent above the standard

Plus an addition of 3 per cent on the standard for every 6d in the price realised. There was no maximum, but 15 per cent below the standard was a minimum to apply whenever the price was below 8s 6d a ton. *The standard* of wages in each colliery should be at the rates paid in 1869 plus 5 per cent.

Source: Schools Council Committee for Wales: *Topics in Welsh History.*

The sliding scale created many difficulties and led to many disputes. Eventually in 1897 miners gave six months notice to their employers that the Sliding Scale should end. This led to a lock-out of the men for three months in 1898. It also led to the formation of one of the most important trade unions in Welsh history, the South Wales Miners' Federation.

In 1900 Keir Hardie was elected M.P. for Merthyr Tydfil. He belonged to the Labour Party. In 1906 six Labour M.P.s were elected for Wales. Some people in Wales were beginning to change their politics and their attitudes. Up until now there had generally been co-operation between owners and workers in the coal industry. The owner of the Cambrian Collieries, D. A. Thomas was a Liberal M.P. Miners' leaders in the South Wales Miners' Federation were usually Liberals too. They certainly championed the workers' cause, but they believed in co-operation and consultation and they were always prepared to see the coal-owners' point of view. They believed in negotiation. They did not want confrontation. There were other people in the South Wales Miners' Federation who believed just as strongly that it was no good trying to compromise with the coal owners. Can you think of reasons why they should take this view?

There was one more complication in the industry. Although the coal industry of south Wales was still of world importance when the

South Wales Miners' Federation was founded in 1898 there were growing problems. South Wales coal is not easy to mine because of difficulties in the rock and coal seams, as we have seen. The result was that the amount of coal produced by each miner was not great and when conditions underground got worse the amount miners earned got less. Also, they were normally only paid for the large pieces of coal they cut, not the small coal. But the owners could still sell the small coal. Then, in 1908, a law was passed which seems to be just what the miners should have wanted. It was the Coal Mines Regulation Act which allowed miners to work for only eight hours a day. Can you think of any reason why miners should have *resented* this law, remembering the difficulties of mining good coal? Output per man went down sharply. What do you think was the reaction of the owners?

The Dispute

The Ely colliery in Penygraig, Rhondda, was part of the giant Cambrian Combine which we have seen was owned by D. A. Thomas, the future Lord Rhondda. Managers at the colliery had decided in 1909 to work a new coal seam. When the colliers worked the seam it turned out that there was a lot of stone in the seam. If the men accepted the amount per ton of coal mined which management offered they would not earn enough to live on. From 1 September, 1910 the eighty men involved in the dispute were sacked. The 800 men who worked at the Ely pit found themselves locked out. The Cambrian Combine dispute had begun. It was to last until October, 1911.

What do you think was the reaction of miners in the other Cambrian pits? The leaders of the men's union, the South Wales Miners' Federation, advised against taking action. The men took no notice of this advice. They came out on strike in support of their locked-out colleagues.

You may remember from the work you did on the Penrhyn lock-out of 1900-1903 that the quarry management tried to break the strike. How did they do this? A similar situation could arise in the coal mines. The managers could attempt to bring in non-union labour or 'black-legs' as the miners called them. The striking miners were determined to stop this happening.

Source 78
Question: Why were the men so hostile towards the police, do you know?
Answer: Well, they weren't so bad, as I told you its the black-legging was the cause of the trouble between the workmen and the police. You know, black-legging, by them going up by there it meant then, you see, the men would be quarrelling and the police interfere that was the cause of it, black-legs.
Source: Interview with eye-witness Mr. B. Edwards, Clydach Vale, 23 vii 1973. South Wales Miners Library, University College, Swansea.

Another way in which the strikers could try to make sure that they would win was to see that no staff got into the collieries to operate the pumps which prevented flooding in the mines. In all this there was the distinct possibility that there could be trouble and that force might be used.

How was this to be prevented? The first answer for the authorities was to make sure that there were enough police in the area. 142 were stationed at Llwynypia, a quarter of a mile from Tonypandy. The chief constable of Glamorgan, Captain Lionel Lindsay, was in direct charge of them.

The "Riots"

On Monday, November 7, 1910, the trouble really started. Striking miners made sure that colliery officials did not get to their place of work. Stones were thrown at officials at the Cambrian Colliery and at mounted police. At only one colliery did the strikers have no effect. This was the Glamorgan colliery. During the evening of 7 November large numbers of strikers gathered outside the colliery gates. For about three hours around midnight there were many fights between strikers and police.

Captain Lindsay wanted reinforcements, not of police but of troops. For troops to be sent there had to be an order from the Home Secretary. The Home Secretary was Winston Churchill, the man who became Prime Minister during the second World War. The Home Office received a telegram from Lindsay at 10 a.m. on 8 November. Lindsay asked for cavalry and infantry to be sent.

Source 79
All the Cambrian collieries menaced last night. The Llwynypia Colliery savagely attacked by large crowd of strikers. Many

casualties on both sides. Am expecting two companies of infantry and 200 cavalry today . . . Position grave.

Source: Reproduced in David Smith, 'From Riot to Revolt: Tonypandy and the *Miners' Next Step'* in T. Herbert and G. E. Jones, eds., *Welsh History and its Sources: Wales 1880-1914* (Open University in Wales Pilot Project, 1983).

Churchill refused this request. What he did was this.

Source 80

Your request for military. Infantry should not be used till all other means have failed. Following arrangements have therefore been made. 10 mounted constables and 200 foot constables of Metropolitan Police will come to Pontypridd by special train . . . Expect these forces will be sufficient, but as further precautionary measure 200 cavalry will be moved into the district tonight and remain there pending cessation of trouble. Infantry meanwhile will be at Swindon. General Macready will command the military . . . (who) . . . will not however be available unless it is clear that the police reinforcements are unable to cope with the situation.

(Telegram from Churchill to Lindsay, sent at 1.30 p.m. on 8th November).

Source: Open University in Wales Pilot Project, *Wales 1880-1914.*

This was how these events were reported in a newspaper.

Source 81 *(See opposite column)*

On the afternoon of November 8, 1910, there was another big demonstration outside the Glamorgan Colliery, involving between 7,000 and 9,000 strikers. The demonstrators threw stones at the machinery which was pumping the water out of the colliery. There was fighting between the crowd and the 120 police who were present. From about 6.00 p.m. on the evening of 8 November there was serious fighting. At 7.45 p.m. the paid magistrate for Pontypridd and Rhondda, Daniel Lleufer Thomas, sent a telegram to the Home Office.

Source 82

Police cannot cope with rioters at Llwynypia, Rhondda Valley. Troops at Cardiff absolutely necessary for further protection. Will you order them to proceed forthwith.

Source: Open University in Wales Pilot Project, *Wales 1880-1914.*

The police had to return to base to regroup so that between 8.00 p.m. and 10 p.m. there was

Source 81

THE WAR OFFICE AND THE CAVALRY.

ORDERS FOR THE MEN TO BE DETAINED AT CARDIFF.

TO BE READY IN CASE THEIR PRESENCE SHOULD BE WANTED!!

ONE SQUADRON LEAVES FOR THE RHONDDA.

METROPOLITAN POLICE SENT ON TO PONTYPRIDD.

The following official statement was issued from the Home Office on Tuesday night:—

A request was addressed last night by the chief-constable of Glamorgan to the local military authorities for the assistance of 200 cavalry and two companies of infantry in keeping order in the Cambrian Collieries.

The Home Secretary, in consultation with Mr. Haldane, decided to send instead a contingent of the Metropolitan police, consisting of 70 mounted and 200 foot constables, to the district to carry out the instructions of the chief-constable, under their own officers. This force was sent by special trains, and will arrive in the early evening.

In the meanwhile, the cavalry and infantry which had been despatched in response to the chief-constable's request have with his concurrence, been detained—the infantry at Swindon and the cavalry at Cardiff, where they will remain for a few days in case their presence should prove to be necessary.

CAVALRY AT CARDIFF.

ANIMATED SCENES AT THE RAILWAY STATION.

The Great Western Railway station at Cardiff on Tuesday evening presented the appearance of an Army headquarters on a minia-

the officers arriving by each train. They all immediately waited upon General Macready, and at one time eight were in the stationmaster's room, the consultation lasting until eight o'clock. A quartermaster-sergeant of the Welsh Regiment from Cardiff Barracks was in attendance the whole time, and there were also a number of orderlies.

The railway officials were also present in full force, among them being Mr. J. J. Leaning, divisional superintendent; Mr. J. Carter, assistant divisional superintendent; Mr Hulin, the stationmaster, &c., while an interested attendant was Mr. C. A. G. Pullin, Mr. D. A. Thomas's private secretary.

When the Hussars arrived the orders for the officer commanding were that he must not proceed further than Cardiff until he received a communication from the War Office. He was also informed by telegram that General Macready was on his way from London to command operations.

It was very evident that even General Macready was under orders not to proceed further than Cardiff until receiving instructions from the War Office.

By the 7.30 train another batch of officers arrived from Bristol, and after acquainting the general of the fact they left the station.

At 8.3 the first contingent consisting of 200 foot police arrived from London. These men were under the charge of Superintendent Powell, and an hour and a half later a special arrived with 100 men and their horses. These forces were immediately despatched

Source: Glamorgan Record Office. Reproduced in D. Egan, *Coal Society*, Gomer Press, 1986.

virtually no police opposition in Tonypandy. At 8.10 p.m. the Home Secretary responded to the magistrate's telegram by himself sending a telegram to General Macready who was in command of the troops on standby.

Source 83

As the situation appears to have become more serious you should if the Chief Constable . . . desires it move all the cavalry into the disturbed district without delay.

Source: Open University in Wales Pilot Project, *Wales 1880-1914.*

The troops were soon in Rhondda to stay, as this photograph taken later in 1910 shows.

Source 84

Source: Cyril Batstone, *Old Rhondda.*

Between 7.00 p.m. and 8.00 p.m. a large group—'thousands' according to the *Western Mail* newspaper—moved off from the colliery to the station in Tonypandy. This took them down the main street. Here is how one eyewitness remembers what happened.

Source 85

They came down into the square. Well a short time after that there appeared on the square an Inspector or something of police on a horseback, and he had a paper and he read the Riot Act. But before he could get very far, somebody threw a brick, and this being the Pandy Inn, and in between the Pandy Inn and this shop was a little passageway, into this fairground, and somebody threw a stone or half a brick or something and caught this Inspector clean under the ear. And that was the man who was killed, you see.

*　　　*　　　*

Well then they smashed this shop here, J. O. Jones a millinery shop, that was on the other corner, they smashed the windows there. We saw that being smashed and the next door to the millinery J. O. Jones, there was a shop and they smashed the window there. Next to that was the De Winton Hotel you see. Well the windows were pretty small there and quite a number went into the De Winton Hotel. But on the other side here, there was Richards the Chemist, the Chemist Shop is still there, who owns it now I don't know, you see, but they smashed that. And they smashed the windows of those three small shops here, one was a greengrocer, the other one was fancy goods and the other one was a barbers shop, and I know the name of the barber quite well, it was Salter. Because we used to think it swanky to go to Salters to have a hair cut, you see. Then they smashed Richard the Chemist, then there was the boot shop next door to it, and that was a

great shop at that time, because they put up all the football results in the window of all the local teams, like Rhondda United, the All Blacks, the team from Lewis Merthyr, football team down there, a great side, amateur side of course. And next to that there was Watkin the flannel merchant had a shop you see, they smashed that and they stole the shoes out of Boots, flannel out of Watkins, and greengrocery well they only picked up there. Well next to that there was a few steps up and there was a dentist and one or two private houses. Well they didn't smash. We didn't see anything that happened below the bridge, because we couldn't because we were afraid to go down there in front of the crowd. But we ran up to Clydach Road you see and on the way up my mother and sister of the other chap who was with me, who is dead today, were coming down to look for us. They knew where we were you see, coming down to look for us. Well keeping this New Inn, it was a very big pub. *Question:* Just one thing I want to ask you there. How many men were actually taking part in this smashing of shops and looting?

Oh there was a huge crowd.

Source: Interview with Mr. Bryn Lewis, Cardiff. 28 January, 1973. South Wales Miners' Library, University College of Swansea.

Source 86

Source: South Wales Miners' Library, University College, Swansea.

There can be no question that on the evening of November 8, 1910 there was fighting, looting and smashing of shop windows in Tonypandy. What is far more difficult is to be sure of the exact sequence of events. Far more difficult still is to be sure of who was responsible. Most difficult of all is to decide why these events took place.

We have already tested the memory of someone who was actually there at the time. Let us look now at some more accounts. Here is the assessment of the commander of the troops who were ordered into the Rhondda, General Macready.

Source 87

Investigations on the spot convinced me that the original reports regarding the attacks on the mines on November 8th had been exaggerated (by the police). What were described as "desperate attempts" to sack the power house at Llwynypia proved to have been an attempt to force the gateway . . . and a good deal of stone throwing . . . and had the mob been as numerous or so determined as the reports implied, there was nothing to have prevented them from overrunning the whole premises. That they did not was due less to the action of the police than to the want of leading or inclination to proceed to extremities on the part of the strikers.

Source: General Macready, *Annals of an Active Life*, Vol. 1, 1924. Quoted in Open University in Wales Pilot Project, *Wales 1880-1914.*

We have an eyewitness account from one of the policemen involved, though he was recalling the event many years later.

Source 88

Yes, yes, they were trying to get in on the colliery premises to wreck the colliery premises. Well this went on for some hours, the same thing went on again the next day, in the afternoon and again in the night. Then on the third night it was really hell. We had a terrible job there, driving them back to the Square, well we only could get them as far as the Square. On that night then, that was the night they wrecked all the shops, buildings there. One shop in particular they skint it out, that was Mr. T. P. Jenkin's shop, drapers shop, gents and one thing and another. There they were then parading about there, white waistcoats, top hats and God knows what, like a lot of showmen. And the whole of the time we could do nothing about it, we could not drive them further than the square. They drove us back every time. And on this night, they ripped down all the hoardings, the boarding that was running from the bottom, by the Thistle Hotel, the bottom of Tonypandy Square, right up to the Colliery entrances. Boardings about nine feet high, enclosing the colliery you see. Well they pulled all these and ripped them up in the roadway, so that stopped all traffic and it stopped us. Well after that night there then, when it did quieten down, oh it took us till the early part of the morning to clear the road. Well on that night the Bristol Police were there, and the stones were coming down so thick and heavy that we had to crouch down under some little offices that was running alongside the entrances. And amongst us Glamorgan boys there then, the British Police were the other side of the entrance, but on them rushing back into the entrance to the colliery from the stones, the Inspector that was in charge of them, Inspector Rendall, Bristol City Police, instead of him turning left, he turned right and came into our group. And his men were the other side of the entrance. Well he was anxious to get back to his own men but we persuaded him not to, stay until the stones eased down a bit. So it did seem to ease down a little bit and he said, "I'm going", although P.C. Evans and myself we did our best to try and stop him from going across, the stones were still flying down. But he had hardly gone two paces before one caught him at the back of the head and down he went. Well we had to go and rescue him then and we carried him into the engine-room, down in the Colliery premises. We waited and eventually an ambulance did come but before he got to hospital he died. Big fine fellow, well that was the first casualty.

Source: Interview with W. Knipe, 2 February, 1973. South Wales Miners' Library.

We also have the account written by David Evans and published only one year afterwards.

Source 89

Immediately after the repulse of the attack on the Glamorgan colliery came the sack of Tonypandy . . . In their flight from Llwynypia, and under the impression that the victorious police were still at their heels, the rioters, desperate at the defeat of their plans to take the colliery, gave vent to their rage by smashing the windows of every shop that came within reach.

Source: David Evans, *Labour Strife in the South Wales Coalfield*, 1911.

There are newspaper accounts. Here is one from the *Western Mail* of 9 November, 1910.

Source 90 *(See page 47)*

The modern historian who has investigated the Tonypandy riots most fully provides this account of what happened. He includes some information from primary sources.

Source 91

The crowd which stoned windows after 8.00 p.m. did so to a "stop and start" pattern of whistling, so that "the absence of the police and other important events" were "notified by members of the apparently inoffensive crowd to the aggressors". Dummies and finery, silks and top hats, were thrown on to the road in contempt or worn in mockery. Jars of sweets, cigarettes, pans of ice cream and packets of tobacco were scattered around and raided by children. Sixty-three shops were damaged. Some were completely ransacked—J. W. Richards, chemist; J. Owen Jones, draper and milliner; J. Haydn Jones, gents' outfitter; T. P. Jenkins, draper; M. A. Phillips, gents' clothier;

Source 90

MAD SCENES IN THE RHONDDA.

DESPERATE ONSLAUGHTS BY STRIKERS.

CHARGE AFTER CHARGE BY THE POLICE.

SERIOUS INJURIES ON BOTH SIDES.

CROWDS WREAK VENGEANCE ON BUSINESS HOUSES.

After ominous murmurings and mutterings during the day the Cambrian Combine strikers again broke into a mad din of riot as soon as darkness fell last evening. Desperate onslaughts were made by the miners upon the police, who replied with equally desperate baton charges. Stormy scenes likewise occurred at Aberdare, where many strikers were wounded and also some police. Pitched battles of a furious character took place in both the Rhondda and Aberdare Valleys.

And meanwhile where were the military? Someone had bungled! If the soldiers had been hurried on to the affected area yesterday morning there would have been no strife at night. Mr. D. Lleufer Thomas, stipendiary magistrate, was in attendance all day at the Thistle Hotel, Llwynypia, to read the Riot Act, if necessary, but the troops did not arrive.

The strikers seemed to recognise that this was their last chance, and such shouts were heard as, " Come on, boys, we'll make the fight of our lives to-night. The military will be here to-morrow, and they'll stop us with their guns. We can beat the police, who have only their batons." Others were heard to say that they would not occupy the places of the police that night for all the gold in the world, but, as a matter of fact, the advantage in the fighting was always with the protectors of law and order, from whom the mob fled helter-skelter at every charge.

In their numerous rushes the police were no respecters of persons, and for this they could not be blamed, because in the darkness they could hardly be expected to pick and choose their victims. Thus, any male person who came within reach of their batons received stunning blows on the head, and after the officers had retired from each charge men and youths were left lying in the roadway till their friends crept up in the darkness and carried them away to the surgery of Drs. Morgan, Jones, and Morgan, the medical attendants to the Cambrian workmen.

The valuable power-house was made a special mark of. This contains £25,000 worth of machinery, and there were repeated appeals to the police from within to put a stop to the stone-throwing, as there was constant fear of serious damage being done.

Eventually finding the power-station an unassailable point, the crowd ran riot in the town of Tonypandy itself. General destruction of shop windows and looting followed, particular attention being paid to clothiers', chemists', and tobacconists' shops. Charge after charge was made by the police through the main streets, and the mob were scattered in all directions.

BATTLE SCENES.

STRIKERS' MAD RUSHES IN THE RHONDDA.

[BY OUR OWN CORRESPONDENT.]

MID-RHONDDA, Tuesday Night.
Mid-Rhondda is in a state of anarchy. Such scenes as those witnessed to-night are almost …

WESTERN MAIL. WEDNESDAY. NOVEMBER 9. 1910.

PRESENCE OF MILITARY NEEDED

ARRIVAL OF LONDON POLICE.

A HOPE OF SETTLEMENT.

RIOTING AT ABERDARE.

ATTACK ON POWER STATION.

DRIVEN BACK BY POLICE.

A FUSILLADE OF STONES.

MEN, WOMEN, CHILDREN IN CANAL.

OVER SIXTY PERSONS INJURED.

[BY OUR OWN CORRESPONDENT.]

SCENES IN A SURGERY.

VISITS OF WOUNDED MEN BY THE SCORE.

J. R. Evans, draper; and four refreshment houses, including two owned by the Bracchi Bros. whose name became eponymous for all Italian cafés in south Wales. Butchers, grocers, furniture shops and others suffered less or minor damage. T. P. Jenkins, the magistrate whose shop was the first to go, said that the crowd made "wild threats both in Welsh and English and then went on their work of destruction". The windows of the twinned draper shops of Mr. and Mrs. Phillips were knocked in at 7.45 p.m. The crowd returned at 9.15 p.m. and systematically broke all the windows as they tore apart the shop, which they had illuminated by lighting the gas jets. Mrs. Phillips told an outraged reporter for the drapers' profession:

People were seen inside the counter handing goods out. They were afterwards walking on the Square wearing various articles of clothing which had been stolen and asking each other how they looked. They were not a bit ashamed, and they actually had the audacity to see how things fitted them in the shop itself. They were in the shop somewhere about three hours and women were as bad as men . . . Everything was done openly and the din was something horrible.

One outfitters was completely denuded of its extensive stock of mufflers. At 10.00 p.m., and although the recently-arrived Metropolitan police were housed in the skating-rink only one hundred yards away, Haydn Jones's drapery, already "smashed to atoms", was now further reduced as "collars, straw hats, braces and caps were passed from hand to hand openly in the street and exchanges were indulged in between the looters".

Source: David Smith, 'Tonypandy 1910: Definitions of Community' in *Past and Present*, No. 87, May 1980.

One shop was not touched. It was a chemist's shop belonging to a famous rugby international, Willie Llewellyn. He had played for Wales in one of the most famous games of all time when, in 1905, Wales beat the New Zealand 'All Blacks'. Other chemists' shops were damaged.

Does this suggest anything to you about the rioting?

Finally, we have the evidence of photographs. Here is the scene after the riots, with shops boarded up.

Source 92

Source 93

Source: Cyril Batstone.

Source 94

Source: National Museum of Wales.

We can see now, therefore, that there were two parts to the troubles in Tonypandy in 1910 even though they were closely connected. There was the dispute and the violence connected with it over work and wages in the collieries. There was also the rioting and smashing of shops. We have looked at some of the reasons why the colliery dispute occurred. But why did the crowds in Tonypandy attack the shops on the night of November 8, 1910? Before you read on can *you* think of any reasons which might account for this? Then you can see whether the evidence supports those ideas or not.

Obviously the mood of the crowd was tense on 7 and 8 November. We have evidence of this from the commander of the troops who was soon to be on the scene. It is interesting, incidentally, to see who he blamed for producing the tension.

Source 95
A factor which greatly contributed towards maintaining and developing the atmosphere of tension and excitement in the strike areas was the attitude of the local press. I ascertained that the confidential secretary of one of the principal mine managers had been a newspaper reporter, and was the instigator of much of the highly coloured propaganda that was being scattered broadcast to prejudice the public mind. A threat to deport the gentleman

from the area had the desired effect of curbing his activities in this direction . . .

   *   *   *

There was no difficulty in obtaining the point of view of the employers, for I had not been many hours in the locality before I was inundated with information and advice as to what I should do, all tending towards one conclusion. viz. that the employers were entirely blameless for what was occurring, and that the men should be coerced into submission by force . . .
Source: General Macready, *Annals of an Active Life*, London, 1924. Printed in *Topics in Welsh History.*

Was it then that a tense and excited crowd just got out of hand and damaged property for the sake of it? Certainly there were youngsters celebrating the event in Tonypandy streets a week later as they sang:

Source 96

Every nice girl loves a collier
In the Rhondda valley war
Every nice girl loves a striker
And you know what strikers are
In Tonypandy they're very handy
With their sticks and their stones and boot
Walking down the street with Jane
Breaking every window pane
Thats loot! Pom pom. That's loot!

Source: South Wales Daily News, 24 November, 1910. Quoted in David Smith, *Past and Present,* May 1980.

This was a useful explanation for the 'respectable' people in the Rhondda and outside who wanted to explain the whole thing away because they felt embarrassed by it.

Source 97

For the editor of the Rhondda's newspaper the riots, instigated and carried out by thoughtless youths and women from further afield, "the mania for loot strong upon them", meant that "a national obloquy has come upon Wales through the roughness of the times". "Tonypandy", he wailed, "is no longer an unknown township . . . The pity of it all is that Tonypandy has to bear the brunt of the defamation and for years the ill repute will stick to it".

Source: David Smith, *Past and Present*, May 1980.

If this was a blot on the good name of the Rhondda it was also felt to be a blot on the good name of Wales. The popular view of Wales which Welshmen like magistrate Daniel Lleufer Thomas wanted people to have was that of a Wales in which people went to chapel, did not drink alcohol and obeyed the law. Wales, for them, was the 'land of the white gloves'— those gloves which judges put on when they had no serious cases to try at the assizes. Wales was a country in which only six years before the Tonypandy riots one of the greatest religious revivals had taken place. There were half a million chapel members in Wales and many more people who were not members attended chapel regularly. If respectable Wales was the true Wales the riots would have to be explained away. One way of doing this was to make it seem as if the riots were the work of a small number of drunken louts.

Source 98

From all responsible quarters, with concerned clergymen, editors and even local tradesmen agreeing, came the concerted view that the shops had been smashed by "a gang of about 150, chiefly youths and men let loose from the public houses" or was "the work of . . . not one hundred . . . many . . . were strangers" and, combining both, "half-drunken, irresponsible persons . . . from outside the . . . district . . . the mad outbreak of 150". This verbal diminution of a crowd of thousands as well as the shuffling aside of the violent events of the nights of 7th and 8th November outside the colliery itself is inextricably related to what was the apparently unacceptable though that a very large number of people had been actively involved in the destruction of Tonypandy's commercial life. Instead a tirade of arraignment was directed against the outcast groups of youths, drunks and strangers. Youths there certainly were (around 14 per cent of the entire mining work-force in the coalfield was under sixteen years of age) but those same youths who stoned the Glamorgan Colliery were also rescued from the clutches of the police by "young men of apparently from twenty to thirty years of age". Men in drink there were, too, though the fact that the magistrate had closed the pubs early (at dusk) might have kept some from being drunk, while the bulk of the crowd had been at a mass meeting in the afternoon or on the streets for hours.

Source: David Smith, *Past and Present*, May, 1980.

Another way to get across the idea that this was not typical of Wales was to blame a small number of people who were socialist, who were not members of the Liberal party for which most people in Wales voted.

Source 99

'The impression conveyed to my mind in regard to the action of the strikers themselves throughout those disturbances, and the motives for rioting, is that the doctrine of extreme socialism preached by a small but energetic section is entirely responsible for the premeditated attempts to destroy property.'

Source: General Macready, *Memorandum* to Home Office, January 1911. Printed in Open University in Wales, *Wales 1880-1914.*

The voice of authority and respectability comes through loud and clear from magistrate Daniel Lleufer Thomas. Violence was not 'respectable' and was 'reprehensible'.

Source 100

I want to say, clearly and emphatically, as a believer in trades unionism, that the state of things which has prevailed in mid-Rhondda, the violence which has been resorted to under the pretence of peaceful persuasion, the treatment as blacklegs of men who were not blacklegs in the ordinary sense of the term, or who would be so regarded by the Executive of any respectable trades union, the too ready acceptance by responsible leaders of the doctrine that the end justified the means, even though the means included rioting, assaults on the police, intimidation, and violence practised on so-called 'officials' or permanent workers engaged in keeping the mines open, the degradation of the women-folk by allowing them to take a leading part in these and like acts of violence—all these constitute a serious indictment against trades union organisations in the district and in the South Wales coalfield. Nor is there any use disguising the fact that there is a widespread impression that the trades union concerned—the South Wales

Miners' Federation—has willingly or unwillingly thrown its cloak, so to speak, over these reprehensible actions, so that, instead of punishing within its own ranks those who disgrace the labour cause by such conduct, it used its trust funds, not merely for the defence of offenders, but for the payment of the penalties imposed upon them, even in cases where no substantial denial of the offence was put forward.

Source: Comments of Stipendiary Magistrate when passing sentence on men convicted of intimidation, October 4, 1911.

It was from official statements like this that there came great pressure on the Liberal members of the South Wales Miners' Federation to oppose the use of violence. Perhaps we should use a stronger word than 'pressure'. What would you suggest?

Source 101

But it is a question of the utmost public interest whether a body is habitually stepping into the breach to shield those who are found guilty of violence and intimidation from the consequences of their guilt, and, by paying their fines, relieving them of the punishment which the Court and the law intends should be borne by the offenders themselves. Any such systematic shifting of the penalty from the right shoulders to those of some other public body will inevitably result in my not giving the option of a fine in cases of assault, intimidation, or the like offence, but in sentencing those convicted to a term of imprisonment without such an option.

Source: Stipendiary Magistrate's statement, 1911.

Socialists looked at things in a rather different way. They emphasised a Wales in which they saw poverty, bad health, grim housing conditions, bad sanitation, extremely dangerous working conditions. Study this photograph of Tonypandy, taken just after the riots.

Source 102 *See bottom of page)*

We have seen that the coal industry in Wales was of world importance. Such an industry produces wealth. Some of that wealth went into the homes and communities of the valleys of south Wales. There was not, at this time, desperate poverty for most of the population in and around Tonypandy. But what wealth there was was not evenly distributed. Miners had to work in difficult and dangerous conditions to earn their money. They were not the only people who worked hard. Shop assistants often worked for eighty hours and more a week.

For the miners and the shop assistants, especially in bad times, poverty was *relative*, that is they did not have anything like enough money to buy the clothes and the goods which were plentiful in the shops. One answer, in the

Source 102

Source: Cyril Batstone.

years before the Tonypandy riots was to go into debt to the shopkeepers. Here is an account, written in 1969, of a grocer's shop which gave credit.

Source 103

'We lived for years behind and above our busy shop; a living room, pantry and scullery behind, three bedrooms above. It was a 'credit' shop and a history of family fortunes. On a lectern desk panelled with a frosted glass screen lay an enormous black ledger, six inches thick, a double page for each customer. Its chronicle of strike-time debts was my mother's bible and bane . . .'

Source: Rhys Davies's autobiography, *Print of a Hare's Foot,* 1969.

If people were in debt to shopkeepers what do you think their attitude to shopkeepers might be? And what would be the attitude of shop-keepers to the debtors? We might remember, too, that some the shopowners were wealthy and this gave them a lot of power in the community. Many shopowners owned houses as well and they rented these houses to tenants. It was not always just a straightforward deal.

Source 104

'There are . . . cases in respect of whom the inspectors are informed that houses are only obtainable on certain conditions, such as an undertaking or promise on the part of the incoming tenant to purchase goods such as furniture or groceries from the owners. Some house-owners . . . object to tenants with many children, while some provision merchants are said to prefer tenants with large families, because every additional child helps to swell the bill for provisions.'

Source: Report of Mr. J. D. Jenkins, Medical Officer of Health for Rhondda, July 1911. Printed in Open University in Wales, *Wales 1880-1914.*

Does the evidence of sources 103 and 104 suggest to you that the smashing of shop windows and the looting of shops may have been more than the efforts of a small, drunken group. If so, why?

Someone who was to become one of the best-known of Welsh trade-unionists believed that events in Tonypandy were far more than the work of a small minority, drunk or sober. He thought they were part of a widespread struggle for the rights of workers.

Source 105

'I saw in action that day the vicious alliance of the Government and the coal owners, backed by police and armed troops, against miners who asked no more than a wage little over starvation level. I never forgot that lesson.'

Source: Arthur Horner in his autobiography, *Incorrigible Rebel* (1960). Printed in Open University in Wales Pilot Project, *Wales 1880-1914.*

We can be certain of one thing; the Tonypandy riots of November 1910 were not just a two-night problem which then went away. There were some more small-scale demonstrations later in 1910 and in 1911. The strike went on. There was an attempt to settle it in April 1911, but the men threw out the terms of the settlement which were no better than what they had been offered originally. As the strike went on so did the hardship—for the men, their wives and their families.

Some miners dug up coal from the hillsides. They could use it themselves or sell some for a few shillings.

Source 106 *(See page 53)*

But despite all the hardships the miners kept their sense of purpose. Their feelings are summed up in their manifesto of June, 1911.

Source 107

Through all the long dark night of years,
The people's cry ascendeth,
And earth is wet with blood and tears
But our meek sufferance endeth.
The few shall not for ever sway
The many toil in sorrow,
The powers of hell are strong today
Our kingdom comes tomorrow.

Fellow workers, we need your support in this strenuous struggle . . .
On behalf of the Cambrian Combine strikers

William John: Chairman
Councillor Noah Rees: Vice-Chairman
James Ivins: Treasurer
Councillor Mark Harcombe: Secretary

Source: E. D. Lewis, *The Rhondda Valley,* Phoenix, 1963.
Printed in *Topics in Welsh History.*

In July, 1911 the last of the mid-Rhondda riots took place at . . .

Source 108

'. . . Penygraig . . . The strikers had taken umbrage at the action of certain workmen in accepting employment at the pits of the Naval Company and marched in procession, 3,000 strong, towards Penygraig . . . One of the leaders addressed the strikers. He complained that they had been refused permission to see the blacklegs, and had been advised to see Mr.

Source 106

Source: Cyril Batstone.

Llewelyn. But they had had enough of deputations, and were determined to remain there and have an understanding with the blacklegs when they came out. By this time, a large proportion of the strikers had got completely out of hand . . . stone throwing became general, and urgent messages were sent to the police headquarters at Tonypandy for reinforcements . . . This force arrived at the Ely colliery soon after . . . and brought the total number of police . . . to over 100. Against between 3,000 and 4,000 desperate rioters spread out along the mountainside, well out of reach of the police and employed in rolling down huge boulders in the direction of the colliery, the police force was hopelessly inadequate, and it became necessary to call in the aid of the military. At 5 o'clock a company of the Somerset Light Infantry, under the command of Major Thickness, surprised the rioters by appearing in extended order on the mountain top armed with fixed bayonets and ball cartridge. They carried their rifles in their hands . . . The troops drove the rioters into the town, where they were charged and dispersed . . . The presence of the military in the district had a decisive influence on the general situation, and after their arrival the police experienced very little difficulty in clearing the streets.'

Source: David Evans, *Labour Strife in the South Wales Coalfield 1910-1911*, 1911.

All was in vain. In October 1911 the men of the Cambrian Combine returned to work. They did so on the terms which they had been offered at the beginning of the strike. These were the owners' terms.

The importance of events in Tonypandy

It might seem as if the whole episode achieved nothing, and meant nothing. That is not the case. It would hardly be remembered now if it had been of no importance.

The first way in which events in Tonypandy made an impact was that the miners were determined to take action for what they believed to be just. They believed that they were entitled to a fair deal and a greater share in the wealth which they were producing for the colliery owners. This was the battle. It was the workers against the owners. They fought this battle in Tonypandy against the advice of their Union. But the rank and file movement in Tonypandy helped to strengthen the purpose of the miners' union in Great Britain. That union called a strike in 1912 and this led to an agreement on a minimum wage for all miners.

The second effect was that some important members of the South Wales Miners' Federation were even more convinced that the old ways of co-operation and negotiation with the owners over pay and safety and conditions of work were not getting them anywhere. They believed that the South Wales Miners' Federation must change its ideas and work towards a different goal. These people, the most important of whom was Noah Ablett, distrusted leaders, especially of the moderate kind who had been against the Tonypandy strike. They distrusted also the Labour Party's idea of the government at some time taking over ownership of the mines by nationalisation. They argued that this would not give the miners direct local control.

This is how Noah Ablett put forward these ideas in a debate held in Tonypandy in November, 1912.

Source 109

'. . . the future does not lie in the direction of bureaucracy. The roadway to emancipation lies in a different direction than the offices of a Minister of Mines (operating state nationalisation). It lies in the democratic organisation, and eventually control of the industries by the workers themselves in their organised capacity as trustees for a working-class world. No minister of Mines will lead us to our emancipation. That must be the work of the workers themselves from the bottom upward, and not from the top downwards, which latter means the servile state'. (Applause).

Source: Printed in Open University in Wales Pilot Project, *Wales, 1880-1914.*

Source 110

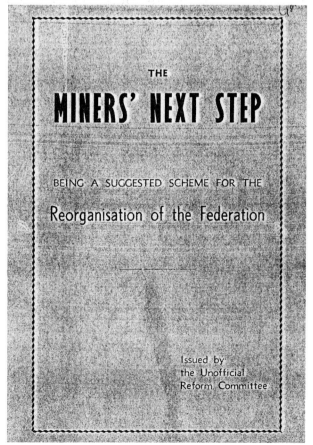

We can get a better idea of what men like Noah Ablett wanted from this pamphlet, *The Miners' Next Step.* Ablett was one of the people who wrote it and it was a very important document in the history of political and workers' ideas in Wales.

Source 111

CONCILIATION AND LEADERS

But we have here to point out why there is discontent with "leaders". The policy of conciliation gives the real power of the men into the hands of a few leaders.

The employers respect them. Why? Because they have the men—the real power—in the hollow of their hands. They, the leaders, become "gentlemen", they become M.P.s, and have considerable social prestige because of this power.

The sectional character of the organisation in the mining industry renders concerted action almost impossible, and thus every section helps to hinder and often defeat the other. What then is necessary to remedy the present evils?

PREAMBLE

I.—A united industrial organisation, which, recognising the war of interest between workers and employers, is constructed on fighting lines, allowing for a rapid and simultaneous stoppage of wheels throughout the mining industry.

II.—A constitution giving free and rapid control by the rank and file acting in such a way that conditions will be unified throughout the coalfield; so that pressure at one point would automatically affect all others and thus readily command united action and resistance.

IMMEDIATE STEPS—INDUSTRIAL

I.—That a minimum wage of 8/- per day, for all workmen employed in or about the mines, constitute a demand to be striven for nationally at once.

II.—That, subject to the foregoing having been obtained, we demand and use our power to obtain a 7 hour day.

PROGRAMME—POLITICAL

That the organisation shall engage in political action, both local and national, on the basis of complete independence of, and hostility to all capitalist parties, with an avowed policy of wresting whatever advantage it can for the working class.

Political action must go on side by side with industrial action. Such measures as the Mines Bill, Workmen's Compensation Acts, proposals for nationalising the Mines.

POLICY

I.—The old policy of identity of interest between employers and ourselves be abolished and a policy of open hostility installed.

XIII.—That a continual agitation be carried on in favour of increasing the minimum wage and shortening the hours of work, until we have extracted the whole of the employers' profits.

XIV—.That our objective be to build up an organisation that will ultimately take over the mining industry and carry it on in the interest of the workers.

THE ELIMINATION OF THE EMPLOYER

This can only be obtained gradually and in one way. We cannot get rid of employers and slave-driving in the mining industry until all other industries have organised for, and progressed towards, the same objective. Their rate of progress conditions ours. All we can do is to set an example and the pace.

Our only concern is to see to it that those who create the value receive it. And if by the force of a more perfect organisation and more militant policy we reduce profits, we shall at the same time tend to eliminate the share-holders who own the coalfield.

Our objective begins to take shape before your eyes. Every industry thoroughly organised, in the first place, to fight, to gain control of, and then to administer that industry. The co-ordination of all industries on a Central Production Board who, with a statistical department to ascertain the needs of the people, will issue its demands on the different departments of industry, leaving to the men themselves to determine under what conditions, and how, the work should be done. This would mean real democracy in real life, making for real manhood and womanhood. Any other form of democracy is a delusion and a snare.

Source: Unofficial Reform Committee, *The Miners' Next Step*, Tonypandy, 1912.

We know that the members of the South Wales Miners' Federation who wrote this did not get their way. Union leaders stayed moderate and did not take up the ideas in the pamphlet. The Miners' Federation of Great Britain and the S.W.M.F. continued to support the idea of nationalisation of the mines, nothing more. Less than three years after the end of the riots royalty visited Tonypandy. Prince and Princess Alexander of Teck had an arch of coal built for them.

Source 112 *(See page 56)*

It might seem that the strike had changed nothing. However, the third point of import-ance is that events in Tonypandy give us evidence that the way political parties and labour relations operated were very different from the way things appeared on the surface. In this Tonypandy was rather like Penrhyn. The problems which, on the surface, mattered most to the people of Wales before the first World War were those connected with the Liberal party. In 1906 all the Welsh Members of Parliament except one were Liberals. The Liberals were fighting hard for Welsh causes. They wanted justice for members of Nonconformist chapels in Wales so that, for example, they did not have to send their children to Church of England schools. They wanted Wales to be recognised as a respectable and important partner in Great Britain, needing proper recognition for the Welsh language and culture. The Liberal party was less concerned with social or working-class problems in the metal and coal-mining parts of Wales. Their M.P.s there, including miners, believed in careful, slow progress in co-operation with owners like D. A. Thomas who was a fellow Liberal M.P. The new Labour party, generally, agreed with a moderate approach and co-operated with the Liberal party. The quarrymen of Penrhyn were staunch Liberals. The first President of the South Wales Miners' Federation, in office at the time of the Tonypandy riots, was William Abraham. He was a Liberal M.P. until, in 1908, he reluctantly joined the Labour members in Parliament. Yet, despite all this, the great strike in Penrhyn and the riots in Tonypandy and the ideas contained in *The Miners' Next Step* were unlike anything in the ideas of the Liberal Party. These ideas were about oppos-ition, not agreement. Tonypandy seemed to point to a change of issues and a change in politics in Wales.

Then, finally, Tonypandy is important because people have *remembered* it as being important. People at the time and since realised that events in Tonypandy were about a basic struggle—that is, how society should be organised. Nearly 70 years after what had happened in Tonypandy, in 1978, the Prime Minister, Jim Callaghan, accused Winston Churchill, M.P., grandson of the Home Secretary at the time of the Tonypandy riots and one of the most famous Prime Ministers in British history, of carrying on his grandfather's attitude of vindictiveness towards the miners. Callaghan mentioned Tonypandy, 1910. There were angry scenes, accusations and counter-

Source 112

Source: Cyril Batstone.

accusations. B.B.C. radio had interviews with a Tory M.P., taking the side of the Churchills, and Dr. Kenneth O. Morgan was interviewed to give his view on whether Winston Churchill (Home Secretary) actually had sent troops to Tonypandy. Dr. Morgan actually gave some evidence. He quoted from the telegrams which you will have already read. (Sources 80, 83). In 1978 the Tonypandy riots of 1910 were still national news. One reason was because a famous historical personality was involved. But that, by itself, would not be enough to make news. Why do *you* think that these events in Tonypandy in 1910-11 have not been forgotten?

Further work on the evidence

Sources 70 and 71: Using just these photographs as evidence, make a list of some of the industries and trades which were operating in Tonypandy in 1910.

Sources 73-76: Just on the basis of this evidence, was coal-mining any safer in south Wales in 1900-1910 than in 1880-1890?

Source 77: What crucial piece of information is *missing* in this source? Can you think of any *kinds* of sources which might give this information?

Source 78: This is oral evidence. There are a few examples of this kind of evidence in this book. Mr. Edwards was present at the Tonypandy riots and was being interviewed about them over sixty years later. What do you think are the (a) strengths and (b) weaknesses of oral evidence such as this?

Source 79: Imagine yourself in the position of the Home Secretary receiving this telegram. What more would you want to know? How do you think you would have acted and why?

Sources 80 and 81: Compare the information given in these two sources. There is one very important point of difference. Which would you regard as more reliable? Give examples, saying whether Churchill's actions were accurately reported in the newspaper.

Source 84: The author states here: 'The troops were soon in Rhondda to stay, as this photograph taken late in 1910 shows''. Does the photograph show this?

Source 85: Compare this interview with P.C. Knipe's statement, Source 88. Would you expect Lewis and Knipe to be biased? In what way? Does this evidence on the death of a policeman agree?

Source 87: Are there any reasons why you would trust Macready's evidence? If so, what reasons might the police have for exaggerating?

Source 89: Look closely at the words Evans uses to describe events. Is there any indication of whose side he was on during this dispute?

Source 90: Before using this as a source of information about the Tonypandy riots what *further* information would it be useful to have about the reporter, the newspaper and its owner?

Source 91: What impression do you get of the riots from this passage?

Sources 92 and 93: Do these photographs tell you anything about the way photographers worked in the period around 1910?

Source 95: Remembering that General Macready was in charge of the troops used in the Rhondda, do you think you could rely on what he says here? Why?

Sources 97 and 98: Why do you think Dr. Smith uses so many quotations from primary sources here?

Source 98: Does Dr. Smith believe that the riots were the work of small number of young drunkards?

Sources 99 and 100: Do Macready and the magistrates provide the same reasons for the violence in Tonypandy?

Source 102: What is the evidence for saying that this photograph was taken soon after the riots? Are there any reasons for thinking that things were back to normal?

Sources 103 and 105: Both these extracts are taken from autobiographies. Is there any difference in the *kind* of evidence the extracts give? How much trust would you put in autobiography as evidence?

Source 108: What would you need to know about the author of this extract before using this evidence? Do you think this is a good source of evidence?

Source 111: Try to summarise in your own words the programme set out in *The Miners Next Step*.

Follow-up exercise

There were other serious riots in South Wales in 1910-11. Find out as much as you can about these. How do they compare with events in Tonypandy? Why do you think they are less well remembered?

The General Strike and Miners Lockout

Background to the Strike

Once the dispute of 1910-1911 was settled, Tonypandy and other towns in the Rhondda got back to prosperity quite quickly. This is evident from coal production figures. In 1913 the south Wales coalfield produced its record output of 56,830,000 tons.

In 1914 came the Great War which lasted until 1918. This caused some problems for the coal industry as some export markets were affected, and so many miners served in the army that there was a labour shortage. But steam coal, which was produced in the eastern part of the coalfield, was in great demand. Why do you think this was?

A few years after the end of the first World War the Welsh coal industry faced the kind of problems which would never have seemed possible in the second half of the 19th century when the industry was growing at such an incredible rate. There were two main problems, closely linked, which led to a crisis.

The first problem was that of control. Do you remember any document in the previous section on Tonypandy which shows that the problem of who should control the coal industry was very important in 1910-11? During the war there was a change in control. There were disputes between the miners and the coalowners, as there had been before the war. Because it was wartime the coalminers were in a much stronger position. Why?

The result was that in 1916 government decided to take control of the coal industry. More than this, the government decided to set up an inquiry to decide whether the state should run the industry permanently, rather than hand it back to the coalowners. The official report, known as the Sankey Commission Report, came out in 1919. You can see what it recommended.

Source 113

COAL INDUSTRY COMMISSION ACT, 1919

REPORT

BY

THE HONOURABLE MR. JUSTICE SANKEY, G.B.E. (*Chairman*).

TO THE KING'S MOST EXCELLENT MAJESTY

MAY IT PLEASE YOUR MAJESTY.

I HAVE the honour to present a further Report in pursuance of the Coal Industry Commission Act, 1919.

1. RECOMMENDATIONS

I

I recommend that Parliament be invited immediately to pass legislation acquiring the Coal Royalties for the State and paying fair and just compensation to the owners.

II

I recommend on the evidence before me that the principle of State ownership of the coal mines be accepted.

5. METHOD OF PURCHASE AND CARRYING ON OF THE COAL MINES

XXXV

It is suggested that the State should purchase all the collieries, including colliery buildings, plant, machinery, stores and other effects in and about the colliery at a fair value subject to the next paragraph.

Source: Report and Minutes of Evidence of the Royal Commission on the Coal Industry, 1919.

It seemed now the government would nationalise the mines and pay off the coal owners. Instead, in 1921, the government gave back the mines to the coalowners. The miners felt betrayed. Feeling was particularly high in the south Wales area.

By 1921 it was also beginning to become clear that the great prosperity which there had been in south Wales for so long, largely due to the ever-expanding coal industry, was threatened. From the end of 1920 foreign trade in coal was going down and this made it inevitable that unemployment would go up. The south Wales coalfield had prospered because of its superb quality steam coal, the most suitable fuel for the steamships of the British navy which had sailed the world. But coal was being replaced.

Source 114
Again, the great steamship companies, whether for passenger or cargo purposes, are steadily adopting oil fuel instead of coal. Increase in running costs has speeded up this tendency, and, despite the greater price of petroleum, steamship owners are, in view of other economies, having vessels built to burn oil. Furthermore, at the Dockers' Enquiry, and elsewhere, there have been continuous complaints about the congestion prevailing at the docks and in the harbours of this country. The building of new docks would be a long and extremely costly affair. The alternative economy is to "turn the ship round," i.e., to bring in, unload, load and send her out more expeditiously. Here, oil fuel is a god-send. The following are comparative figures regarding the "Olympic," the largest of British ships:— When using coal she had 246 stokers; now, using oil, she has sixty, twenty on each shift. When using coal, it required on each trip 300 men, working four to four and a half days, or

9,600 of labour, to coal her; now, 10 men, working for eight hours each, or 80 hours in all, can oil her. She burns 600 tons of oil a day as against 840 to 920 tons of coal.

Source: J. T. W. Newbold, *The Doom of a Coalfield*, London, 1921.

The effects were not immediate. Production in the south Wales coalfield was high until 1923 but prospects for the future were obviously not good. Two tables will help explain why.

Source 115

Best Admiralty Large, per ton, f.o.b. Cardiff.
Sept., 1920.   Nov., 1920.   Dec., 1920.
115/-, 120/-.   107/6, 115/-.   95/-, 115/-.
Jan., 1921.   Aug., 1921.
57/6, 85/-.   32/6, 45/-.

No. 3 Rhondda Large, per ton, f.o.b. Cardiff.
Aug., 1920.   Nov., 1920.   Dec., 1920.
112/6, 115/-.   110/-, 115/-.   110/-,115/-.
Jan., 1921.   Aug., 1921.
70/-, 110/-.   42/6, 50/-.

Source: Newbold, *Doom of a Coalfield*, p. 15.

Source 116

Monthly Average of Coal from Bristol Channel Ports.

To	1913	1925
Germany	34,552	2,950
Netherlands	9,612	5,535
Italy	463,780	271,110

Source: Quoted in David Egan, *Coal Society*, 1986.

Thinking particularly of source 114 what do you think would be the reaction of the coal-owners as soon as they regained control of the industry?

The reaction of the miners in 1921 to the fact that:
(a) they had been denied the nationalisation of their industry and
(b) they were faced with big cuts in wages
was not at all surprising. There was a national coal strike from March to July, 1921. In some ways the situation was a bit like that ten years earlier in Tonypandy, although there were no incidents like the attack on shops. But the government had not forgotten Tonypandy.

Source 117

Conclusions of a Conference of Ministers at 10 Downing Street, 9 April, 1921.
"Situation in Wales: The Conference were informed that the situation in South Wales was dangerous and the population of Tonypandy was restive . . . The G.O.C. Western Command had despatched 3 Comp-anies of the Yorkshire and Lancashire Regiment to Cardiff. These troops were not sufficient to enable guards to be placed at the pit heads. The opinion was expressed that unless the disturbed areas in South Wales were taken in hand, serious trouble would arise and that action should be taken immediately . . . Agreed
(1) That the Admiralty should immediately form a battalion for service on land from such naval ratings as were available . . .
(2) That in view of the expected arrival of troops from Silesia one battalion should be moved immediately by railway from London to Wales for the purpose of freeing the 3 companies at Cardiff for use in the disturbed areas."
Source: P.R.O. CAB/23/25/22. Reproduced in *The Age of the People*, No. 3 of Document Pack, The Dragon has Two Tongues, H.T.V. Doc. No. 4.

There were other resemblances to Tonypandy, 1910. The police were out in force.

Source 118 *(See page 60)*

In the end the miners were defeated and were forced to go back to work in July. But the situation did not improve, in fact it got worse. Demand for coal continued to go down and productivity also went down.

Source 119

Our export coal tonnage decreased by over 10 millions in the 11 months, Jan.-Nov., 1925, compared with the same period in 1924.

Tonnage exported	Average f.o.b. Price per ton.
Eleven months, 1924—56,483,748	. . . 23/7
Eleven months, 1925—46,185,067	. . . 20/-

The decrease of tonnage and prices represent a loss of over £20 million in 1925 compared with 1924. In South Wales, the export tonnage decreased by over 4 millions in the same period, while prices declined by over 2/- per ton.

These figures do not present a very cheerful picture, but if the prospects for the future were bright, we could afford to forget the gloomy past. Unfortunately, the future looks as dark as the past has been, and no one can hold out any hope that the new year will show any substantial improvement. The coal trade the world over is in a parlous state, and while Britain, as the greatest coal exporting country, has been hardest hit, all the other great coal producing countries are suffering also.

Source: The Colliery Workers' Magazine, Vol. 4, 1926, p.3.

The last sentence of source 119 leads us to realise that competition from other coal-producing countries was very fierce.

Source 118

Source: South Wales Miners' Library, University College of Swansea.

Source 120

In the coal export trade in 1925, the United Kingdom experienced a year of exceptional competition. Europe takes about 80 per cent of the British coal exports, so that the state of the European coal markets largely determines the degree of activity in the British coal export trade. In 1925 there was more coal in Europe than could be absorbed. Keen competition prevailed and prices were cut.

French Coal Imports

From	1924 M. Tons	1925 M. Tons
United Kingdom	13,019,711	9,936,764
Belgium-Luxembourg	1,710,694	1,897,713
Germany	4,265,179	5,517,944
Holland	509,028	563,677
United States	344,648	204,199
Other Countries	43,294	176,120
Total	19,892,554	18,296,417

Source: Coal Year Book 1925, pp. 37-39.

Against this background the coalowners insisted in 1925 that the miners must take a big cut in wages and they wanted to put an extra hour on the working day—from 7 hours to 8 hours. It looked as if a coal strike was inevitable. Then the government gave way. They gave a subsidy to the owners and at the same time set up a Royal Commission to inquire into the state of the industry. In the end the commission solved nothing. The owners were still insisting on large wage cuts. Workers in the industry were very worried at the beginning of 1926 and saw that there was trouble ahead.

Source 121

What of 1926?

We are only four months away from May 1st, when the present wage arrangement terminates, and unless the subsidy is continued beyond that date, a conflict appears inevitable. It may be significant that a leading London paper recently stated that the subsidy may have to be continued beyond the period originally contemplated. With an extension of the subsidy, it is to be hoped that the Government will take steps to place the industry on a better economic basis. The position has become considerably worse since the subsidy has been in operation. Apart from the subsidy, every coalfield in the country, with the exception of the small district of Somerset, worked at a loss during the three months, August, September and October, the average loss for the whole country being 1/10 per ton;

Source: The Colliery Workers' Magazine, Vol. 4, 1926, p. 3.

If the subsidy given by the government was to be withdrawn south Wales would suffer particularly badly.

Source 122 *(See page 61)*

If the subsidy stopped there would obviously be a savage reduction in wages. The coalowners proposed that from April 30, 1926 wages should be decided on a district basis. This was a particularly serious threat for south Wales miners. Why?

Source 122

The Coal Industry Subvention.

Claims Paid to the end of the Year 1925.

The following statement has been issued by the Mines Department, showing the claims paid to 31st December, 1925, under the Coal Mining Industry Subvention.—

Area.	In respect of the months of Aug. & Sept. £	Oct. £	Nov. £	Total. £
Scotland ...	636,443	411,261	412,206	1,459,910
Northumberland	238,554	172,885	184,409	595,848
Durham ...	588,626	415,759	431,943	1,436,328
South Wales and Monmouthshire	759,887	677,385	707,303	2,144,575
Eastern Division of the Federated Area ...	608,638	526,483	473,149	1,608,270
Lancs., N. Staffs. & Cheshire ...	383,223	304,387	292,475	980,085
North Wales ...	58,792	44,463	46,873	150,128
South Staffs. & Salop	38,223	26,322	26,373	90,918
Cumberland ...	59,548	41,239	43,832	144,619
Bristol ...	3,757	2,892	3,702	10,351
Forest of Dean	22,860	16,364	16,932	56,156
Somerset ...	3,864	2,333	2,986	9,183
Kent ...	4,854	3,207	4,026	12,087
	£3,407,269	2,644,980	2,646,209	8,698,458

Source: Colliery Workers' Magazine, Vol 4, 1926, p.42.

The General Strike

The government refused to go on paying a subsidy. From 30 April 1926 miners who refused to accept the wage cuts were locked out. Miners all over Britain stopped work. From 4th May, 1926 there was a general strike, with the miners joined by all members of trade unions. The country came to a standstill. Newspapers could not publish, though the *South Wales Argus* tried to get some information out.

Source 123 *(See page 62)*

South Wales miners were very much to the forefront of the strike. We saw when we were studying Tonypandy in 1910-11 that some miners' leaders wanted to take over their industry and control it themselves. Indeed they believed that this was the way all industry in the country should be run. Such men were now in office in the South Wales Miners' Federation. One was the Vice-President S. O. Davies. But the best-known and most important miner at the time of the General Strike was Arthur Cook, the general secretary of the Miners' Federation of Great Britain. He was a superb

speaker and an inspiring leader. Although he was born in Somerset in 1883 he came to work in the South Wales Coalfield as a young man. He had learned the art of public speaking as a Baptist preacher and Band of Hope speaker when he was young. He thought up some of the best-known slogans of the dispute. In one of his speeches he said: ''We are going to be slaves no longer and our men will starve before they accept any reductions in wages.'' He also said: ''not a penny off the pay, not a minute on the day'' and the miners supported him wholeheartedly in this. Here is a photograph of him.

Source 124

Source: South Wales Miners' Library.

The effect of the strike in the whole of Britain was dramatic. It was particularly so in Wales because support was so widespread. In the port of Holyhead in Anglesey, which linked the area with Ireland, work was brought to a halt. In the rest of north Wales railwaymen and other transport workers played a vital part in making sure the strike was effective. In south Wales, which had such a strong union tradition through the miners' union, the strike was solid. The organisation making sure of this, and the job of organising communities to see that basic food and other supplies were available, was in the hands of strike committees.

Source 125 *(See page 63)*

For nine days normal life was more or less halted. Newspapers were not published, trains and buses were at a standstill, factories were shut down and, of course, there was no-one at work in the pits. The strike committees made sure that there were supplies of essential

Source 123

South Wales Argus

Coal Crisis Emergency Issue.

OUR EXPLANATION.

Because of the General Strike we are unable to publish the "South Wales Argus" in the usual form, we therefore give the news in brief as best we can.

10,477. NEWPORT, TUESDAY, MAY 4, 1926. ONE PENNY

At midnight the "cease work" instruction of the Trades Union Congress came into effective operation; and in city, town and hamlet the wheels of industry began to slow down.

There was a march through the West End of London. One demonstrator who carried a red flag came in for police attention, and after a sharp struggle, was deprived of his emblem.

In the final message just as the strike commenced the Trades Union Council stated that the Trade Unions were fighting in defence of the mine workers. They declared that the responsibility for the national crisis lay on the Government. With the people the trades unions had no quarrel. They were assured that the trades unionists of the country would stand loyally by their leaders until victory and an honourable peace had been won.

Crazy looking contraptions of very ancient orders rattled noisily along the streets of London, graced in many cases with fair passengers perched precariously upon hastily constructed strings of boxes and wooden cases. A few pirate buses in London gleaned a rich harvest. Each time a bus drew up at a stopping place there was a wild though good natured stampede to mount it.

No trams are running at Manchester and but for the volunteer service the whole transport organisation of the city is dead. The principal Manchester stations were picketed.

All the iron and steel works closed at Hanley. A number of potteries stopped for want of coal.

The London and North Eastern Railway announce a skeleton service of trains.

The transport services for the supply of milk in London is working according to scheme. Drivers are working and all is quiet.

On the G.W.R. all milk and fish trains have arrived at Paddington.

A skeleton service of trains and buses was run by volunteers at Glasgow.

The stations at Pontypool were closed, and Pontypool Road, particularly, presented a very desolate appearance.

Newport was like Sunday with the shops open. There was a curious crowd of persons at Newport Station but there was nothing for them to see except a train in a siding. A good percentage of railway clerks have remained at work at Newport.

At Abertillery at midnight hundreds of young colliers marched the streets singing the "Red Flag." Abertillery Tinworks (500 employees) and Abercarn Tinworks (700) closed down.

Woolwich Arsenal is involved in the strike. Several thousand men are said to be affected, and strike pickets are on duty outside the Arsenal gates.

A destroyer passed Woolwich Arsenal going up the Thames, carrying a large number of naval ratings.

A statement issued by Mr. John Moxon, Chairman for Newport and Monmouthshire, says volunteers' services are required which to handle food, fuel, light and power, etc., essential to the well-being of the community. They will not act as strikebreakers. All engaging volunteer labour will be held responsible that this instruction is adhered to. Any complaint should be addressed to "Civil Commissioner, Ministry of Health, Cardiff," who will investigate and take action.

Ebbw Vale Sheet Mills on Tuesday (2200 employees) are idle. Ebbw Vale-Cwm bus service was running this morning.

All gunpowder stores at collieries in the Eastern Valley have been removed to Cardiff.

Nineteen men were sworn as special constables at Pontypool to serve on the Great Western Railway.

The Railway Co., Du Midi, France, received a telegram from the Southern Railway, asking it not to accept any goods destined for England.

The "Echo de Paris" says that the strike affects the very existence of England, while the "Matin" declares that the outcome of the struggle will have its effect outside the frontiers of Great Britain, and expresses the fear that the political and social evolution of other countries may be gravely affected thereby.

At Blackwood, all the railwaymen ceased work. Omnibus service suspended. A number of business vans, lorries and private cars were running.

A special meeting of Tredegar Valley District of the Miners' Federation was held at Blackwood. It was decided to hold a mass meeting of miners and members of all other Trades Union organisations at Blackwood on Tuesday afternoon.

Blackwood Trades and Labour Council have made arrangements for setting up a joint council of action under Blackwood and Mynyddislwyn Trades and Labour Council. A meeting for this purpose is to be held this evening.

"This conduct in these times is doubly dangerous," said Mr. J. J. Finston at Pontypool on Tuesday, when Thomas and William Allen labourers, were sent to a month's hard labour each for being drunk and assaulting police.

Train and train services were completely paralysed at Newcastle.

Bristol dockers ceased work.

Large ironworks at Ilfreton have ceased work.

A skeleton tram service is running a local service.

A trainload of stranded passengers went from Carlisle to London.

The ex-Labour Member for Norwich, Mr. G. H. Roberts, formerly Secretary of Typographical Association, declared at Toronto that the action of the printing staffs of London newspapers in ceasing work was entirely unnecessary and the liberty of the Press. The Government must not yield, declared Mr. Roberts. If it does, the Country will be driven into bankruptcy.

By the closing down of Blaenavon Company's blast furnace the last of the Blaenavon industries is at a standstill. Blaenavon workmen numbering between 3,000 and 4,000, are idle, except a small number engaged in safety work at the colliery. The mechanics were locked out on Friday.

Almost complete industrial paralysis.

Almost complete industrial paralysis prevails in the Nottingham district.

At Swansea idle workers are patrolling the streets. The Mumbles Railway is included in the stoppage.

Hull Docks and Railways are at a complete standstill. Motor transport has been arranged for fish supplies.

The Midland Railway are running no trains.

GENERAL NEWS.

Sir John Holden, Bart., of Sharples Hall, Leigh, Lancs., died after a long illness aged 60.

An empty passenger train left the metals at Newport Station last night, through a parcel which fell on the level crossing. No one was injured. Traffic slightly delayed.

The Prince of Wales has arrived in Paris but nothing has been fixed in regard to his journey to London.

Henry Cecil Hales, of Danbury Road, Pontnewynydd, was taken to Pontypool Hospital suffering from head injuries received by being knocked down by a motor car on the Abergavenny Road, near Pontypool.

Mrs. Tom Jones, president, Mrs. A. J. Harries, J.P., chairman, and Mr. E. L. Boulter, treasurer, have been elected officers of Newport Liberal Women's Association.

A case of sleepy sickness has been reported by the Medical Officer for Newport.

A deficiency of £2,680 7s. is shown by Wm. John Davies, builder and contractor, of Yorkrd, Newport, at a meeting of creditors on Tuesday. Liabilities were £3,383 12s. 7d., and assets £697 4s.

The House of Commons Standing Committee on the Electricity Bill adjourned until next Tuesday.

Business on the Stock Exchange is practically purely a matter of negotiation for dealers continue loath to market prices. Railway prices Great Western 82, Brunner 82. Southern deferred 43, are quite nominal.

Neath Watch Committee appointed Sergt. Keefe, Swansea Borough Police Force as Chief Constable.

Garage proprietors at Caerphilly are reaping a rich harvest by motors being hired in Caerphilly.

Men employed in motor manufactures at Birmingham are still at work.

Derby industries are in a state of chaos.

The London Midland and Scottish Railway managed to run one train to Manchester and one to Sheffield.

Boot factories are running as usual at Northampton.

Over fifty thousand men are out in Sheffield. Traffic is maintained in North Derbyshire bus services.

A Cabinet meeting was held at the Home Office. The Miners' Executive re-assembled with their officials, but there was no actual meeting of the Executive, the miners' case having passed into the hands of the T.U.C. General Council.

The Great Western Bus Service, from Crickhowell to Abergavenny, carried on till noon. Pickets were then successful in getting the men to abandon the buses.

There is no road transport between Abergavenny and Crickhowell. The bus service from Raglan to Abergavenny, from Ponty road to Abergavenny are being maintained.

Monmouthshire County Council to-day protested against the Budget proposals for taking money from the Road Fund.

Mon County Council have decided to make application for a loan of £11,320 for the erection of a boys' school at Newbridge and for another similar sum for funds for a new infants' school at Bedwas and for land for the Agricultural Institute, Usk.

Newport docks were completely at a standstill to-day.

Mr. W. J. Watkins, chairman of the Mon County Council, has appealed for everyone, whatever his opinion, to accept the responsibilities which fall upon him in this crisis.

It is anticipated that the milk supply to hospitals, institutions, schools, hotels, restaurants and private consumers will be maintained. Owing to the increased cost of emergency measures, the prices will be increased by 8d. per gallon wholesale and 2s. per quart retail.

The T.U.C. Council, which met at Eccleston Square, was joined by Mr. Herbert Smith, Mr. Cook and Mr. Richardson. Mr. Ramsay MacDonald and Mr. Henderson arrived later. Great privacy was observed and the outer door was closed.

The Executive Council of the Miners' Federation were summoned to the House of Commons for a conference with the General Council of the T.U.C.

Wholesalers in Newport have raised the price of frozen meat by 2d. per lb.

That railway repair shops at Caerphilly are closed.

Saklatvala, the Communist M.P. for North Battersea, was arrested in Highgate and will be brought up at Bow Street charged with making a seditious speech in Hyde Park.

COUNTY CRICKET.

Australians 336 (Gregory 120), Leicester 4 for 3.

Lancashire 179 and 153 for 5. Warwickshire 140.

Yorkshire 357 (Rhodes 132). Essex 110 and 95 for 4.

Notts 180, Northants 144 and 179 for 3. Surrey 245 and 44 for 0. Hampshire 182. Cambridge U. and Middlesex abandoned owing to strike.

TO-DAY'S SPORTING.

Chester.

2.0 1, Cabbage. 2, Little Grey. 3, Bayonet. First two.

Betting: 6-1, 11 to 10, 8-1.

2.30 1, Bouge. 2, Phaethon. 3, John.

2.30 Betting: 6-1, 10-1, 11-4.

3.0 Chester Betting: 5-1, 6-1, 8-2.

3.30 1, Swift and Sure. 2, Bearboar. 3, Lancaster.

Pershore.

4.0 1, Golden Hero. 2, Glamorous Light. Only two runners. 7-4 on Golden Hero.

Printed and published by the South Wales Argus.

Source: South Wales Miners' Library.

DIAGRAM ILLUSTRATING ORGANISATION OF GENERAL STRIKE COMMITTEE.

Source 125

Source: David Egan, Coal Society, 1986.

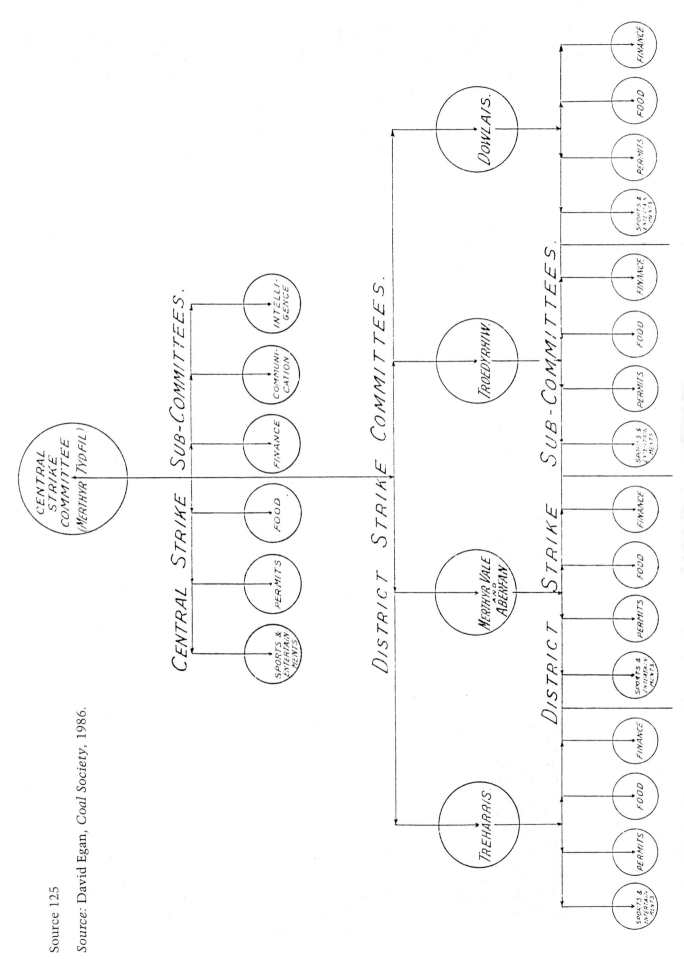

electricity and food. Volunteers tried to fill in some of the other gaps. These were middle-class volunteers. Businessmen tried their hand at being engine-drivers. University students, particularly from Oxford and Cambridge, tried various forms of work but got tired very quickly.

After nine days the nerve of the Trade Union Congress broke. T.U.C. leaders now argued that the government was prepared to negotiate so people should go back to work. They called off the strike on 12 May, 1926. Welsh workers took no such view. They were extremely angry that the T.U.C. was giving in like this. Some groups of workers in Wales debated whether to accept the T.U.C.'s order or not.

Source 126

The decision of the General Council to call off the General Strike came as a surprise, and created something like bewilderment. In the main the workers were standing firm, and the men who were still working were expecting every day to receive the call to take a stand alongside their fellows. Like a "bolt from the blue" came the order to resume work. Large masses of men refused for some time to believe it, they suspected that the news was only another trick of the Government for the purpose of breaking down the strike; they had had so much "news" over the wireless which they knew from personal knowledge to be false that they were justified in their scepticism.

Source: The Colliery Workers' Magazine, Vol. 4, 1926.

Source 127

Was there any disappointment, there must have been. How do you measure the disappointment among the working class of Aberdare for instance . . .

Well, it was a disappointment, and when the order to go back to work came, the several unions that the people backed in the localities were disappointed. They were in the mood to stay out much longer than the ten days you see.

Source: Transcript of recording of Mr. D. J. Davies, South Wales Miners' Library.

However, such people were in an impossible position, given T.U.C. instructions and within a week most people were back at work.

The Miners' Lockout

The miners did not go back. The coalowners now locked them out. For another six months the miners fought on.

Source 128

Source: Reproduced in *The Age of the People*, No. 3 of Document Packs, The Dragon has Two Tongues, H.T.V. Document No. 7.

Their spirit of defiance and their determination to keep their spirits up in the face of terrible shortages and hardship is summed up in sources 128 to 130.

Source 129

Now the '26 strike everybody was happy, a peculiar thing, happy. Why because we were utilising our time, we had carnivals, we had sports, we had concerts, we had whist drives and I was the sec. of the entertainment committee at that time, and we organised all these things. We used to have some of the finest runners now in our sports coming here, you had concerts, you had artists coming here you had everything. We had, the whist drives that we had, was the first prize would be a tin of corned beef, and mind you think of that as a wonderful prize, a tin of corned beef or a parcel of food that some sympathetic grocer was prepared to give us you see, or a pound of butter from somebody else. Now those were the prizes that we had in the whist drive, and you would have about 24 tables playing whist, surprising you know and that was in the old hall by here. Just here then, now they've converted it into houses now, have you been down Trefleming that old road over there. On the right hand side you'll see an old building that used to be the church hall before they built the new one, that used to be the Church hall, and the activities of the strike organised there. Dramas, concerts of all descriptions, whist drives and everything. Then in the day we'd have sports, carnivals and we used to have a carnival here it was a treat, and we were the first to introduce to this place the Jazz Band and they came over from Glynneath.

Source: Interview with Mr. Henry John. Transcript in South Wales Miners' Library, University College of Swansea.

Source 130

Can you tell me much about 1926 and the Character Band and Jazz Band?

Oh yes the Character Bands and Jazz Bands, well they were formed you see, more than anything, to take our minds off the real struggle you know. Well I myself was in the character band, what you call a Sheik Band you know, Harem Band, they were all dressed up as Harem Ladies, veils on their faces and the beads etc., etc. And we had the slaves in front, of course the sheik first and slaves, stripped to the half and all black, and behind them was the slave driver with the whip and he was cracking the whip you know as you were going along. And instruments we had was the gazoots, some had gazoots, and some of us had what do you call, eumaniphones what you blow through your nose. So we used to play a tune you know going all over South Wales. We went

to Cardiff and other parts of South Wales and very successful.

Source: Interview with Mr. Reg Fine, 2/7/1973. Transcript in South Wales Miners' Library, University College, Swansea.

Despite the attempts to raise funds and the methods of keeping spirits up there was real hardship and suffering as the dispute went on.

Miners and their wives fought back and tried to get their views across in a variety of ways. Some of these ways become clear from the *South Wales News* and *Western Mail.*

Source 131

May 18th
Rhondda men before Pontypridd magistrates:
Frank Bright (35) Colliery repairer, Ynyshir.
Emrys Llewellyn (24) Labourer.
D. J. Lewis (22)
Isaac Lewis (17) Colliers, Llwyncelyn, Porth.

All charged with being in possession of seditious literature likely to cause disaffection amongst the troops, police, fire brigades and civilian population (under the Emergency Powers Regulations).

May 22nd
Thousands of demonstrators from *Risca, Abercarn, Cross Keys, Nine Mile Point, Pontymister, Bedwas, Machen.* Marching to Newport to protest to the Board of Guardians on lack of relief. Prevented by Emergency Powers Regulations from entering Newport.

May 25
In *Mardy* . . . . the Communists are establishing a reign of terror and violence with a trade boycott which is creating an amazing state of affairs. There are hundreds of avowed Communists who christen their town 'Little Moscow' and try by intimidation and organised interference to live up to the name.

One Mardy professional gentleman made the following statement "I go about during the day but I dare not show myself after dark."

The Strike and Distress Committee . . . runs Mardy. It intimidates newsagents not to sell the "yellow press".

May 31st
Merfyn Payne, a well known *Pencoed* miners' leader, was charged under the Emergency Regulations with doing an act calculated to impede means of locomotion. Fined £50 or 2 months prison.

June 25th
3,000 men and women from all parts of *Eastern Valley* march to *Griffithstown* demanding increased relief. Board of Guardians decide to feed women and children.

June 25th
Rev. Edward Teilo Owen of *Cwmgwrach* fined £20 or 2 months prison. Alleged to have said in a Welsh sermon during the General

Strike, ''We have been squeezed. It is time to rebel. I have turned a rebel.'' Prosecution said it was likely to cause disaffection.

June 30th
300 *Pontypool* miners march to Race Mountain to stop outcrop workers who sell coal at a profit.

August 6th
March from *Llanhilleth* stopped by police at *Hafodyrynys*. Protesting over poor relief.

August 25th
One *Ton Pentre* blackleg escorted home from Ton Pit by police because of violent crowd.

33 returned to work at *New Tredegar* and *Elliots*. Subjected to booing on way home particularly by women at Elliotstown and Phillipstown who were armed with white shirts and a supply of whitewash.

August 31st
Baton charge at *Pontypool* where miners under Arthur Jenkins and William Coldrick (both on the S.W.M.F. E.C.) were protesting against outcrop working.

September 17th
5 women and 15 men on trial at Bridgend for unlawful assembly, intimidation of blacklegs at *Heol-y-Cyw* on August 12th-13th.

September 18th
Ogmore miners' agent (E. J. Williams) committed for trial for unlawful assembly, along with 4 others on August 25th. 6 others for intimidation of blacklegs on August 22nd.

September 24th
29 defendants from *Ogmore Vale* charged with 120 offences of unlawful assembly and intimidation. Crowds assembled to stop blacklegs after a bugle call. Sent for trial.

November 3rd
Mrs. Elvira Bailey (*Treorchy*) given 2 months for throwing stone at policeman. Rhondda Stipendiary said ''I find that the women have been taking too prominent a part in these disturbances and I must impose a penalty that will be a deterrent to others.''

November 24th
Trials begin of Arthur Jenkins and William Coldrick (both Labour County Councillors and on S.W.M.F. E.C.). Also 4 others including Tchitaro Mishayawa, a Japanese labourer. Jenkins charged with inciting his co-defendants to riot, to incite workmen to do damage and riotous assembly on October 30th outside *Pontypool*.

Source: South Wales News and *Western Mail*, 1926.

Whatever the attempts to get funds, to get publicity for their cause and to stop any working by 'blacklegs' the miners were forced steadily into a situation in which they and their families could no longer survive. They had to give in. They returned to work in December, 1926. They had lost.

As with Tonypandy, the individuals and the communities involved in the General Strike and the Miners' Lockout never forgot. Of course they remembered different aspects of it in different ways.

Some consider it as a time when Britain came close to revolution.

Source 132

Well the nearest time we were to revolution was unquestionably the general strike. Now in the General Strike every Trades Council became the local representatives of the T.U.C. We became strike committees, now in Brynmawr and Nantyglo the same, we prevented any stuff being carried from the railway station which was the means of getting stuff in, unless they had sanction of the trades council. In other words we had accepted Lenin's thesis ''Every factory is a fortress'', and we said then at that time, the power was in the employed workers not the unemployed workers because they were the ones in contact with the economy of the country, and could wreck it if necessary and we said and you've read undoubtedly the St. Petersburgh Councils of Action in 1905, now we modelled ourselves in those days on the Councils of Action that were set up in St. Petersburgh in the 1905 abortive revolution and it was a very similar situation here, you know you couldn't move anything, you couldn't move a ton of coal, you couldn't move a bag of flour, you couldn't do anything without a licence from the trades council who was sitting daily as a council of action. That was the nearest time to me that we were to a revolution.

Source: Interview with Phil Abraham, 1973. South Wales Miners' Library.

Others remembered the defeat, first for the Trades Union and then for the miners. The miners believed that they had been deceived by the government and that the Trade Union leadership had been duped.

Source 133

The rank and file were not defeated, the leadership was defeated, but at least you had there a rank and file willing and able to carry on the struggle.

Source: Interview with Phil Arthur, 1973. South Wales Miners' Library.

Source 134

Looking back, the whole situation of the nineteen twenty six strike is that the T.U.C. had got itself into a position that when it came to the General Strike itself you know, they got into a situation that they were frightened really, and were hoping that they could have made a settlement with the government then so as to put an end to it. Because its said that old Jimmy Thomas himself who could see now that it was becoming a challenge to the constitution as it were, and old Jimmy said, ''Well I hope that if this struggle keeps on that the constitution will win.'' Which showed of course that Jimmy had no notion of using what you might call a revolutionary situation, and although I don't think that we could have made a challenge at that time myself even if we'd had better leadership, but it did show that the leadership of the T.U.C. were, you know, their ideas were limited merely to trade union activity, and what they would have liked of course would have been to see Baldwin and Co. succumb and come to a settlement, instead of which, they succumbed.

Source: Interview with D. J. Davies, 1973. South Wales Miners Library.

So, nearly fifty years later people who took part in the General Strike saw it in very different ways. We can be certain of one thing. The troubles of the coal industry were not over.

Further work on the evidence

Source 115: Give the information available in this Source in graph form.

Source 120: From the information given here write a sentence or two about what was happening to French coal imports in 1924 and 1925.

Source 123: What kind of primary source is this? It is a one page issue. What can you tell about people's *interests* in 1926 from this one page?

Source 124: Just on the evidence of this photograph would it be possible to tell where the photograph was taken? Why?

Source 128: What different kinds of information does this picture give to an historian?

Source 130: Is there anything you can learn from this document which you do not already know from Source 128?

Source 131: Is there any evidence in the Report for May 25th that the *Western Mail* might be biased in its reporting of events in Maerdy?

Source 132 This is oral evidence. It was recorded in 1973 about events in 1926, by someone who was actually involved. What are (a) the strengths (b) the weaknesses of this evidence?

Company Unionism

In December 1926, the miners' lock-out officially came to an end in Wales. The end came because sheer hardship had driven thousands of miners back to work throughout November. The south Wales miners had to accept one of those district agreements which they hated and which had been one of the reasons for the original strike. The men went back on the owners' terms.

This was a big defeat for the union, the South Wales Miners' Federation.

Source 135

The owners were determined to follow up the advantage now that the Union was in a much weaker position than before the strike. Many miners who had been active in the strike were purposely not re-employed. Managers changed the customary rules by which miners had previously operated. Some miners who had served on branch (lodge) committees of the Union were kept out of work for twenty years or more. Before the end of the strike thousands of members of the S.W.M.F. had left the Union. Some pits never re-opened after the strike. The miners' Union was down and, some thought, nearly out. What made matters worse was that the parent union, the Miners' Federation of Great Britain, was in a worse state and not capable of giving any real leadership.

In the north Wales coalfield an industrial union, that is a breakaway union approved of by the colliery management, started at Point of Ayr colliery in Flintshire. During the course of the 1926 strike miners at a new pit at Trelewis,

run by the Taff-Merthyr coal company, held a meeting at which they decided to break away from the S.W.M.F. and form a new union. The owners would not then employ members of the S.W.M.F. By November 1926 a new coalminers' union was in existence. It was called the South Wales Miners' Industrial Union. Colliery officials immediately accepted the new union. Why? The new union promised not to concern itself with politics. In the light of what you remember about the chapter on 'Tonypandy' what was the importance of this promise?

The new union grew quickly, helped by colliery officials who allowed it in the collieries free of any of the restrictions placed on the S.W.M.F. The S.W.M.F., undermined by the despair left over from the 1926 strike, could do very little to stop the new union. Colliery management made life more difficult by victimising, or refusing to employ, miners who did not join the new union in pits where it had a hold. It was also the case that the S.W.M.F. did not take the new union seriously enough, believing that it would die out of its own accord.

By the end of 1927 the S.W.M.F. *had* to take the new union seriously. During 1927 membership of the S.W.M.F. had fallen by about half, from 136,000 to 73,000. So, in 1928, the S.W.M.F. passed a resolution at its annual conference:

> Source 136
>
> "That this annual Conference instructs the Executive Council to conduct a campaign throughout the Coalfield against the non-Political Union which is being supported by the Owners. This Campaign should be a preliminary to the handing in of Notices for a Coalfield strike in an effort to destroy the last vestige of Non-Political Unionism, and also get the Non-Unionists to re-join the Federation."
>
> *Source:* Quoted in Hywel Francis and David Smith, *The Fed a history of the South Wales Miners in the twentieth century*, London, 1980, p. 97.

The worst years for the S.W.M.F. were from 1927 to 1934. As we shall see, these were terrible years of growing unemployment and closure of pits. Appalling poverty hit the south Wales mining valleys.

One well-known historian has called these years 'Wales's locust years'. What point was he making? During these years membership of the new coal union, the S.W.M.I.U., increased, especially early on, though support for it was never widespread. In 1927 the union claimed to have up to 150 branches, and had four full-time organisers based in Cardiff. At the same time the S.W.M.F. made it clear that it would not accept the weakening of the mineworkers' position which the new union was bringing. One of the leaders of the S.W.M.F. wrote in the *Western Mail* in 1927:

Source 137

"The responsibility of coalowners or others who may seek to foster disruptive influences will be a very grave one indeed. No matter how long it may take, nor what losses may be involved to the coal industry or the community, the work of re-establishing the undisputed supremacy of the Miners' Federation as the sole representative and champion of the Mineworkers shall be done, and done right thoroughly."
Source: Quoted in Francis and Smith, *The Fed*, p. 127.

The *Western Mail* newspaper allowed Vernon Hartshorn to put the S.W.M.F. case. At the same time the paper gave strong support to the S.W.M.I.U.:

Source 138

". . . these organisations (breakaway unions) are not fostered or planted by the coalowners but are the voluntary unions of men who have grown disgusted with the policy of the Federation and who have risen in revolt against the methods which have involved them and the Federation in financial ruin."
Source: Quoted in Francis and Smith, *The Fed*, p. 128.

There were constant clashes between the unions in the late 1920s and the early 1930s, with colliery managements always supporting the company union. The battle was a bitter one. We have seen that the S.W.M.I.U. started in the Taff-Merthyr colliery of Trelewis and was always centred around a few collieries where it was very strong. Another stronghold was Nine Mile Point colliery, Cwmfelinfach. The S.W.M.F. could make very little progress in Taff-Merthyr pits because the company sacked men who did not join the new union.

Source 139

And so you began work in 1929? Yes.
This was at the Taff Merthyr Pit under the Powell Duffryn. Had you by this time been . . .
They wouldn't call it P.D., Powell Duffryn, because when I went back and I had to sign on

again like, and I asked them what should I put here, P.D. "No, no, you put Taff Merthyr Colliery Company". Now the Ocean people had the selling rights of that pit see, and the Powell Duffryn sunk it see, that is what happened.
So then, was the Industrial Union there at that time?
At that time yes, until 1934-35.
So when you went to work there you joined that?
Yes you had to join it of course, when you are speaking when we went back see, 1929. Well now there was a strike in South Wales, it was the old South Wales Miners Federation then mind, it wasn't the N.U.M. then, and in 1931 they came out on strike for an increase in wages. Taff Merthyr worked, Bedwas worked, and all the people worked, they had I think it was a pound each we had for working at that time. And look at the bother they made when they wanted to change the Union there, and they all worked that time, for more wages.

Source: Interview with Mr. Haydn Thomas, 1974. South Wales Miners Library, University College of Swansea.

There were demonstrations and a running propaganda battle between the two sides.

Source 140

The South Wales Miners' Industrial Union.

To the Taff Merthyr Workmen,

Bedwas is now going through a period identical with that which you have gone through. The tyranny of the South Wales Miners' Federation did not break you in 1934 and it will not break Bedwas in 1936, whatever lying literature might say. The Federation's claim of its increase of membership is on a par with all the lying statements they have made at Taff Merthyr.

At Taff Merthyr, the ranks of the Miners' Industrial Union are whole and steady, in spite of the mass intimidation and physical violence which you have endured.

During the next few weeks the South Wales Miners' Federation will try your patience in many ways, hoping to cause trouble and strife at the Colliery. They will try to break through our ranks with unscrupulous propaganda, but together we can hold back this Red tide of Communism.

TAFF MERTHYR COMMITTEE,

The South Wales Miners' Industrial Union.

Source 140 Continued

Taff Merthyr Lodge, S.W.M.F.

INDUSTRIAL UNION RECORD.

Extracts from Balance Sheets of M.I.U.

IS THIS WHERE THE FOURPENCES GO ?

1934	One Motor Car	-	-	£325
1935	One Motor Car	-	-	£468
1936	The Price of a Hearse ?			
1934	Legal Charges - Compensation			Nil
1935	Legal Charges - Compensation			£4 7 0
1934	Pit Examinations	-	-	£12 0 0
1935	Pit Examinations	-	-	£5 10 0
1934	Vacuum Cleaner	-	-	£20 0 0
1935	Vacuum Cleaner, Balance			£8 0 0

More spent on a Vacuum Cleaner than on Pit Examinations.

200 times more spent on Motor Cars than on Compensation Cases.

What was spent on Negotiations for Wages Increases? NOTHING !

What was spent on Conferences for Members? NOTHING !

To-morrow we will give the record of the SOUTH WALES MINERS' FEDERATION - the only Organisation that is fighting for the South Wales M

JOIN THE FEDERATION

Source: Printed in Document Pack 3 published in association with 'The Dragon has two tongues' H.T.V. series.

Source 141

GARW DISTRICT, S.W.M.F.
NOTICE.
A
MONSTER CAMPAIGN

Against Non-Unionism in the Garw Valley

Has been inaugurated with the joint support of the Executive Council of the S.W.M.F.; the Garw District S.W.M.F.; and the Garw Valley Joint Committee.

The Campaign will proceed until the

Scourge of Non-Unionism

has been COMPLETELY WIPED OUT from the Valley.

Look out for Posters announcing Meetings and for Explanatory Literature.

SUPPORT THE HOUSE-TO-HOUSE CANVASSERS

Miners' Wives specially invited to co-operate.

(Signed) RICHARD BENNETTA, Miners' Agent.

Inevitably the atmosphere in mining communities was poisoned by these bitter rivalries.

Source 142

There was enough bitterness engendered to split the village asunder, socially, culturally, and even religiously. People who had been friends and neighbours for years now became bitter enemies. Women refused to sing in choirs with those whose husbands were members of the "scab" union and not of the S.W.M.F. Such enmity was even carried into chapel services. There, if a family had an attachment to the new "Industrial Union" and stood to sing the hymn the minister had announced, those who favoured the official miners' union promptly sat down in protest. Vindictiveness even went to such lengths as daubing paint on "enemy" houses, damaging rival property, and even (so it was rumoured) throwing snails from one garden into the other

as an expression of animosity and disgust with those who could not agree as to union membership.

Source: Walter Haydn Davies, quoted in David Egan, *Coal Society.*

Members of the S.W.M.I.U. had to be given police protection on their way to work.

Source 143 *(See page 71)*

To one of the members of the S.W.M.I.U. at the time memories remained vivid of the bad feeling in the mining communities over company unionism.

Source 144

Oh yes and the police were watching you in the morning going to work and all, yes. But they were dirty, throwing stones at our front door and things like that you know, marking the door and all things like that. Well the old

Source 143

man and woman were living and they nearly went crackers then, but there you are. So anyhow all that finished and I was very friendly with the manager then, because he was a bit on the musical side although he couldn't sing much himself. And any time I wanted an hour or two off to go to a concert I mean he always used to let me go. Well anyhow it came now that they started back to work, and the funny thing about it they had to go down to the manager and ask for work of course, but half of them didn't have the guts to go down. They would ask my father, and my father was friendly with the manager as well, and they would ask my father if he would go see. I've seen men offering him £2 to go down to the manager and ask if they could start work.

What would happen then, you would come out from the shift . . .

Oh they were all watching you, all watching you at the station. Women and all. But they wasn't doing nothing to you only (hissing) of ''Scab'', and all the rest you see, hissing at you they were, doing things like that see. But I was very fortunate I only had to go round the corner and I was in the house. Well there were people working up at the very top of the village, they used to follow them and hiss them, and shout at them and all the rest of it. And oh there was a Court case remember and they had jail, they had jail remember for it. Down there throwing stones and things at the colliery and at the men

too, and at the trains. They caught one fellow trying to put one of these stones from off the bridge to drop on the Rhymney train when it was going.

A lot of women in the village they wouldn't speak to your wife would they?

No, they wouldn't speak to her no. Even sisters in laws, and brothers, they had a brother living here, two brothers, and that was one who gave my father £2 her oldest brother, to see if he could get his work back.

Source: Interview with Mr. Haydn Thomas, Bedlinog, 1974. South Wales Miners Library, University College of Swansea.

The historians of the S.W.M.F. show just how far the divisions had spread into all aspects of community life:

Source 145

''In a more generalised way a 'social boycott' of almost all those connected with the Industrial Union now took place. In Bedlinog shopkeepers, milkmen and bakers who had dealings with the S.W.M.I.U. were boycotted; the secretary of a local singing festival had to resign because he had a relative in the pit; whole cinema audiences walked out if blacklegs were found there, until the management co-operated by refusing entrance to blacklegs or their relatives; school children were kept away from those classes where teachers refused to discriminate against Industrial

Union children, and in Nelson a hairdresser's trade plummeted because of his son's membership of the S.W.M.I.U.''
Source: Francis and Smith, *The Fed*, p. 224.

Despite the terrible unemployment in the coal industry the S.W.M.F. began to go on the attack again from about 1934. It now had a better, more democratic, organisation and it started recruiting more members. But the real success against company unionism came in October, 1935. At Nine Mile Point colliery in Bedwas in Monmouthshire, members of the S.W.M.F. won a famous victory. At this colliery the management recognised the two rival unions. On Saturday, 12 October, 1935, the Industrial Union members came up to the surface early so as to make sure that there were no clashes with S.W.M.F. members. The Federation members decided that they would stay underground on hunger strike until only their members were allowed to work at the colliery. The Federation members were convinced that the following week the management was going to get rid of them and allow only Industrial Union members to work there.

The men acted and organised secretly. This is apparent from the memories of school-teacher Mavis Llewellyn.

Source 146
. . . Fred (her uncle) had been to a combine meeting on this Saturday evening. He came home, didn't say anything. My father was working nights in the pit, so he went to work on the Sunday night. Monday morning he would normally be home before I would get up. Father would come in, light the fire and call when it was time to get up. My mother came and said, 'Mav, your father's not come home from work.' 'Oh he's working on.' 'That's unusual, because if he's working on he sends a message.' Well, I didn't pay much attention, I went on getting the breakfast. Mother kept on going back and fore to the front door, she was uneasy because he hadn't come home from work. And presently she said, 'Hey, have a look, the boys are coming home!' The pit was at the top here and the youngsters were coming down the road. So she said, 'What's happened?' 'Oh, they're staying down.' 'Staying down?' 'Yes, and they've sent us up, we're too young. So we've given them our food and our water.' Well, it was the first we knew. Fred had come home, he had confided in my father, and—what I always felt was so interesting—in the old days, if there was a dispute, and they'd have a pithead meeting, one man had to take the cork out of his bottle or his can, and empty his water, and once they started emptying

their water, that meant 'We're not going down.' That was it, it was settled, once you started. But that time instead of saying 'Empty your water', he said 'Take care of your water'. That was Dad's job then at the bottom of the pit to tell the men when they got down, 'Go easy with your water.' And when they sent out the old men and those who were ill, they all left their water down with them. Well, that was such a complete change and it was a new way of fighting the bosses.
Source: Quoted in Francis and Smith, *The Fed*, p. 283.

The men also acted unofficially. They had to, because the executive council of the S.W.M.F. was in a very difficult position. When members of the executive council heard of the idea there was a problem.

Source 147
''This confronted me, and the Executive Council, with a dilemma. It was a breach of the Coal Mines Act to stay down the mine beyond the permitted hours. If we called upon our men to stay down we would be in breach of an Act of Parliament designed to protect our safety. To this some of the enthusiasts had an answer. 'You close your eyes—we will do it on our own'.
Source: Recollections of Jim Griffiths. Quoted in Francis and Smith, *The Fed*, p. 280.

There had been 'stay-downs' before in Wales but nothing as important as this. Men in other pits stayed underground, too, or came out on strike in sympathy.

Source 148 *(See page 73)*

This picture is of miners from Treorchy who stayed underground for eight days to get rid of Company Unionism in their pit.

Other pits where the Industrial Union was particularly strong were the adjoining Parc and Dare pits in Cwmparc. Here are the Parc miners after their eight-day stay-down.

Source 149 *(See page 73)*

The men at Nine Mile Point were underground for 7½ days. For over 24 hours they had no food but then the coal company allowed tea, sandwiches and cakes to be sent down the pit. They came up when the managers undertook in writing that there would be no victimisation. They agreed also that only the S.W.M.F. would negotiate with them over opening up the pit again. The Parc and Dare miners came up when, in effect, the management agreed to their terms.

Source 148

Source: Cyril Batstone.

Source 149

Source: Printed in Francis and Smith, *The Fed*, after p. 108.

It is difficult to imagine what it must have been like to be stuck underground for this length of time. But the miners felt the fight was worth it. They got enormous publicity.

Source 150

Source: Reproduced in Document pack 3 produced in association with 'The Dragon had Two Tongues' H.T.V. series.

The S.W.M.F. pressed home its advantage after these stay-down strikes had proved successful. By the end of the following year, 1936, company unionism had far less support in the south Wales coalfield. The Fed had won its greatest battle. But in the coalfield and in the rest of industrial south Wales unemployment was as bad as ever.

You have now worked on the events of 1926 and the events which followed in the coalfields.

You are now able to consider some questions which historians still ask about these events. Why had the coalowners run into such serious financial difficulties by 1926? Was there bound to be a strike in 1926? Was the Miners' Federation of Great Britain wise to carry on with the battle when the other unions were no longer involved? Why do you think some people joined the South Wales Miners' Industrial Union? Why did others oppose it so bitterly?

Further work on the evidence

Source 135: What does this Source tell you about coal-mining?

Sources 137, 138: What do these two Sources tell you about the *Western Mail* newspaper from which they are both taken?

Source 141 What information vital to the historian is missing from this Source?

Source 144 What information would you like to have about Mr. Haydn Thomas before making full use of this Source?

Sources 147, 150: In what way is the newspaper account (Source 150) 'Stay In' misleading? The answer is in Source 147.

Unemployed Movements

We have seen that the demand for coal went down dramatically in the late 1920s. In the 1930s the situation became far worse and many more collieries closed. Coal was not the only industry which was in difficulties in the 1920s and 1930s. In north west Wales you will remember that the greatest industry of the 19th century was the slate industry. Apart from the catastrophic strike of 1903 do you remember what was the main cause of the drop in demand for slate? Even if you cannot remember, try to deduce the cause.

There was also great difficulty in the steel industry in Wales. There was strong foreign competition. It came mainly from France, Germany and America. The steel industry of south Wales, particularly, was not in a good position to deal with this competition. This statement is *literally* true! The iron industries of Wales had grown up around Merthyr and other towns at the top end of the south Wales valleys. They had been very prosperous in the 19th century because there was so much demand for iron—especially for building railways—and later steel. It did not matter that getting the finished iron down to the coast for export was expensive. At least the iron stone or iron ore was available locally. Later in the century high-grade iron ore had to be imported. What effect did this have on costs?

When competition increased, and when the works got old and out-of-date, and transport costs increased, they could not compete. Almost all the steel works had to move down to the coast to survive. This meant that the original big iron works of the 19th century closed. The great Merthyr works closed— Cyfarthfa in 1921, most of Dowlais in 1930. Thousands of workers in the valleys were unemployed as a result. This is how an official report summed up the situation.

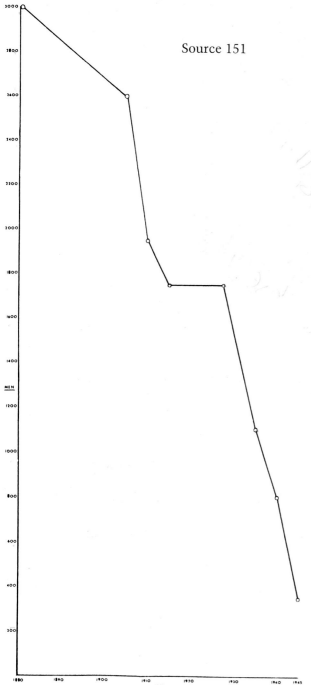

Source 151

Decline in the number of slate quarrymen employed in the Nantlle Valley, Caernarvonshire, 1880-1945.

Source: Documentary pack no. 3 produced in conjunction with H.T.V.'s series, 'The Dragon has Two Tongues'.

Source 152

Numbers and Percentage unemployed, including temporarily stopped, Steel-workers in Industrial Region, 1929–1936[1]

Month.	1929.		1930.		1931.		1932.	
	No.	Per cent.	No.	Per cent.	No.	Per cent.	No.	Per cent.
June	5,661	21·4	11,768	45·1	11,862	49·0	13,564	56·0
Dec.	6,674	25·2	16,482	63·1	13,204	54·4	12,557	51·7

Month.	1933.		1934.		1935.		1936.	
	No.	Per cent.	No.	Per cent.	No.	Per cent.	No.	Per cent.
June..	11,359	46·5	7,092	28·0	7,895	33·6	6,069	
Dec.	7,844	32·1	7,201	29·0	5,977	25·4		

[1] Up to and including June, 1933, these figures do not include workers in the Tredegar district.

The peak of unemployment was reached in December, 1930, during the very early stages of the depression, when there were 16,482 or 63.1 per cent. of the steel-workers unemployed. After that unemployment remained high, though falling slightly, until a considerable improvement took place in 1933 and 1934. There were about 1,500 more steel-workers unemployed in 1934 than in 1929.

Approximate numbers employed in Iron and Steel Industry in the Industrial Region of South Wales in June of each year[1]

Year	Estimated Total Numbers Insured (July).	Numbers " in Employment " (June)[2].	
		Excluding Temporarily Stopped.	Including Temporarily Stopped.
1923	27,940	26,000	26,005
1924	28,440	25,931	25,931
1927	28,400	24,016	26,323
1929	26,440	20,779	24,922
1930	26,090	14,322	22,328
1931	24,120	12,368	19,226
1932	24,270	10,686	18,433
1933	24,940	13,051	19,151
1934	25,030	17,418	21,042
1935	23,510	15,615	19,990

Source: Second Industrial Survey of South Wales, Cardiff, 1937, pp. 97, 98.

In the Monmouthshire valleys it was the same story. The Blaenavon works closed in 1922. They have now re-opened—as a museum, one of the best-preserved of the great iron works of 19th century Wales.

A short distance from the Blaenavon iron works museum is Big Pit, Blaenavon. That too is a museum. It is a coalmine which is now one of the most important tourist attractions in Wales. Big Pit did not close until the 1960s, but it is a useful reminder of the other basic industry which came crashing down in the 1920s and 1930s. Welsh wealth in the second half of the 19th century had been based on coal. Just after the first World War all seemed well. Over a quarter of a million men worked in Welsh collieries. We have seen that overseas competition, general lack of demand over the whole industrial world, lack of investment and the difficult conditions for mining coal in south Wales, resulted in a slump.

Between 1920 and 1921 coal exports from Britain slumped by two thirds. Collieries started to close on a big scale. Here is a list of collieries closed in the Afan valley between 1924 and 1931.

In 1904 south Wales produced over 30% of the world's coal exports. By 1929 it produced 3%. Coal had largely been replaced by oil in the world's ships and source 154 shows how dramatically coal production and trade slumped.

Source 153

Colliery.	Colly.	No. Employed in 1924	No. now Employed	Date Colly. Closed	Is Colly. Abandoned?
Corrwg Vale	Corrwg Vale Colliery Co.	80	None	1925	Yes
Cwmmawr	Britton Ferry Colls. Ltd.	120	20	1925	No
Glyncymmer	Glenavon Garw Colls Ltd	140	None	Oct. 1927	Yes
Glyncorrwg Pits	Glyncorrwg Colly. Co.	550	None	July 1925	Yes
Abergwynfi Pits	do.	500	None	July 1925	Yes
Merthyr Llantwit	Merthyr Llantwit Colly Co	80	None	1924	Yes
Corrwg Rhondda	Glenavon Garw Colls. Ltd.	40	None	1924	Yes
Duffryn Rhondda No. 2	Imperial Nav Coal Co Ltd	140	None	1925	Yes
Argoed	H. Hudson Ltd.	120	None	July 1927	Yes
Talbot Merthyr	T.M. Colly Co.	40	None	1924	Yes
Oakwood	Oakwood C. Co.	200	None	1927	Yes
Oakland	Oakland C.C.	50	None	1928	Yes
Ynyslas	Ynyslas C. Co.	30	None	April 1926	Yes
Craiglyn	Craiglyn C. Co.	25	None	1925	Yes
Maesmelyn	H. Hudson Ltd.	40	None	1925	Yes
Llwynffynon	Llwynffynon Colly Co.	30	None	1926	Yes
Bwlch	Bwlch C. Co.	20	None	1925	Yes
Court Herbert	Main Coll Co.	180	None	1927	Yes
Brynderwen	do.	350	None	1924	Yes
Bryncoch	do.	250	None	1924	Yes
Villiers	do.	60	None	1924	Yes
Glyn Merthyr	Ynisarwed Co.	90	None	1926	Yes
Glyn Merthyr	G.M. Coll Co.	130	None	1930	Yes
Gored Merthyr	G.M. Coll Co.	160	None	1926	Yes
Cilfrew	Cilfrew C. Co.	160	None	1931	Yes
Premier Merthyr	P.M. Col Co.	130	None	1926	Yes
Blaengwrach	Cory Bros.	60	None	1927	Yes
		3770			

Source: South Wales Miners' Library, University College of Swansea.

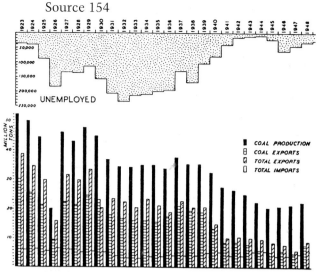

Source 154

Source: Margaret Davies, *Wales in Maps.* Reproduced in Document Pack 3 of *The Dragon has Two Tongues*—H.T.V. series.

The result of these economic and industrial changes was massive unemployment. At the end of 1925 unemployment in Wales was 13.4%. Two years later it was 23.2%. In 1932 there were 150,000 people out of work in south Wales. In 1935 nearly 50% of Merthyr's population was unemployed. In the eastern part of the south Wales coalfield, in eastern Glamorgan and Monmouthshire, about 45% of people had no work. Here are the figures provided by an official report.

Source 155

In the area as a whole the average percentage of unemployed men in the coal-industry was 32.5 in 1931, rose to 42.4 in 1932, and fell steadily in subsequent years to 34.4 in 1935. Expressed in numbers these percentages represent 65,853 in 1931, 81,507 in 1932, and 62,155 in 1935. These figures include both wholly unemployed and temporarily stopped.

Numbers of Coal-miners (men only) insured (July), Unemployed[1] (June), and approximate numbers employed in June of each year from 1931 to 1935

District.	Status.	1931	1932	1933	1934	1935
Monmouth, East and West	Insured	39,253	37,031	36,587	35,410	33,974
	Unemployed	8,988	16,252	15,644	15,969	9,313
	Employed	30,265	20,879	21,943	20,441	24,661
Rhymney, Merthyr and Aberdare	Insured	57,716	55,011	54,414	54,017	51,689
	Unemployed	21,554	28,355	27.168	29,258	20,266
	Employed	36,162	26,656	26,246	24,759	31,423
Rhondda and Port Talbot	Insured	69,237	65,770	65,075	63,090	59,943
	Unemployed	34,586	39,610	32,940	31,995	26,511
	Employed	34,651	36,160	32,135	31,095	33,432
Neath, Swansea, Amman	Insured	36,002	34,198	33,723	34,111	34,769
	Unemployed	7,880	5,590	5,361	5,934	5,232
	Employed	28,122	28,608	28,362	28,177	29,537
Whole Region	Insured	202,208	192,020	189,790	186,728	180,275
	Unemployed	72,608	89,816	80,913	83,146	61,332
	Employed	129,600	102,204	108,877	103,582	118,943

1 Wholly unemployed and temporarily stopped.

Source: Second Industrial Survey of South Wales, Cardiff, 1937, pp. 68, 69.

Look at the heading to the table. Why was the actual situation even worse than it seems from the figures in the table? Here was disaster on a grand scale. The unemployment was long-term with all the terrible effects that has on people's lives when they want to be working.

Source 156

It is not too much to say that every thoughtful person with whom we have talked has expressed greater concern at the destructive effect of idleness upon the character and morale of the unemployed than at the hardships involved in the scant supply of the necessaries of life. It is a common observation that work is needed rather than food or clothing. We feel that there is much justification for this view. From the first we were struck more by the aspect of depression among the unemployed men and their listlessness than by any other signs of poverty.

Source: Report on Investigation in the Coalfield of South Wales and Monmouth. Cmd. 3272, H.M.S.O., 1929.

This document recognises that people take pride in their work as well as depending on it for an income to keep themselves and their families. See if you can find out what benefits unemployed people get now. We know that they do not have a comfortable standard of living now but it is much better than what was possible in the 1930s. This is how a recent book sums up the situation for individuals and communities in the 1930s.

Source 157

For the population that remained in the valleys to battle out the depression, the quality of life cannot have been anything other than meagre. Life on the dole was desperate indeed for an unemployed worker in south Wales, indeed a struggle for bare existence. At the end of the twenties, an unemployed man received 23s. a week for himself and his family, plus 2s. per child. From this, perhaps 6s. to 7s. had to be paid out as rent for what accommodation he was able to obtain. From what money remained, all food, clothing, and other necessities had somehow to be found.

* * *

Meanwhile, the Unemployment Assistance Board set up in 1934 created enormous resentment in south Wales as in other industrial areas, for its bureaucratic and seemingly inhuman approach. The full indignities of the 'genuinely seeking work' provision, often accompanied by financial and even moral inquisitions of the unemployed man, the rigours of the means test which entailed minute investigation of the savings,

kinship structure, marital status, and other aspects of a working man's existence provoked frequent explosions of anger. Being kept alive on these terms was scarcely worth while.
Source: Kenneth O. Morgan, *Rebirth of a Nation Wales 1880-1980*, Oxford and Cardiff, 1981, pp. 231, 232.

As a result of this terrible poverty there were some things which families and communities could do nothing about. For example, they could do very little to change their poor diet.

Source 158 *(See opposite column)*

Source 159

Co-operative Wholesale Society
Food Prices June 1937

Butter	1sh 4d lb	Flour	3½d lb
Lard	7d lb	Currants	6d lb
Cheese	9d lb	Sultanas	8d lb
Bacon	1sh 4d lb	Biscuits	6d lb
Eggs	1sh 4d Dozen	Cereals	5½d lb
Margarine	6d lb	Green peas	4d lb
Tea	2sh 2d lb	Salt	2½d lb
Sugar	2½ lb	Rice	3d lb
Jam	7½d pot	Salmon	1sh 2d tin
Potatoes	1½d lb	Milk	3½d tin

Source: The South Wales Miner, June 1937.

They could do nothing about the effect of bad diet on their health.

Source 160

Malnutrition is, of course, difficult to assess as a separate factor apart from the incidence of definite disease. The personal equation of the observer must always come in and there are all degrees of failure of nutrition and no definite standard. From the observations which we made personally in the houses we visited, observations which were confirmed by what has been told us by various informants, the diet in the households of the unemployed men comprised little beyond white bread, butter or margarine, potatoes, sugar, jam, tea and bacon in limited quantity. Meat was seldom eaten except in very small amounts on Sundays, very often not more than a shillingsworth for the whole family. Fresh milk was not seen by us except when supplied from a welfare clinic, the usual milk being skimmed condensed. Fresh vegetables other than potatoes were seldom eaten, and it was noticeable that almost invariably the bread was not baked at home.

Source: Report on Investigation in the Coalfield of South Wales and Monmouth, 1929.

Some diseases resulted from bad diet. Rickets was one.

Source 161

As regards what are specially termed "deficiency diseases," there was no evidence

Source 158

Weekly Income and Expenditure for Unemployed and Employed Miners and Their Families

Two Case Studies from Blaina, Summer 1937

1. Unemployed miner, wife and 4 children: Income 39/- per week from Unemployment Assistance Board.

Expenditure:	s.	d.
Rent	10.	4.
Doctor		1.
Hospital		1.
Light	1.	0.
Coal		6.
Soap		9½.
Starch		1½.
Blue		1.
Cleaning things, polish, etc.		4½.
Insurance		8.
Clothes and Boots for children	1.	6.
Bread	4.	0.
3 lbs. butter	3.	6.
Meat (Sunday only)	1.	6.
1 lb. cheese		11.
2 tins of milk		7.
1 lb. bacon	1.	2.
2 qutrs of tea	1.	1.
4 lbs sugar		11½.
1 lb margarine		7.
½ lb lard		4½.
1 tin cocoa		5½.
Potatoes	2.	6.
Other vegatables	1.	0.
Jam		7½.
Tin of fruit and cream for Sunday	1.	0.
Baby milk food	2.	0.
	37.	9½.

Comment 1. Total food bill – £1. 2. 3d.

2. Balance of only 1s. 2½d. for extra food, biscuits, amusements, breakages, emergencies etc.

3. Coal bill eased by unemployed working eight hours at a level for 4 bags.

4. Excluding baby, 1¾d. spent per person per meal.

2. Employed Miner, wife and 2 children: Net Income £2.12.2d.

Expenditure:	s.	d.
Fares	1.	9.
Carbon for Lamp		10.
Rent and rates	6.	0.
Clothes	3.	0.
Food	25.	0.
Milk		–
Fuel	2.	6.
Nursing		1.
Insurance	1.	8.
Newspapers		8.
Trade Union		6.
Household replacements and cleaning things	2.	6.
Pocket money	3.	0.
Furniture	2.	6.
Children	1.	2.
Amusements	1.	4.
Radio		3.
	£2. 12.	9.

Comment 1. Total food bill £1.5.0d.

2. Expenditure exceeds income.

3. 3¼d. spent per person per meal.

Source Philip Massey, Portrait of a Mining Town (Published in Fact, November, 1937.)

Source: Reprinted in Document pack 3, produced for H.T.V.'s The Dragon has Two Tongues.

of the existence of scurvy, and the only form belonging to this category which appeared to have shown signs of increase was rickets. This disease, according to the evidence which we could obtain, has until recent years not been common in South Wales and Monmouth. We thought it of importance, for two reasons, to explore with some care the question whether there has been a recent increase. In the first place, apart from the deformity which may result from the disease, it indicates directly a low health standard among children affected and therefore of the rising generation. In the second place, an extended prevalence of the disease may be regarded as a warning of a lowering of the standard of nutrition generally. From the investigations we have made, it is clear to us that in some districts, but not uniformly, there is an increase in the occurrence of rickets.

Source: Report on Investigation in the Coalfield, 1929, p. 5.

See if you can find out more about this disease and how it was cured.

Serious diseases were made worse by lack of good, nourishing food. Tuberculosis was one of the most serious. Find out what you can about it and how it was conquered. It was one of the most feared diseases of the 1920s and 1930s. Why? But common diseases like colds and flu tend to affect people far more and last longer when people are undernourished. It did not help when families had so little money to buy clothing and children often walked around without shoes on, even to school.

Source 162

Apart from diet, another factor which must tend to impair the physical condition of the poorest of the population is the insufficiency of proper clothing and footwear. The existence of this deficiency is more immediately obvious than that of insufficient food, and shabby outer garments and worn-out boots were often to be seen in public. In the houses we visited we frequently found the bed clothing and under-clothing far from adequate, and the boots not enough for the school children, to say nothing of the adults and infants.

Source: Report on Investigation in Coalfield of South Wales and Monmouth, p. 7.

Faced with this kind of situation, and with no obvious signs of improvement for years on end what do you think the response of individuals and communities might be? Before you read on try to think what some of the alternative courses of action might be.

*   *   *

Many individuals and their families left the depressed areas. This was particularly so after about 1934 when, in parts of England, newer industries offered well-paid work. There was plenty of official encouragement for them to leave in search of work. But there was official recognition, too, that this was not going to solve the problem.

Source 163

'We have met nobody who doubts that the policy adopted on the recommendation of the Industrial Transference Board is the right one, but it is pointed out that without something like a miracle it will be several years before the many thousands who must leave the area can be transferred to work elsewhere, and that in the meantime a large number of men, even if a steadily diminishing one, must remain exposed to the demoralising effects of idleness. That the danger is serious is clear when it is realised that a considerable number of the unemployed have not worked in a mine since 1921, while many more have been idle since May, 1926. Even now there are men who regard it as in the natural order that they should for all time be provided with the necessaries of life without working for them.'

Source: Report on Investigation in Coalfield of South Wales and Monmouth, 1929, p. 9.

Still, 430,000 people left Wales between 1920 and 1940. This was about a fifth of total population. Most of those people came from the valleys of south Wales.

Source 164

'There was a steady drift of younger Welshmen and their families to the newer industries of the south-east of England and to the Midlands. There was a more planned migration, too, orchestrated by Neville Chamberlain after 1931 and assisted by the Ministry of Labour, in the transfer of tens of thousands of Welsh workers to the London suburbs of Hounslow or Dagenham, to the engineering works at Coventry, the light industries of Watford and Slough, and the Morris motor-car works at Cowley, Oxford.'

Source: Kenneth O. Morgan, Rebirth of a Nation, Wales 1880-1980, Oxford and Cardiff, 1981, p. 231.

Another response could have been to have given up in the face of a problem on such a scale. In fact, individuals and communities did not give up. Many fought back. Some did what they could to help themselves. They grew vegetables in local allotments. They went out to the coaltips and collected waste coal.

Source 165

Source: Reproduced in D. Egan, *Coal Society*, p. 262.

Collecting coal in this way was dangerous and could end in tragedy.

Source 166 *(See bottom of page)*

There was some escape in the small amount of entertainment which people could afford. This included going to the cinema. How might you find evidence of the popularity of the cinema in your area during this period? There were cheaper alternatives which showed the spirit in these valley communities. There were jazz bands and carnivals.

Source 167 *(See page 81)*

Source 166

They Die to Give Their Children Warmth!

Death on the Tips

Every day, fresh reports of death and accidents in the search for coal. Tips and outcrop levels are reaping an increasingly heavier toll of life and limb. The whole valley was horrified when the other day news came through that an unemployed man was killed in a Ystrad outcrop level.

We had scarcely recovered from the shock when we learned that another young unemployed man had been horribly mutilated and killed on the Tylorstown tip, grimly referred to as the "Death-tip." It has been a scene of many tragic accidents.

Source 167

Source: Reproduced in D. Egan, *Coal Society*.

There were traditional Welsh eisteddfodau, too.

Source 168

BLACKWOOD MINERS' WELFARE INSTITUTE and LIBRARY, LM.

The First Annual
CHAIR EISTEDDFOD
(In connection with the above), WILL BE HELD ON
SATURDAY, 21st JANUARY, 1933
In the Wesley Hall, Blackwood

Musical Adjudicators—MATTHEW DAVIES, Esq., B.A., MUS.BAC. (Neath);
GEO. A. JAMES, Esq., A.R.C.O., MUS BAC. (Leicester)
Literary and Poems—E. PHILLIPS, Esq. (Tredegar), Blackwood

Source: David Egan, *Coal Society.*

Some observers fought back in print. Some of the bitterness which Welsh people felt is evident in this extract.

Source 169

'The English dilute all doctrines and render them harmless; the Welsh swallow them neat. That is what has made the recovery of the Welsh coalfield impossible. Once you insist on pricing men—the majority of men, not a few chosen ones—above commodities, once you seek to apply brotherhood and equality neat to all and sundry, once you admit that merely because men exist they have human rights against the world, and must neither be slaughtered nor starved, then economic war is inevitable and bankruptcy not improbable.

It is 10 Downing Street which is the distressed area. So many remedies have been tried in vain. South Wales has become a bore.

It is like a crying baby in the arms of an ignorant mother. It is smacked by one department and kissed by another. Why won't it go to sleep like Dorsetshire?'

Source: Anon, *What's Wrong with South Wales*, Published by the *New Statesman*, 1935, pp. 14, 15.

Some unemployed people of Wales protested by taking part in marching and demonstrating. There were local marches.

Source 170

At 2.30 p.m. on the 29th of August 1933, the first contingent to take the road assembled at Brynmawr. After a few words from the leaders the Marchers took the road that would lead to Newport. Every Marcher carried a "kit" containing a blanket, plate, cup, knife, etc., and soap and towel. In addition each Marcher carried a stick. The March was in columns of "fours" with a leader to each section of four ranks. With banners held high, with firm step and determined expression, the Marchers, the representatives of all the Mon. workers, were determined to show the Mon. County Council that the days of poverty and suffering must come to an end. At Garn Nantyglo the Brynmawr Marchers were met by the North Monmouthshire Marchers and their Band. The March, growing stronger with each mile, came swinging into Blaina where the workers were, en masse, on the streets to acclaim their champions and where a strong contingent of 50 Marchers fell in behind the Brynmawr and Nantyglo Marchers. Now the long stretch to Abertillery which is accomplished to the playing of the Band and the singing of the Red Flag and the International. Abertillery is a sight never to be forgotten. Workers massing the streets, cheers from the Marchers and on-lookers produces a sound like thunder. The Abertillery contingent fall in behind Blaina and the March takes on the aspect of a triumphant procession of working-class solidarity.

Destitute Blaina, poverty stricken Abertillery, shout their challenge to the powers that be.

Through Abertillery, Llanhilleth! On they come with firm step and iron determination. Newport is their objective and Newport it shall be!

That is the spirit of the Marchers.

Source: Monmouthshire Marchers Council, *Monmouthshire Hunger March*, August, 1935, pp. 8, 9.

There were marches to Bristol.

Source 171

South Wales Hunger March to Bristol T.U.C. 1931
Source: South Wales Miners Library, University College of Swansea.

Above all, there were marches to London.

Source 172 *(See page 84)*

Source 173 *(See page 85)*

Why did the march become such a popular form of protest? These hunger marches, like all other pressure on the National Government to do something about unemployment, had very little direct effect. This was not the case with one protest in the south Wales of the Depression.

In 1931 the National Government decided that local authorities such as counties and county boroughs should set up Public Assistance Committees. These committees would take over giving out unemployment benefit or 'dole' money. First, they would give a 'means test', that is, find out exactly what every member of the family was earning and then they would pay out the 'dole' entitlement. These committees in Wales could see at close quarters the grim state of the communities around them. They were as generous as they could be in their Means Test and tried to give as much benefit as they could. The result was that different Committees gave different rates.

The government in London wanted to know precisely what was going on and wanted standard rates. In 1934, therefore, the government passed an Act of Parliament which, in effect, replaced local scales of payment by national scales. The means test was to be put into force rigidly. One estimate was that unemployed people in Glamorgan would lose, in total, about £1 million as a result of these changes.

The communities of Glamorgan and Monmouthshire rose up in protest against this further assault on their dignity. On 20 January, 1935, 50,000 people marched to a vast meeting in Tonypandy. On Sunday, 3 February, 300,000 people gathered in various parts of Glamorgan and Monmouthshire to protest against this new law. The protesters were in their best clothes.

Source 174

But it was Sunday afternoon and all this arose from the peculiar psychology of the Welsh miner and his family in regard to the sartorial requirements of the Sabbath. That 'well-dressed' atmosphere of the procession did nothing to obscure the issue that a man and his wife cannot live on 8s. 3d. a week each after

Source 172

South Wales Marchers' Organising Council.

SOUTH WALES MINERS'
MARCH to LONDON

CALL TO ACTION! VOLUNTEERS WANTED!

Arising out of the pronouncement by A. J. COOK, 18/9/27, a Miners' March to London from S. Wales is being organised. The March will commence on the day Parliament opens--Nov. 8th, and the Marchers will arrive in London on Nov. 20th, where they will be received by an <u>All London</u> Working Class Demonstration.

The object of the March shall be two-fold, to arouse a Nation-wide feeling concerning the Appalling Conditions in the Minefields created by the policy of the Government and the Coal-owners, and to seek an interview with the Prime Minister, the Minister of Mines, the Minister of Labour, and the Minister of Health.

The purpose of such interview shall be :

1. To draw attention to the Chronic Destitution affecting Unemployed and Employed Miners arising out of the Failure of Private Enterprise in the Mining Industry.

2. To draw the attention of the Government to the persistent Closing of Mines, thus causing further widespread Unemployment.

3. To point out the consequences of the 8-hour Day.

4. To urge the Government to make Satisfactory Provision for the Employment of those Unemployed.

5. To demand State Aid to permit Guardians to more effectively Relieve Distress.

6. To protest against the Continuous Disqualification of Men and Women from Benefit at the Labour Exchange, and to urge More Adequate Scales of Benefit.

7. To press for a system of Adequate Pensioning of Miners over Sixty Years of age as a means of Reducing the Number of Unemployed.

☞ Those wishing to Enrol as Recruits for this Historic March should make application at once to :

THE TRAGEDY OF THE MINEFIELDS **MUST** BE MADE KNOWN !

Thomas Bros., Printers, &c. Pandy Square, Tonypandy

Source 173

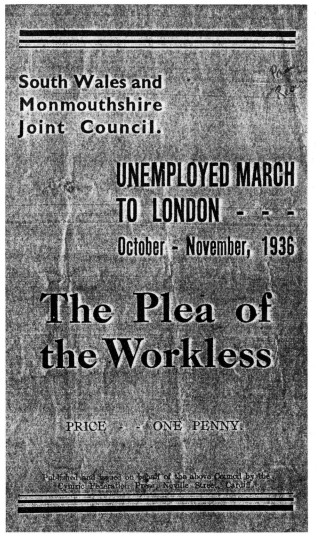

South Wales and
Monmouthshire
Joint Council.

UNEMPLOYED MARCH
TO LONDON - - -

October - November, 1936

The Plea of
the Workless

PRICE - - ONE PENNY.

Published and issued on behalf of the above Council by the
Cymric Federation Press, Neville Street, Cardiff.

Source: Title-page of pamphlet in South Wales Miners Library, University College, Swansea.

paying the rent; that to expect a young man over 21 to exist (apart from live!) on 10s. or 8s. a week is colossal vanity on the part of our country's Government. The miracle of it all was that such good-looking clothes could ever have been obtained by many of the marchers.

There was no mistaking the procession as a vividly unified protest against the regulations, for in the march, in addition to miners, employed and unemployed, were teachers, tradesmen, UDC employees, printers, shop assistants, Salvation Army officers, British Legionnaires, Co-op employees, many women's organisations, representatives of Churches and Sunday Schools, indeed no section of the community one felt was disassociated from the march.

. . . It was for all its pathos a magnificent gesture of protest; a cry from humanity for humanity. The Government cannot refuse to listen to the cry of the people . . .

When one remembers that thousands of these people, including women and children,

had walked to Mountain Ash from Hirwaun, Llwydcoed, Cwmdare, Trecynon and had to walk back again—many of them tramping 16 miles all told in the wind and rain one is impressed by the determination of the people in making this great protest. The Government *must* listen.

Source: Aberdare Leader, 9 February, 1935. Quoted in Hywel Francis and David Smith, *The Fed*, London, 1980, p. 259.

On 4 February, 1,000 women and 2,000 men visited the Unemployment Assistance Board office in Merthyr. They destroyed the records there.

Source 175

But now the Act took effect, and they were knocking them off, I remember I was knocked from fifteen shillings . . . (to) five shillings I received that week. And everybody was the same you know . . . We had a meeting for a further demonstration and this was to be a women's demonstration to Merthyr, Iscoed House . . . I remember us starting off from Pengarnddu with banners and all the rest of it, there was about thirty started from Pengarnddu. We stopped at Dowlais, there was people there with banners. By the time we reached South Street they were coming in from Pant, Caeracae, and all the rest of it. Then down on the new road . . . they were coming from all directions, well down through the town, you could see it was a huge demonstration. Then when we reached Pontmorlais, they came up from below, from Twyn, Penyard and Swansea Road . . . Well the place was packed . . . But I remember when they were all crowded there the actual gate of Iscoed House gave in and they started moving in . . . Well when we got in the garden somebody threw a stone, through the window you know, that started it off . . . some clerks upstairs had been making faces at us . . . and there were stones flying from all directions . . . well they smashed all the windows, all the windows were in. And the police came there but they were helpless. They (the demonstrators) went inside, through the windows, they pulled the stairs away, ripped everything, all the fittings, phone and everything and tried to burn the papers there. Well the papers were all flung in a heap. And at that time they had some speakers there, John Dennithorne, the Quaker now, and John he got up to speak on the window sill. They called him down, they called him 'Old Bug Whiskers' and all the rest of it. 'Get down from there.' John appealed to them of course, not to carry on, against violence and all the rest of it, that we would make a special appeal, we would march up to London to see the Government and all the rest of it. But they wouldn't have it see. 'Get down.' And there was a fellow with us, he was with the Party at that time, George

Nicholas, a Greek. George got up to speak. No good. A few others got up to speak, they wouldn't have it, the only ones who could speak were Jack Williams and Crid Brown from Aberdare. They spoke.

Source: Interview with Griff Jones, 1972. South Wales Miners Library, University College of Swansea.

The following day came an announcement that the unemployed would be entitled to claim benefit on either the old or the new rates. Everyone who had lost money in the meantime would have it restored. Community dignity and community spirit had told the government that the people of south Wales had suffered enough blows to their pride and spirit. They forced the government to change their mind for once.

Further work on the evidence

Source 151: Put into words the information contained in this graph.

Source 152: What had happened to employment in the steel industry between 1923 and 1935?

Source 154: Put into words the history of coal production from 1923 to 1948.

Source 165: How useful is this photograph as a historical source? What would you need to know before answering that question?

Source 166: Are there any clues in this document as to how it might be biased?

Source 170: How reliable do you think the evidence in this Document is?

Wales and the Spanish Civil War

Spain in 1936 was a poor country but one in which there were some extremely rich people. Spanish farming and its industry were backward and inefficient. The country had been a Republic since 1931 but there were still grim social and political problems. Most of the land was owned by wealthy proprietors who paid very little tax and employed as much casual, part-time labour as they could. Even where peasants owned land they had such small plots that they were hardly able to make a living. Industrial workers were very badly paid. So the majority of the population on the land and in industry lived in real poverty.

The Roman Catholic Church was very important. The Republican government had tried to control the Church but this had upset the Church's powerful, aristocratic supporters. The situation was made worse by some opponents who had burned down churches.

Spain is a large country in which there are strong regional loyalties which still produce political problems today. The strongest of these loyalties in the 1930s were among the Catalonians and the Basques who wanted independence for their regions.

The army had always played an important part in government in Spain. Army officers believed they had a right to interfere in politics. The Republican government had tried to control the army which had, in the past, been used to suppress any critical groups in the population. Not surprisingly this led to strong army opposition to the Republic.

With so many different groups in opposition to each other the political situation in 1936 was very unstable indeed.

In February 1936 there was a general election in Spain. It was won by a grouping of republicans (people who do not believe in a monarchy). The group won 267 seats in the Spanish parliament. Its opponents were monarchists, many of the military, and people who did not want change in Spanish society. This grouping won 132 seats. The republicans formed a government and had the support of socialists and communists. For some years Spain had experienced violence between opposing political movements. Shootings, bombings and strikes had taken place. Now things got worse. Without a strong government Spain drifted towards civil war.

On July 13, 1936, an important right-wing politician, Calvo Sotela, was murdered. This sparked off a revolt of the army against the government which had already been planned. The leader of the group of army officers was General Sonjurjo. He died in a plane accident and his place as leader was taken by General Francisco Franco. The generals hoped that they would take over Spain in a very short time. In fact, despite all the advantages, they did not succeed for over three years. What do you think their main advantage was?

One advantage they had was that they got immediate, massive support from the dictator rulers of Germany and Italy, Hitler and Mussolini. They sent planes, tanks, arms, soldiers and advisers—80,000 Italians, 30,000 Germans.

There were two main reasons why, despite this help, Franco's forces did not succeed quickly. First, there was the heroic resistance of some of the ordinary people of Spain. It is evident from this letter from Bill Paynter who was the official representative of the South Wales Miners Federation in Spain at the time.

Source 176

Dear Arthur,
    You have probably been expecting to hear from me before now, but the fact is, as you can well imagine, the state of things out here keeps a fellow pretty well occupied. The full story of what is happening to, and with, our lads out here will probably not be fully told until it is all over. This war, I suppose, has the same scenes of devastation, desolation, misery and suffering, that are characteristic of all wars. To those who are close to it, it is real and moving, and it appears more clearly, not merely as a conflict of armies, but as a conflict in which masses of men, women and children take part.
    To read the newspapers in England, one gets the mental picture of uniformed soldiers, the rattle of machine gun fire, the hum of aeroplanes and the crash of bombs. Such is a very incomplete picture. The real picture is seen more in the drab scenes, in the less inspiring and less terrifying aspects. To see twenty or thirty little children in a small peaceful railway station, fatherless and motherless, awaiting transportation to a centre where they can be better cared for, is to get a picture of misery. To see middle aged and old women with their worldly belongings tied within the four corners of a blanket, seeking refuge from a town or village that has been bombed, is to get a picture of the havoc and desolation. To see long queues of women and children outside the shops patiently waiting to get perhaps a half a bar of soap or a bit of butter, is to get a picture of the privation and suffering entailed.
    Yet, even this is not complete, because despite this, and as a result of it, you see the quiet courage and determination of the people

as a whole. It is a common sight to see the peasant farmer working in the olive grove, or the plough field within the range of rifle or machine gun fire; to see gangs of men right behind the lines who are tirelessly working to build new roads, etc.; to see men and women who remain in villages under Fascist artillery fire in order to care for the wounded. Everywhere you see a people who by courage, self sacrifice and ceaseless labour, are welded together by the common aim of maintaining their freedom and liberty from Fascist barbarism.

Havoc and ruin caused by Franco and the combined Fascist powers, but over and above it, the unconquerable loyalty and devotion of the Spanish people to the cause of democracy. This is crystalised vividly in the events in Spain today. There is a section who would promote disloyalty and disunity, but they are substantially uninfluential and futile. The vast support for the new Government is proof of this. This section will be crushed, not merely in the formal sense by the Government, but by the invincible loyalty of the whole people.

It is when you see all this that you realise what the war is, and what it is all about. It is here that you can feel the terrible menace to France and the people of Britain if the Fascists are not crushed at this point. It is here that you really feel that the people of all countries have an obligation in rendering the maximum of assistance to the Spanish people. It is here that you really feel that the International Brigade is a necessary part of that assistance. It is here that you realise that a battle is in progress not merely to defend a people from a savage aggressor, but to destroy something that, if allowed to advance, will eventually crush the people of all democratic countries.

In other words your own senses compel you to realise that for the anti-Fascist everywhere this is a fight of self preservation. More so, it is a fight of self preservation for all those in democratic countries who would continue the small rights and liberties they are at present afforded. For those who would have the greater freedom and life under Socialism it is certainly their battleground and testing place. Because if defeat is recorded in this partial fight, then the prospects of victory for the whole is indeed pushed further into the background of abandoned hopes.

This I suppose has all been said or written before, but here it is symbolised in the most commonplace event and in the most ordinary place. It is for that reason that it becomes outstanding in one's consciousness and has to be repeated.

From it all emerges one thing at least, and that is that the International Brigade, and the British Battalion as part of it, is not some noble and gallant band of crusaders come to succour an helpless people from an injustice, it is just the logical expression of the conscious urge of democratic peoples for self preservation. No one will deny but that the Brigade has had a tremendous and inspiring effect upon the morale and fighting capacity of the Spanish people. Yet no one would claim that it was done out of pity, or as a chivalrous gesture of an advanced democratic peoples. The Brigades is the historic answer of the democratic peoples of the world to protect *their* democracy, and the urgency of the need for that protection would warrant an even greater response. The people who have organised and built the Brigade are those who have clearly seen the need, and who strive to direct the progress of history to the advantage of the common people.

The people of Britain should be proud of the British Battalion. It is their weapon of self preservation. Those who donate their pennies and pounds, those who give their gifts of food, those who have given their sons, brothers and husbands, to build and maintain the Battalion, are the real defenders of democracy and progress. Their sacrifice and devotion is only surpassed by that of the men who make up the Battalion and by those who have already spilled their blood.

Best wishes,
Bill Paynter.

Source: Quoted in Hywel Francis, *Miners Against Facism, Wales and the Spanish Civil War*, London, 1984.

Second, the republicans got help from socialists, communists and other sympathisers from many countries. About 40,000 people went to Spain to help the republican democratic cause. About 2,000 were from Great Britain. These people formed the International Brigade and they were all volunteers. No government sent official help to the republicans. Of the British battalion of the International Brigade the biggest number, proportionately, was from Wales—174. 122 of these were miners. Here are some of the Welsh volunteers before a battle of 1938.

Source 177 *(See page 89)*

Most of the volunteers were from south Wales. 32 were miners from the Rhondda and most of these from the areas which had been active in the Tonypandy riots and the movements against company unionism. Can you think of any reason for this?

There were north Walians, too. It was a north Walian, Tom Jones, of Rhos, who was the last Welsh prisoner to be released when the war eventually ended.

Source 177

Source: South Wales Miners Library, University College of Swansea.

Source 178 *(See page 90)*

Why should men from Wales be prepared to risk and often sacrifice their lives to help to preserve democracy in a country as far away as Spain?

There were many reasons. One was that the left-wing political tradition of the south Wales miners was opposed to any kind of fascist dictatorship. Their union, the South Wales Miners' Federation, was totally committed to the people's fight in Spain. This is one of the posters they published in support.

Source 179 *(See opposite column)*

The union and its members saw a cruel injustice which the National Government in Britain was not prepared to do anything about. A Spanish government which had been properly elected by the people was in danger from military might.

It is amazing how involved ordinary people got in what was a war *within* a country far away from Britain. Why was Spain a much more 'remote' country than it is today? The war divided people in Wales, and in Britain generally.

In this situation the workers of Wales, who had a strong tradition of protest as we have seen, could only do something about the situation by direct action because there was no lead from the government. They saw an anti-democratic injustice and determined to do

Source 179

THIS MAP SHOWS THAT:

1.—British Trade Routes are Menaced.—Starvation can Follow.
2.—Naval and Air Bases in Northern Spain.—French Sea-Board Valueless.
3.—France Encircled by Fascist Forces.—A Weakened Ally.
4.—Air Bases in Northern Spain.—France and South Wales at Mercy of Bombers.
5.—Fascist Naval Bases in Spain.—Render Ineffective Co-operation Between Democracies.
6.—DEFEAT OF SPANISH REPUBLIC.—PROBABLE DEFEAT OF DEMOCRACY IN BRITAIN AND EUROPE.

Stop the Fascist Dictators before they conquer the Democracies of Britain, France & Central Europe

Printed by the Cymric Federation Press, Cardiff, and Published by the South Wales Miners' Federation

Source: South Wales Miners Library, University College, Swansea.

something. This is how Will Paynter, in Spain to help with individual problems of the British members of the International Brigade, saw Welsh participation (Source 180).

Source 178

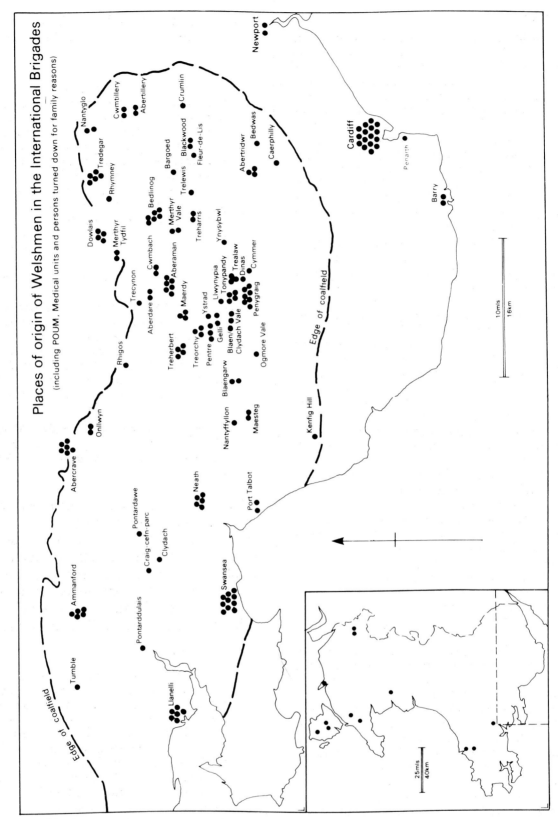

Places of origin of Welshmen in the International Brigades
(including POUM. Medical units and persons turned down for family reasons)

Source: Francis, Miners against Fascism, pp. 184, 5.

Source 180

'Although there was a vast difference in the stage of historical development reached in Spain compared with the industrial regions of Wales, the people had much in common. They both had long experience of poverty, oppression and persecution. Both had long experience of bitter struggles to bring about radical social change. The landless peasants of Spain in their fight for land reform faced the power of tyrannical landlords aided by the ruthless militarized Civil Guards. Bitter clashes on the issue of land reform occurred in the years immediately preceding the election of the Popular Front Government in February 1936. The miners of Asturias in their struggle for fundamental social change faced the guns of the military, led by Franco, and suffered hundreds killed and thousands wounded in 1934.

Obviously, the intensity of poverty and repression was greater in backward agrarian Spain than in the mining valleys of South Wales. But the basic conditions were similar. The wages of Welsh miners were severely and continuously butchered in 1921, 1926 and 1931 and reduced to a bare subsistence level. The intimidating presence of the military and police were prominent in the struggles of the miners against the attacks of the coalowners and government.

Mass unemployment was widespread with unemployment benefit below subsistence level. Harassment was rife by the use of the 'not genuinely seeking work' rule which denied benefit to thousands of the unemployed. The operation of the family 'means and needs' test following on benefits cuts of 10% and wholesale economies in the social and health services in 1931 intensified the poverty of the unemployed. Unemployment benefit for a man and wife was a paltry twenty-four shillings (£1.20) a week. The family means and need test meant that the earnings of employed members were assessed in fixing the benefit for those unemployed in the family. The fightback of the unemployed was by demonstrations to local administrative bodies and National Hunger Marches to London to lobby Parliament. The first of these national marches was in November 1922 and included strong contingents of unemployed miners and ex-soldiers. Such marches were a feature of unemployed struggles until 1936 and are recurring today as unemployment again reaches massive and chronic proportions.

Source: W. Paynter's Foreword to H. Francis, *Miners against Fascism.* pp. 19, 20.

There were other kinds of fellow feeling between the Welsh and the Spaniards. One link was that Spanish people came to live in Wales in the 19th century and the early 20th century to work in the iron industry. This is what the family memory was of one of these arrivals.

Source 181

'(When my aunt) arrived in Dowlais she was nine years of age. But she remembers living in Baracaldo . . . and then suddenly as a young girl, beginning this new life . . . coming over on board ship, one family and one mattress . . . with their bits and pieces, and then coming to Cardiff, and Cardiff to Dowlais.

Now Dowlais, really . . . was not so strange. Because the steel owners . . . built for them a Spain within Wales . . . They were recruiting labour and so they built a street which was for the Spaniards alone . . . it was King Alphonso Street.

I can remember Spaniards . . . worked in the furnaces . . . their clothes were smouldering, they had to have people to throw water on them to keep down the heat . . . Of course in Dowlais at this time you had the Irish, you had all kinds of . . . nationalities. Now during the lock-out in Dowlais (they decided) 'Well why don't we go to Abercrave. There's a French company there, they'll find us housing, we'll have good conditions there . . .'

Source: Memories of Leandro Macho, of Abercrave, who grew up there in the 1930s. Quoted in H. Francis, *Miners against Fascism,* p. 35.

For these reasons Welshmen started volunteering to go to Spain from December 1936. Volunteering was not an easy decision. Why? It certainly required the volunteers to be wholeheartedly convinced that what they were doing was right. Tom Jones of Rhos, for example, was a former pacifist who went to fight. This is how he justified his decision.

Source 182

'I went to fight and take part in the Civil War in Spain firstly because I am a democrat and an anti-fascist and that my sympathies were with the legally elected government of Spain. Secondly because fascist Italy and Germany were sending hundreds of thousands of troops and large quantities of war material to the aid of the rebel General Franco to try to crush the young Spanish Democratic Republic. Thirdly I knew that if fascism won in Spain it would encourage it to spread to other nations in Europe and would cause world conflict.'

Source: Quoted in Francis, *Miners against Fascism,* p. 212.

When they had volunteered the International Brigaders went straight off to Spain. This is how W. J. Davies of Ammanford remembered his journey.

Source 183

'After having breakfast with my parents, I went up to Sam's, we understood each other. At the weekend we went to Cardiff and saw Idris Cox and Len Jefferies. We were sent to London and saw Willie Gallacher at King Street. We were directed to Victoria Station to get a 33/- return to Paris. Pat Murphy was already in Paris. There were about a dozen Britons there including Dunbar, Tony Ireland and Ronnie Burgess who was (J.B.S.) Haldane's step-son. We stayed in Perpignan a night. The French border police let us through without even looking at our passports. Then on to Barcelona where we met a lot of Canadians in barracks there. We took part in a parade the following day through Barcelona. Two days later we were in Valencia . . . Albacete, one night later.'

Source: Quoted in Francis, *Miners against Fascism*, p. 164.

They were then issued with identity cards. Here is part of the one issued to Tom Glyn Evans.

Source 184

Source: Reproduced in Francis, *Miners against Fascism*.

They were well received in Spain. There is evidence of this in this extract from a letter from Jim Brewer to his former teacher in Coleg Harlech, Wales's first and only adult residential college, shows.

Source 185

'Now that the tide has turned in favour of the government it is possible for us to be trained. Since I've been here, I've met comrades of the same age and lack of experiences as myself from every principal country in the world. Here too one meets the finest type of Spaniard. Not the cafe-lizard type who made trouble in Barcelona the other day, ably seconded by the half-dozen ILPers present in Spain. One thing is clear, that the Fascists will never pass here except it be over the dead bodies of every man on the front. Here there are none of those whom Houseman designated in his epitaph on an Army of Mercenaries. We get good food, 10 cigarettes a day and plenty of newspapers, good guns and ammo and pay—6 pesetas a day. The regular army gets 15 a day. It must be disappointing to England's gutter press to know that. Most of us look upon the matter of pay with indifference. One or two people have gone back to England and spread all sorts of lying reports. The *truth* about them is that they deserted in the most trying hours. Some of them absconded with money that belonged to dead comrades. One in the course of an advance is known to have stopped, taken a few pounds from the pocket of a comrade who had failed and quit. Later he wrote a letter to the Times about rotten treatment by the Spanish authorities. I hope you'll use my remarks to counteract any such reports you may hear. Someday those quitters will get what's coming to them. In our experience the Spanish authorities and the people are embarrassingly helpful and kind. And its impossible to refuse them. Appropos of this matter of desertions, etc. It appears that the only way to get help from British consular authorities is to complain of bad treatment by the Spanish authorities. On the other hand, worth while people would hardly need the help of our consular authorities. All of us I believe are quite content to leave our destinies at large, in the hands of the Spanish authorities.'

Source: Letter of 20 June, 1937. Reproduced in Francis, *Miners against Fascism*, p. 275.

The volunteers were soon in action in the crucial defence of the capital of Spain, Madrid. They joined a war which was a particularly cruel one. There was ruthlessness on both sides. The military, in particular, were merciless. When they captured a republican town they made prisoners dig a large trench for their own grave before shooting them.

Back in south Wales there were many kinds of back-up support for the soldiers in Spain and for the war effort generally. The South Wales Miners Federation was wholehearted in its support.

Source 186
South Wales Miners' Federation.

AID FOR THE SPANISH PEOPLE
AN APPEAL.

The dreadful sufferings of the Spanish people, the ruthless slaughter of men, women and children, and the destruction of their homes by the rebel Franco and his **FASCIST** accomplices, **ITALY** and **GERMANY**, call for the active sympathy of **ALL** Workers.

The Fight of the **SPANISH WORKERS** against Fascism **IS YOUR FIGHT.**

The success of Fascism in Spain would endanger the liberties of the Workers in all Countries.

Fascism means the horrors of the Concentration Camps, Imprisonment and Death.

Help the Spanish People in their heroic struggle.

A Collection will be taken at your Colliery on **FRIDAY NEXT, JULY 16th,** to help to relieve distress caused by the Civil War.

THE SPANISH PEOPLE ARE GIVING THEIR LIVES, WE ASK YOU TO GIVE A GENEROUS CONTRIBUTION.   THE EXECUTIVE COUNCIL.

Source: Reproduced in Pack 3 of the Documents packs produced in conjunction with H.T.V.'s The Dragon Has Two Tongues.

Source 187

Our policy as a federation has always been clear. We are for the defence of Republican Spain and we accept the contingent upon this in terms of men and resources. We still have faith in the undying courage and inventiveness of the Spanish people to win victory, subject to the world working-class securing for the Spanish Government the right to buy arms to defend its people . . .

Source: Speech by Arthur Horner, *Miners Monthly*, 1937. Reprinted in Francis and Smith, *The Fed*, p. 364.

The S.W.M.F. looked after Welshmen who were wounded fighting in Spain. Most members of the union gave money directly to relief and medical funds, and continued to do this throughout the war.

The efforts of the ordinary families, suffering themselves, were amazing in the circumstances.

Source 188

'. . . going into the streets of Trealaw and Tonypandy, in Trehafod and Porth, with a trolley, knocking on the door of people, most of whom were unemployed and destitute, pleading for a tin of milk or a pound of sugar, and there wasn't a home, facing the impoverishment that they were facing, that wouldn't make a contribution, during that period, to help the fight of the Spanish people.'

Source: Recollections of Will Paynter, 1976. Printed in Francis and Smith, *The Fed*, p. 355.

There were fund-raising efforts, house-to-house collections, concerts, football matches and dances. Here is a collection of goods at Pontypridd in 1937.

Source 189

Source: Printed in Francis, *Miners against Fascism.*

Despite support from the working class of many countries who fought in the International Brigade and who contributed generously there was no success in the end. There was often disagreement within the brigade and the heroism of private individuals could not match the backing which Franco got from his fellow dictators. In September, 1938, the members of the International Brigade left Spain. They could do no more. Now all the S.W.M.F. could do was to help Spanish refugees who escaped and came to Wales. These refugees from northern Spain went to a home in Caerleon.

Source 190

Source: Reproduced in Francis, *Miners against Fascism.*

Some Welsh members of the International Brigade did not return immediately (see Source 192). They were prisoners of Franco's victorious armies. They were kept in camps in grim conditions of overcrowding, bad sanitation and, sometimes, ill treatment. They had enough food to keep them alive, but it was a desperately boring diet. This letter from Jack Jones, a prisoner in San Pedro camp, gives some idea of this. It was written in August, 1938.

Source 191

'Thanks a lot for the ten Woodbines. I am smoking one at the time of writing. They are a bit flat, so in future keep them in the packets. One chap here received in a Registered letter four double packets of Woodbines, so if there are any friends who would care to oblige let them know how pleased I would be. We are all happier now that we are receiving letters and money, but I can't understand why I have not heard from Lewis and Charlie. With the money we are able to buy some tobacco and cigarette papers, a sort of chocolate, and occasionally some fruit. My chief luxury is to buy a tin of condensed milk and spread the milk on bread. Our food here consists of beans, beans, and beans, lentils, lentils, lentils, sardines, sardines, sardines and Bread. Of course there is a War on in this country, but may I never see beans, lentils or sardines after I leave this place. Would I like a cup of tea or coffee! Water has been our drink for the past four months. We understand that the 100 fellows who left here two months ago, (on the way home) for Valencia are having a better time. We were told by Colonel Martin representing the British Govt. that the second group would be quickly following the first. However that was over two months ago. If you have any news about our release let me know. Will you please do me another favour. Try sending me two pairs of socks. I believe we will get them especially if they are sent by Registered *Letter* post. We have no reason to believe other than that we get all that is sent to us. I realise this is a bit of a drain on you, but when I return home and work I will make up for it.'

Source: Printed in Francis, *Miners against Fascism*, p. 287.

Source 192

Source: Francis, *Miners against Fascism.*

Thirty three Welsh volunteers never returned. Here is a photograph of one of them and an account of his bravery.

Source 193

The most important military experience for me was the Ebro offensive in the Summer of 1938. It was the biggest and last action for the International Brigades . . . I was given orders to capture a ridge. As I advanced with six other men we were peppered with enemy fire. We would not have achieved our objective had not Harry Dobson of the Rhondda given us cover-fire. Harry and I were caught by shrapnel. He insisted that his wound was not as bad as mine and . . . that I should be taken back on a stretcher first. I was taken back across the river to Cherte. Harry was removed later but he died.

> Morris Davies (Treharris),
> Company Commander,
> interview 12 May 1969.

Source: Printed in Francis, *Miners against Fascism*, p. 223.

Another was Tom Howell Jones, a miner and trade unionist from Aberdare.

Source 194

Mam Cariad a'r teulu,

I . . . write this brief note to you in a small cave, as dry as a house, outside the rain is coming down in torrents . . . Thunder and rain come here in terrific sharp periods. The boots and coats have been a god send. I can laugh at the weather . . .

I wrote an appeal to the Tower Lodge a few days ago. Tell Dai to inform Slavin I want the letter to reach by May Day . . .

Let me have news of yourself. How is your health, how is your spirit. Never let it lag. Please send some Welsh cakes through King Street. Here is a Spanish dish. Fry some sliced potatoes, when done, break 2 or 3 eggs in a dish and whisk. Pour the eggs into the potatoes. The potatoes should solidify through the eggs into a pancake. It is ready to eat. Here it is called totila. You must try one and think of me . . .

Letter from Tom Howell Jones to his family, 30 April 1938.

Tom Howell Jones, frail of body, sensitive of mind, was *a hero of the working class.* He did more than talk of liberty; when the time came that the freedom of the people was threatened by Fascism, he left his home and went to Spain to help the workers there to protect their liberty in the face of all the terrors of modern warfare. Death came to him out of a summer afternoon. Struck on the chest, mortally wounded by a fragment of shell, he died in the arms of another Aberdare man, Edwin Greening, who with two other Welshmen carried his body to the grave where it lies in earth not alone, but with other brave men who gave their lives for liberty. Tears his kinfolk have shed must have been lightened by pride.

Aberdare Leader editorial, 10 September 1938.

Source: Printed in Francis, *Miners against Fascism*, p. 27.

And here are short biographies of three more Welshmen who died for the cause in which they believed.

Source 195 *(See page 97)*

Those who sacrificed their lives in the Spanish Civil War were remembered in Wales. At a Welsh National Memorial meeting at Mountain Ash in December, 1938 there were more than 7,000 people there to pay their tribute. Among them was Paul Robeson, the great black American singer and actor. This is part of what Robeson said.

Source 196

'I have waited a long time to come down to Wales because I know there are friends here. I am here tonight because as I have said many times before, I feel that in the struggle we are waging for a better life, an artist must do his part. I am here because I know that these fellows fought not only for Spain but for me and the whole world. I feel it is my duty to be here.'

Source: Printed in Francis, *Miners against Fascism*, p. 249.

They have also been remembered by a later generation. S4C have made a television programme on the role of Welsh volunteers in the Spanish Civil War. In January, 1976, a plaque was dedicated to their memory at the South Wales Miners' Library. It now stands opposite the main entrance at Hendrefoilan, part of the University College of Swansea, where it serves as a permanent memorial to a story of men who died for a cause in which they believed.

Source 197

ER BYTHOL GOF AM Y CYMRY A ROES EU BYWYD
GYDÁU CYMRODYR O SBAEN AC ERAILL O LAWER CENEDL
YN RHENGOEDD Y BRIGADAU RHYNGWLADOL
ER MWYN CEFNOGI BRWYDR ARWROL
GWERINIAETH SBAEN YN ERBYN FFASGIAETH
1936-1939

TO THE IMMORTAL MEMORY OF THE WELSHMEN WHO WITH
THEIR COMRADES OF SPAIN AND OF MANY NATIONS IN
THE RANKS OF THE INTERNATIONAL BRIGADES GAVE
THEIR LIVES IN SUPPORT OF THE HEROIC STRUGGLE
OF THE SPANISH REPUBLIC AGAINST FASCISM
1936-1939

WILLIAM COLES · Cardiff	SIDNEY JAMES · Treherbert	J. SCOTT · Swansea
ALEC CUMMINGS · Tonypandy	DAVID JONES · Llwynypia	ALWYN SKINNER · Neath
HAROLD DAVIES · Neath	R. JAMADEESIS · Cardiff	BADEN SKINNER · Tredegar & Canada
W.J. DAVIES · Gilfach Goch	TOM HOWELL JONES · Aberdare	H.J.P. STRANGWARD · Onllwyn
HARRY DOBSON · Blaenclydach	A. MORRIS · Cardigan	GILBERT TAYLOR · Cardiff
W.E DURSTON · Aberaman	SAM MORRIS · Ammanford	BRAZELL THOMAS · Llanelli
VICTORIANO ESTEBAN · Abercrave	W. MORRIS · Llanelli	R. TRAILL · Cardiff
GEORGE FRETWELL · Penygroes	DAN MURPHY · Cardiff	JAMES WATTS · Swansea
SID HAMM · Cardiff	FRANK OWEN · Mardy	FRED WHITE · Ogmore Vale
JACK HARRIS · Llanelli	TOM PICTON · Treherbert	J.E. WILLIAMS · Ammanford
RICHARD HORRIDGE · Swansea	ROMAN RODRIGUEZ · Dowlais	FRANK ZAMORRA · Abercrave

CORDOBA · JARAMA · BRUNETE · BELCHITE · SARAGOSSA · TERUEL · ARAGON · GANDESA (2) · EBRO

Tros ryddid daear syrthiodd yn y ffos,
Ai fys yn chwilio diced poeth ei wn.
Daw nodyn dwysa'r byd o glwyf y draen
A chan caniadau'r byd o ingoedd Spaen.

He fell exalting brotherhood and right,
His bleeding visage scorched by fire and smoke.
E'en as the sweetest note is born of pain,
So shall the song of songs be born in Spain.

Source 195

★ *In Memoriam* ★

WILLIE DAVIES

O F Court Street, Blaenclydach, joined the International Brigade in November, 1936. One of the first to volunteer he was on active service until his death. Leaving London, where he was then staying, with Ralph Fox, noted writer and Political Commissar of the International Brigade, Willie was in the first big battles; he was one of those heroes that saved Madrid when the hour was darkest for the people of Spain, when everyone thought that all was lost.

Although wounded, his spirit was unquenchable. All the terrors of Fascism could not break his heroic spirit, and on recovering he was again in the front line, cheering his comrades and playing a magnificent role. Again he was wounded and the Medical Commission offered him his discharge, even providing him with facilities for returning home. He refused, and from his last letter to his mother and father we quote, with grief and pride, his reason:

" I was willing to pay the supreme sacrifice for my ideals and I knew to what I was coming—war, the most loathsome thing ever known. Although I have been wounded I still hold to my views.

" I am not going to pretend to be any kind of a hero by saying that I don't want to come home, because I do wish to return, but as long as the workers of Spain need my services I shall stay."

Comrade Paynter, Political Commissar of the International Brigade, said of Willie Davies: " He was one of our best comrades and his comrades fight on, inspired by his example."

FRANK OWEN

O F Pentre Road, Mardy, had been a member of the Communist Party since 1936 and a member of the committee of the Mardy Lodge, S.W.M.F., since 1935.

He was imprisoned three times for his working-class activities. At the time of joining the International Brigade he was the " Daily Worker " agent for Mardy.

Answering the call for the defence of Spanish Democracy, he joined the Brigade in April of this year, and was killed in the recent big Government offensive on the Madrid front.

Writing to his wife in June, Frank said: " I'll come home sometime. I have no fear that anything will happen to me, but I must leave it to you to impress on the kids that I'll be home sometime. While I'm on this point, I must say that I came here to do a job which I must go through with and am more determined now than ever I was when I started from home. The line which I took and which you, fortunately, were a party to, has been proved correct a dozen times over since I came here. It's an ideal worth fighting for. I fought Fascism back home and read quite a lot concerning it, but you cannot visualise the brutalities of German, Italian and Spanish Fascism until you come here, see it in its most horrible nakedness and hear what the poor people tell you of conditions before and during the civil war. I do not wonder why these people are fighting with a determination previously unknown. Further, it is only a matter of time, as the legal Spanish Government has at its command an army second to none."

Of Comrade Frank Owen, Will Paynter, Political Commissar of the Brigade, said: " He proved himself worthy of the revolutionary traditions of ' Red Mardy.' A disciplined soldier, ready at all times to respond when a job had to be done."

DAVID JONES

O F George Street, Penygraig, was an ex-Grenadier Guardsman and joined anti-Fascist forces in London, where he was then living, in November, 1936. Proceeding to Spain, he joined the International Brigade on its formation and took part in all of its activities until he was killed in action in February last.

Comrade Springhall, leader of the London Communist Party, who was Political Commissar in the International Brigade during this period, said of our late comrade: " He was a splendid comrade, capable and reliable. His previous military training was utilised to the full in helping to train his comrades and sustaining their morale under fire. He carried his political convictions to the uttermost by making the supreme sacrifice."

THEY WHO LIVE IN THIS UNCONQUERABLE SPIRIT CAN NEVER DIE, AND FOR ALL TIME WILL THEIR MEMORY SERVE TO INSPIRE HUMANITY TO LIBERTY AND FREEDOM

Unconquerable

Spirit !

David Jones   Frank Owen   W.Davies
(PENYGRAIG)   (MARDY)   (BLAENCLYDACH)

who died fighting in the

BRITISH BATTALION

of the

International Brigade in Spain

Source: South Wales Miners' Library.

Further work on the evidence

Source 176: What are (a) the strengths (b) the weaknesses of this Document as historical evidence?

Source 177: How do you think you could set about proving that this was a genuine photograph of the time and not a fake?

Source 179: Do you agree that the map shows that points 1 to 6 are true?

Source 183 What further information would be useful to you in using this evidence to describe the experiences of volunteers going from Wales to fight in Spain?

Source 184: What use is this Document to someone who cannot read Spanish?

Source 188: Is there anything in this Document which might make you doubt that it is true in every detail?

Source 191: How might you check up that the information given in this Document is accurate? Is there any reason why it might not be accurate?

Source 194: What does this Document tell you about the *Aberdare Leader* newspaper?

Source 195: Just using the information here, can you say anything *general* about volunteers who fought in the Spanish Civil War?

Source 197: Why should South Wales miners dedicate a memorial to the Welshmen who died in the Spanish Civil War?

Cymru Fydd and Home Rule for Wales

700 years ago the Welsh, at least a large proportion of them, were conquered by the English. Llywelyn ap Gruffydd, who was to be Llywelyn the Last, was killed at Cilmeri, near Builth in mid-Wales. The English king, Edward I, quickly mopped up the rest of Welsh opposition. By the Statute of Wales, signed at Rhuddlan in 1284, Llywelyn's independent Wales was to be ruled over by the English king. Especially in the towns, or boroughs, of Wales, Welsh people were now second-class citizens in their own country.

Just over 100 years later the Welsh had a new hero, Owain Glyndŵr. He did not originally fight for Wales. He started off by pursuing a personal quarrel with Lord Grey of Ruthin. This quarrel developed into an attempt to win back independence for Wales, a Wales which would have a parliament, a university and a separate Church organisation. Owain failed, eventually, and disappeared into legend—no one knows where or when he died. The reality of his defeat was harsh for his fellow Welsh, because during Owain's revolt even harsher laws had been passed against the Welsh in their own country. These laws meant that they were not allowed to own land in certain places, for example.

In 1485 Henry Tudor, grandson of a Welshman from Anglesey, became King as Henry VII and the atmosphere at his court and in England and Wales changed. Welshmen were much more in favour, but the government of Wales was still unco-ordinated and inefficient. For this reason, among others, there were two momentous Acts of Parliament in 1536 and 1543. These were the Acts of Union. These Acts did two things of enormous significance in Welsh history. They united Wales with England, so giving Welsh and English equal rights as citizens.

Source 198

AN ACT FOR LAWS AND JUSTICE TO BE MINISTERED IN WALES IN LIKE FORM AS IT IS IN THIS REALM

That his (the King's) said Country or Dominion of Wales shall be, stand and continue for ever from henceforth incorporated united and annexed to and with this his Realm of England; and that all and singular Person and Persons, born or to be born in the said Principality Country or Dominion of Wales, shall have enjoy and inherit all and singular Freedoms Liberties Rights Privileges and Laws within this his Realm and other the King's Dominions, as other the King's Subjects naturally born within the same have, enjoy and inherit.
Source: Ivor Bowen, *The Statutes of Wales*, London, 1908.

Secondly, and part of the same process, the Acts did away with the Welsh language as an official language in anything to do with the courts and the law and the running of the country.

Source 199

Also be it enacted . . . That all Justices, Commissioners Sheriffs Coroners, Escheators Stewards and their Lieutenants, and all other Officers and Ministers of the Law, shall proclaim and keep the Sessions Courts . . . and all other Courts in the English Tongue; and all Oaths of Officers . . . to be given and done in the English Tongue; and also that from henceforth no Person or Persons that use the Welsh Speech or Language shall have or enjoy any Manner Office or Fees within this Realm of England, Wales, or other the King's Dominion, upon Pain of forfeiting the same Offices or Fees, unless he or they use and exercise the English Speech or Language . . .
Source: Bowen, *Statutes of Wales.*

Once these Acts were passed and put into force there was, in law, no such place as Wales, only a country which covered the area of England and Wales, though no name has ever been thought up for this combination. Of course in practice, Wales still existed. The vast majority of people in Wales still spoke only Welsh, and continued to do so until the 19th century. There was always some concern about the history—at many points a mysterious and half-understood one—of Wales. In the 18th century many writers, historians and scholars were particularly keen to rescue what they could of ancient Welsh poetry and documents. Although there was interest in the language and culture of Wales this had nothing to do with any kind of political or independence movement.

Then in the 19th century, Wales and her people went through dramatic changes, as did all the countries of western Europe. Wales changed more, and more quickly, than England in the 19th century because of the Industrial Revolution. Wales became a country of world importance because of its metal industries and, especially, because of its coal. From being a very poor country, because of the bad quality of its farm land, Wales became much more prosperous, though the Industrial Revolution produced not only wealth, but also squalor and disease and exploitation in the new towns.

Industrialisation changed people's lives in all kinds of ways. One of the most important changes was that by the end of the 19th century eight out of ten Welsh people lived in towns, whereas, a hundred years before, eight out of ten lived in the countryside. The other dramatic change which resulted from industrialisation was a change in politics, or the way power was shared among people in communities, and between those communities and central government in London. When Wales had been united with England in 1536-43 landowners were the most powerful people in Wales. The wealth of the country was in the land and those who owned it made sure that their money gave them political power as well. In the 19th century landowners were still very important in Wales, but there were more ways of being wealthy now. Some of the owners of factories and mines and iron works were just as wealthy as landowners and wanted their share of power, both locally and as Members of Parliament. Slowly and very gradually this came about. With industrialisation and increasing wealth came a much more complicated society and more and more professional people to help run that society—lawyers, doctors, teachers and, eventually, civil servants. This complicated society produced more goods for sale, and more people able to buy them, so that in the industrial areas there were now, in the second half of the 19th century, far more shopkeepers, many of whom became very wealthy by the standards of the incomes of people from the working class. These people also felt they should have more say in how their towns and their country were governed.

The other very important strand in this story is the way in which industrialisation produced conditions which made it possible, even inevitable, for people to protest. They protested against the way in which their wages went up and down without there being any discussion about the matter. They protested against the conditions in which they were forced to live, the rate of disease and accidents which affected them. The government in London was forced to deal with many of these problems, even though the last thing the government wanted was to get involved.

Because of industrialisation, then, government in Great Britain changed. Instead of the House of Commons being made up almost entirely of landowners it gradually became possible for a wider range of people to become M.P.s—solicitors or talented sons of poor farmers, for example. As a result of Reform Acts a far larger number of people had the vote by the end of the 19th century—in effect those people in towns and countryside who owned houses.

It was also the case that everybody was involved in what government did to a much greater extent because the government was forced, in the new conditions of the 19th century, to pass laws controlling health, hours of work, education, the treatment of poverty, safety in factories and a host of other matters affecting the lives of all the people. The state was becoming more and more important.

For Wales this meant that a new kind of politics was possible, with new kinds of people becoming involved. Because of the changes which industrialisation had produced in Wales, middle class people and working class people were now of great importance in politics. Whereas the old landowners had generally been English in their language and their interests, and regarded anything to do with the Welsh language and customs as second-rate, there were now, after about 1860, new champions of the Welsh language and Welsh institutions. Whereas the landowners had been members of the Church of England, the majority of Welsh people were Nonconformists, that is members of Methodist, Baptist and Independent chapels. One of the main movements in Wales in the second half of the 19th century was to bring to an end the privileges of the Church of England as the Established Church in Wales, entitled to a proportion of everybody's income. This opposition to landlords and the Church of England had to be *political* because it involved getting landlords voted out of their parliamentary seats and getting acts of Parliament passed. It also meant thinking of Wales as a different country from England—especially different in its religion.

This political activity centred around the Liberal party, in opposition to the Tory party. (There was no Labour party until the end of the 19th century). In the years after 1868 Wales sent more and more Liberal M.P.s to Parliament in Westminster. Indeed, there were so many Liberal M.P.s by the 1880s and 1890s that they had a great influence on the whole of the British Liberal party and government. In 1881, for the first time since the Acts of Union 350 years before, there was an Act of Parliament which applied only to Wales and so recognised it as different from England. It was an act to close Welsh public houses on Sundays.

Two Welsh Liberal M.P.s became particularly important. Tom Ellis was the son of a tenant-farmer in Bala, the kind of person who could never have hoped to have ended up in Parliament fifty years before. He went on eventually to become Chief Whip in the British Liberal party. The other was Lloyd George, future Prime Minister of Britain, a legend in his lifetime and a man of mystery, then and now, for years one of the most important politicians in the world.

In 1886, the year in which Ellis was elected M.P. for Merioneth, all that lay ahead. Welsh matters were pressing, and in 1887 Ellis founded the first branch of the *Cymru Fydd*—literally, Wales Will Be—movement. Under Ellis's guidance the society produced its Constitution and Rules in 1888.

Source 200
CONSTITUTION AND RULES OF THE 'CYMRU FYDD SOCIETY'

1. That the main purpose of the 'Cymru Fydd Society' be to secure a National Legislature for Wales, dealing exclusively with Welsh affairs, while preserving the relations with the British Parliament upon all questions of Imperial interest.
2. That the Society shall assist in securing the return to the House of Commons of thoroughly representative men, who will in the meantime advocate Welsh reforms, in accordance with the National aspiration.
3. That the Society stimulate the Welsh Party to more united and energetic action with regard to Welsh reforms and the interests of Wales . . .
4. That the Society shall exert its utmost efforts to establish like Societies within and without the Principality, and shall co-operate with other societies for the promotion of these objects.

Source: H.T.V. document pack, *The Dragon Has Two Tongues*, Pack 3, 9, 1.

From this document we can see that Tom Ellis and his supporters were not in favour of separating from the British parliament. The aim was to have a body in Wales to make laws on Welsh matters. Wales would still send Members of Parliament to the House of Commons. They felt that treating Wales in the same way as England would lead to certain injustices. Furthermore, both he and David Lloyd George argued that Wales, as a separate nation, with a separate voice, would have

special qualities which could be of considerable influence for good in the world. Ellis, particularly, saw Wales as a country of co-operating people, giving mutual help and support to each other in their communities. As a nation with a separate identity they could set an example to others.

Source 201
'We have never quarrelled with tyranny as the Irish have done. We have rather turned the other cheek to the smiter . . . This resolution is a fitting climax to this meeting's programme. You have pledged yourselves to—Disestablishment, Land Reform, Local Option and other great reforms. But, however drastic and broad they may appear to be, they after all simply touch the fringe of that vast social question which must be dealt with in the near future. There is a momentous time coming. The dark continent of wrong is being explored and there is a missionary spirit abroad for its reclamation to the realm of right . . . That is why I feel so sanguine that were self-government granted to Wales she would be a model to the nationalities of the earth of a people who have driven oppression from their hillsides, and initiated the glorious reign of freedom, justice and truth.'

Lloyd George, speech to South Wales Liberal Federation, February, 1890.

Source: Kenneth O. Morgan, ed., *Lloyd George Family Letters, 1885-1936.*

Tom Ellis worked hard in the late 1880s and the early 1890s for a limited amount of Home Rule. It was a time when the idea of national identity was becoming more and more important all over Europe. In Wales it did seem that the idea of a national identity was having some good results. The Welsh language was looked on more favourably—where once it had been regarded as a handicap. There was a healthy Welsh literature. Poetry was made available on a wide scale by the National Eisteddfod Association which was formed in 1880 to co-ordinate the most important Welsh folk festival of the arts. In 1889 an act of Parliament gave Wales a system of secondary schools unlike any in England. Perhaps a move towards some sort of political independence might work.

In 1888 Tom Ellis tried to get Parliament to agree to a National Council for Wales. It would be made up of Welsh M.P.s and some representatives from the new County Councils which were being set up.

In 1891 there was actually a bill put forward in Parliament for Welsh Home Rule. It involved setting up a National Council for Wales, with a Secretary of State for Wales and a Welsh education department. The bill was not very well thought out and it was thrown out by a very big majority. However, it does show how the idea of separate institutions for Wales was now a reality.

In the 1890s the aims of the *Cymru Fydd* movement became more obviously political, especially as Lloyd George took control of the movement. Lloyd George and his supporters wanted the British Liberal Party to take up the idea of Home Rule for Wales, and Lloyd George himself was in a good position to pursue his ideas after 1890 when he became an M.P.

By 1894 there was a full-scale organisation for the *Cymru Fydd* movement. There were branches of the movement all over north Wales and mid-Wales, and there were some in south Wales, too. A national *Cymru Fydd* League had been set up to bring together the work of the branches and to co-operate at all levels with the all-powerful Welsh Liberal party. In fact, in 1895 the Federation of Liberals in north Wales actually joined with the *Cymru Fydd* League. This looked like a very powerful organisation indeed. However, the wealth and therefore much of the influence, of Wales lay in the south mainly, the centre of the coal industry, and in the south Wales coastal towns of Newport, Cardiff and Swansea. It was from here that the coal was exported and the shipowners and coal traders had their headquarters.

Then, in 1895, came two disasters for *Cymru Fydd*'s notion of Home Rule for Wales. The first was that in June 1895 the Liberal government at Westminster, which had been so dependent on Welsh M.P.s for support, was defeated in an election. The second disaster, was more basic because it showed a disunited Wales. Lloyd George, as we have seen, was now working flat out for the *Cymru Fydd* cause. He had plenty of support in north Wales but it was absolutely essential that the important south Wales Liberal Federation should support him too. In 1895 Lloyd George went to south Wales to give a series of lectures to try to win support for the Home Rule cause.

The campaign for south Wales support was in full swing in November, 1895, and seemed to be proving successful.

Source 202

'*12 November 1895* (from Ferndale, Rhondda)
Today we had a most successful Cymru Fydd conference at the Café, the best men of the town being present. Elfed & I spoke. Elfed is with us heart & soul. I made the best speech I ever made in my life. The only man who spoke in favour of postponement was the Methodist minister. I adroitly hinted that Herbert Lewis would come down to address their demonstration. This chap then subsided & was instantly put on the Committee.'

20 November 1895 (from Tonypandy)
The Rhondda is coming over to us bodily.
Source: Kenneth O. Morgan, ed., *Lloyd George Family Letters, 1885-1936*, Oxford and Cardiff, 1973, pp. 90, 91.

Yet not everything was to Lloyd George's liking.

Source 203

'*19 November 1895* (from Tredegar)
Got a capital meeting last night altho' the audience in these semi-English districts are not comparable to those I get in the Welsh districts. Here the people have sunk into a morbid footballism.'

Source: Morgan, *Lloyd George Letters*, p. 91.

Lloyd George's worries were to prove right. Two months later he suffered a massive defeat in his fight for Welsh Home Rule. There was a meeting at Newport at which he was hoping to see the South Wales Liberal Federation combine with the *Cymru Fydd* League. This is his account of that meeting.

Source 204

'*16 January 1896* (from Newport)
The meeting of the Federation was a packed one. Associations supposed to be favourable to us were refused representation & men not elected at all received tickets. There were two points of dispute between us. By some oversight they allowed me to speak on one & we carried it—as it turned out not because the majority of the meeting was with us but because they went to the vote immediately after my speech & I can assure you the impression made could be felt. I simply danced upon them. So they refused to allow me to speak on the second point. The majority present were Englishmen from the Newport district. The next step is that we mean to summon a Conference of South Wales & to fight it out. I am in bellicose form & don't know when I can get home.'

Source: Morgan, *Lloyd George Letters*, p. 94.

Effectively, *Cymru Fydd* was dead after this. The business men of south-east Wales had made it clear that they were not interested in the idea of Wales becoming separated politically from England.

The man who started it, and one of its greatest spokesmen, Tom Ellis, died in 1899, still a young man at the height of his powers. Lloyd George went on to be Prime Minister during the Great War and after. Never again did he give his energies to trying to give Home Rule to Wales.

Further work on the evidence

Source 201: What would you say Lloyd George's attitude to Home Rule was in 1890 from the evidence given in this document?

Sources 202, 204: These sources seem to contradict each other. Can you think of any reasons why this should be so?

Plaid Cymru—Foundation and Development

In looking at the *Cymru Fydd* movement we saw that in the early days Tom Ellis's main emphasis was on Welsh culture. The Welsh language is a very ancient one. It goes back about 1200 years, when masterpieces of Welsh poetry were being composed. Welsh traditions and history are equally ancient. Tom Ellis and his supporters at the time were anxious that these traditions, seen in the poetry and the history of the Welsh, should be passed on. In order that this should happen there should be a Welsh university and Welsh secondary schools, a Welsh museum and a Welsh library. So Welshmen who had influence in parliament and in the cultural life of Wales worked for these things.

Cymru Fydd would never have come into existence if Welsh patriotism had not been strong. It continued to be strong. In the second half of the 19th century Wales was a great industrial success, a vital part of the world's economy. The *eisteddfod* was a national festival showing the strength of a widespread popular culture in Wales. Many history books were written which told of great Welsh heroes and painted a picture of Wales as a land of culture and education and good behaviour. The chapels in Wales had a very strong membership. They held meetings, debates, lectures and music festivals. Welsh was the first language of about half the population.

Wales had a national anthem which was enormously popular. It had the same message as the history books—the land of my fathers is dear to me; it is a land of poets and singers, fighters for freedom, a country to which it is worth pledging love and loyalty.

Wales was also getting an identity through sport. This was particularly the case in rugby. In 1893 Wales won the Triple Crown for the first time. Between 1901 and 1912 she won the Triple Crown six times. In 1905 Wales beat the New Zealand 'All Blacks', as much of an achievement then as it is now.

In the 1890s a state system of secondary schools was established which was run on rather different lines from the one which developed in England. In 1893 the University of Wales was set up which allowed the University Colleges of Wales to give Welsh degrees, not degrees of the University of London. In the 1900s there came a National Library and a National Museum. There was also a Welsh Department of the Board of Education, which seemed to acknowledge Wales as requiring some special governmental treatment. And yet for some people there was a feeling of unease about these successes.

Source 205

'The truth has been that the intellectual movement in Wales, while it has been a strong supporter of Welsh nationalism, on its linguistic and literary sides, has hardly created an atmosphere favourable for Welsh Home Rule.'

Source: J. A. Price, 'Is Welsh Home Rule Coming?' *Welsh Outlook*, July 1917, p. 247. Quoted in D. Howell Davies, *The Welsh Nationalist Party 1925-1945*, Cardiff, University of Wales Press, 1983, p. 1.

Cymru Fydd had failed to get Home Rule. It was not a movement which had captured the loyalties of the majority of the Welsh and the kind of home rule it worked for was not well thought out. Things were not going quite so well for the Welsh language. The census of 1901 showed that, for the first time, less than half the people living in Wales could speak Welsh. This drew attention to what was a continuous decline in the proportion of Welsh speakers. There were many people in Wales who believed that without its language Wales was doomed.

Within Welsh Nationalism there have always been these two strands. The first has been cultural nationalism. The second has been political nationalism. They both go right through the story of nationalism in the 20th century. They often seemed to tell different, contradictory stories. There is an example of this at the time of the first World War. E. T. John was a Liberal M.P., and a man held in high regard by all schools of nationalists, as can be seen from this obituary.

Source 206

MR. E. T. JOHN

Gweddus iawn yw i'r DDRAIG GOCH gofnodi gyda galar farwolaeth Mr. Edward Thomas John yn 73 oed. Yr oedd Mr. John yn genedlaetholwr Cymreig gwirioneddol. Treuliodd oes hir yn brwydro dros hawliau gwleidyddol Cymru, cyflwynodd fesur llywodraeth i Gymru yn Nhy'r Cyffredin, cyhoeddodd lyfrau a phamffledi lawer ar y pwnc, astudiodd yn drwyadl agweddau economaidd y mater, ac ymladdodd ei etholiad seneddol olaf yn 1924 fel ymgeisydd dros ''Lafur a Chenedlaetholdeb Cymreig'', ac y mae'n hysbys mai oherwydd y mynnai ef gadw'r ddau air olaf yna yn ei deitl y gwrthododd Mr. Ramsay Macdonald ddyfod i Frycheiniog i siarad dros ei ymgeisiaeth. Yn y blynyddoedd diwethaf hyn rhoes Mr. John gymorth ei wybodaeth helaeth a'i farn ddewr yn hael i'r BLAID GENEDLAETHOL, a bu ei bresenoldeb yn rhai o bwyllgorau'r Blaid yn fantais sylweddol iddi.

Gŵr gonest a da ydoedd. Bu unwaith yn gyfoethog. Ychydig sy'n gwybod am faint dirfawr ei haelioni preifat. Yn ddiweddar, cyn dyfod yr iseldra diwydiannol a cholli ohono filoedd lawer, ni welid ei enw yn aml ar restrau tanysgrifwyr hynod ac enwog. Y rheswm am hynny oedd ei fod yn caru rhoi yn y dirgel; ac ni wyddai ond ychydig ohonom am ei hunan-aberth ef dros rai a ddibynnai arno.

Ofnai rhai ohonom ei fod yn gwastraffu ei amser i raddau gyda'i hoff sefydliad, sef y Gyngres Geltaidd; ond ni ddywedwyd y gair olaf eto ar honno chwaith, ac efallai pan sgrifenner ei hanes y gwelir nad yn gwbl ofer y llafuriodd Mr. John drosti a thrwyddi. Aeth gŵr da i'w orffwystra, a chollodd Cymru fab a'i carodd yn unplyg ac o galon.

S.L.

Source: Ddraig Goch, March 1931.

John actually put forward a Bill in Parliament in 1914 for a government for Wales. In some ways it was based on a more solid foundation than *Cymru Fydd* movements because E. T. John had tried to show that it was *economically* sound to have Welsh self-government. But even of the Welsh M.P.s only eleven supported the Bill and it got nowhere. Then, the year after the war ended, an Act of Parliament was passed which did away in Wales with the greatest grievance of the Welsh Liberal M.P.s, the established Church of England. For non-conformists it was a great victory. For all Christians the setting up of a Church in Wales was another sign of Wales as a distinct, different part of Britain.

For some people, like Lewis Valentine, the man who would be the first President of Plaid Cymru, the terrible First World War seemed to strengthen their belief in Wales and Welsh nationalism.

Source 207

'Having believed the rigmarole of the politicians that it was a war to give freedom to small nations, I accepted it totally. When I came out of the war, I was an out-and-out Welsh nationalist.'

Source: Lewis Valentine, quoted in D. Howell Davies, *the Welsh Nationalist Party 1925-1945*, Cardiff, University of Wales Press, 1983, p. 24.

There were new writers and scholars committed to Wales and to the Welsh language. Some Welsh politicians talked about Home Rule. There was some pressure to give Wales a Secretary of State. There was a report in 1920 which recommended local Parliaments for Scotland and Wales, but there was no enthusiasm for this. Another Bill went before parliament in 1922 which would have set up a government for Wales. But it got nowhere. As had been the case for the last 500 years there was a great difference between the situation in Wales—and in Scotland—to the situation in Ireland. By 1922 much of Ireland had achieved Home Rule. Could it be that the Welsh as a people were content with an inferior status? Why did most of the Welsh feel differently from the Irish about ruling themselves?

Up until 1925 political pressure came mainly from the Liberal Party in Wales. However, there were new types of Welsh nationalist, fearful for the future of the Welsh language, and fed up with all the conferences and talk there had been without any action. They could not stand the situation any more.

Source 208

'My firm opinion is this—that it is necessary also to break every link with the Parliament in England. That is essential to the success of our objectives. The nationalist party must work in Wales, through the local authorities; making Wales Welsh through them, and leaving the parliament of England alone, boycotting Parliament, and thereby making a Welsh Wales a fact . . . Nothing will ever come to Wales through the Parliament of England.'

Source: Saunders Lewis, quoted in Davies, *The Welsh Nationalist Party*, p. 41.

Source 209

'There is a need for Nationalists to represent Wales—not Conservatives and Liberals, but nationalists first; they can be party men second.'

Source: Iorwerth C. Peate, quoted in Davies, *The Welsh Nationalist Party*, p. 28.

It was clear to people like this exactly what must be done.

Source 210

'A Welsh Government is the only thing that will give us a wholly Welsh society, with a Welsh civilisation, Welsh literature, and Welsh life, with the language blossoming in the security that will come from a government which will defend it. Indeed, here, ultimately, is the strongest argument: there is no civilisation without politics. Conclusion? Let us work for home rule. For the time being, politics first.'

Source: Bebb, quoted in Davies, *The Welsh Nationalist Party*, p. 36.

They took a strong line on the Welsh language. Professor Watkin of Cardiff suggested that:

Source 211

'the two languages spoken in Wales should have an equal right to be used in schools, in the administrative departments of the country, in the preparation, debate and publication of every law and every rule and order formulated for the benefit of Wales. The educational institutions of Wales should be so organised that every pupil can receive a substantial proportion of the elements of education in his own natural language.'

Source: M. Watkin, quoted in Davies, *Welsh Nationalist Party*, p. 73.

Saunders Lewis believed that this was not enough.

Source 212

'The Welsh language must be the only official language of Wales, the language of government in Wales, the language of every county and town and district council, of the staffs of the councils, and of courts of law. Every public medium that transmits information, such as wireless, must be in Welsh, and must be used to sustain and promote Welsh identity. In a word, all the social life of Wales, and every instrument of social life, must adapt consistently and unswervingly to one objective: that is, a Welsh civilisation for Wales.'

Source: Saunders Lewis, quoted in *Welsh Nationalist Party*, p. 74.

In order to try to achieve these objectives a new party was founded in 1925. This was *Plaid Genedlaethol Cymru,* later to be called *Plaid Cymru,* the Welsh Nationalist Party. It was founded during the week of the National Eisteddfod at Pwllheli. The Party had its own newspaper and its own emblem.

Source 213

Cenedlaetholdeb a Chyfalaf.
GAN SAUNDERS LEWIS

Y Ddraig Goch

Organ Plaid Genedlaethol Cymru.

CYF. I.   RHIF 1.   MEHEFIN 1926.   PRIS DWY GEINIOG.

Y TRIBAN.

What do you think this emblem was intended to represent? Why?

The aim of the movement was not originally to get self-government for Wales, though from 1932 the Party's policy was dominion status for Wales on the same footing as Canada or Australia.

Source 214

'We demand that Wales should be an equal, free and self-governing member of the British Commonwealth of Nations. This is the status, commonly referred to in political terms as Dominion Status, that is at present enjoyed by the Dominions of Canada, Australia, New Zealand, the Union of South Africa, and that was recently granted to the Irish Free State.'

Source: Party Policy October 1931, quoted in Howell Davies, *The Welsh Nationalist Party*, p. 83.

The immediate concern was to ensure the future of the Welsh language. *Plaid Cymru* wanted Welsh to be made the only official language of Wales. Welsh would also be the language of education at school and university.

Plaid Cymru did not have much impact immediately. Then, in 1936 came an event which focussed attention on the Party. The background was that in 1935 the Air Ministry decided to set up a Royal Air Force base at Penyberth in the Lleyn Peninsula in north Wales. It would specialise in training in bombing techniques. Many people in north Wales welcomed the plan because it would bring jobs to the area. Welsh Nationalists objected to the plan because it would set up a camp of 700 people right in the heart of Welsh-speaking Wales. A previous plan to set the camp up in England had been turned down because of the damage it would cause to bird life in the area! Some nationalists were also pacifists, so they naturally objected.

Here, then was an obvious nationalist cause. It came exactly 400 years after the first Act of Union which bound Wales so closely to England. Many nationalists believed that there should be passive resistance.

Saunders Lewis was determined to do more. At 1.30 a.m., September 8th, 1936, three leaders of the Welsh Nationalist Party, Saunders Lewis, The President, The Rev. Lewis Valentine, its previous President, and D. J. Williams set fire to workmen's huts and some wood on the site.

No other people were involved. The three men went straight to Pwllheli Police Station to report what they had done.

In October 1936 the three men appeared in

court at Caernarfon charged with arson and malicious damage. There were disputes about their use of the Welsh language in court. A dispute which had originally not aroused much public interest was now big news in Wales and had become an extremely significant matter for Wales. Saunders Lewis made it clear that this was *not* part of a campaign of violence.

Source 215

Revd. Lewis Valentine, Saunders Lewis, D. J. Williams

Source: Y Ddraig Goch, March 1936.

Source 216

'I have repeated and publicly declared that the Welsh Nation must gain its political freedom without resort to violence or to physical force. And I submit to you that our action in burning the Penrhos Aerodrome proves the sincerity of this affirmation. Had we wished to follow the methods of violence, with which national minority movements are sometimes taunted, and into which they are often driven, nothing could have been easier for us than to ask some of the generous and spirited young men of the Welsh Nationalist Party to set fire to the aerodrome and get away undiscovered. It would have been the beginning of methods of sabotage and guerilla turmoil.'

Source: Saunders Lewis quoted in Davies, *The Welsh Nationalist Party*, p. 163.

The jury in the Caernarfon court could not agree on their verdict. The Judge had to order a new trial. This time the full weight of English government authority was brought to bear. The new trial was put on in the most famous of courts in England, the Old Bailey. The jury were Londoners. Not surprisingly they were not concerned with the wider issues of nationalism in Wales. They could not understand what all the fuss was about. Why should three men, all highly educated and perfectly fluent in English, refuse to give evidence in English? The

evidence was not disputed. In the heart of London it was an open and shut case. Guilty. Nine months imprisonment.

Source 217 *(See page 108)*

Can you think of reasons why the prisoners and their Party got more support in Wales than they had ever done before? There was a surge of confidence.

Source 218

Y DDRAIG GOCH, MEDI, 1937

y Ddraig Goch

PAPUR PLAID CENEDLAETHOL CYMRU

RHIFYN ARBENNIG Y RHYDDHAU

CYFROL XI, RHIF 9   MEDI 1937   PRIS: DWY GEINIOG

" O GARCHAR OFN DAETH YN RHYDD "

Llun ydyw hwn a dynnwyd gan y Dr. Gwent Jones ar ei ymweliad â Mr. Saunders Lewis yng Ngharchar Wormwood Scrubs. Y mae yn llun nodedig iawn. Tu ol i'r waliau diadlam hyn yr oedd y Tri, ac uwch eu pen adar adwythig Annwfn. Dau simbol effeithiol, y naill o'r ormes oesol a fu ar Gymru, y llall o'i myngeiant hacraf yn ein dyddiau ni. Llun anobaith, darlun o'r pethau sydd yn llethu Cymru, arwyddlun y barbareiddiwch a fu'n ein bygwth ymhob cenhedlaeth.

Ond i'r Blaid Genedlaethol, darlun gobaith ydyw'r darlun hwn, arwyddlun buddugoliaeth. Oblegid darlun ydyw o elyn a wynebwyd ac a goncrwyd, celain bwystfil a laddwyd ydyw. A'r gelyn a'r bwystfil hwnnw

ydyw Ofn. O fewn y muriau hyn y dangoswyd, peth na chredasai neb cyn hyn, fod Cymru yn wlad y gellid dioddef drosti yn ogystal ag elwa arni, ei bod yn wrthrych serch yn ogystal ag yn gyfle uchelgais. O fewn i'r muriau hyn yr achubwyd enw da Cymru gerbron brawdle ei Hanes ei hun ac ar goedd byd. Yn bennaf oll, o fewn i'r muriau hyn y gwisgodd Cymru gig a gwaed, a throi o fod yn breswylydd amgueddfa a chrair yr hanesydd, i fod yn gydymaith byw. Megis yn Odysseia Homer na allai ysbryd y proffwyd marw Teiresias lefaru gair wrth y byw nes yfed o rym gwaed yr aberth, felly y mae llawer na fedrodd "ysbryd" Cymru lefaru gair wrthynt nes i aberth a dioddefaint y

Tri arllwys gwaed i'w wythiennau gwelw a gosod llafar ar ei dafod mud.

Source 219

Croeso Cenedlaetholdeb i'r Tri

Cynhaliwyd Cyfarfod Croeso Cenedlaethol i dderbyn y Tri i'w gwlad yn ôl o Garchar estron Wormwood Scrubbs, nos Sadwrn, Medi 11eg am 6 o'r gloch. Gorlanwyd Pafiliwn Caernarfon, yr adeilad cyhoeddus mwyaf yng Nghymru, sydd yn dal 12,000, a bernir bod tua 5,000 rhagor y tuallan i'r Pafiliwn. Gwasanaethwyd gan Seindorf Llanberis. Arweiniwyd y canu cynulleidfaol gan Mr. Ffowc Williams, Llandudno. Cadeiriwyd gan yr Athro J. E. Daniel. Anerchwyd gan y Tri, yn y drefn hon: Lewis Valentine, D. J. Williams a Saunders Lewis. Pasiwyd yn unfrydol benderfyniadau (a) o groeso, (b) yn cyhoeddi gwrthwynebiad di-ildio i'r Ysgol Fomio, ac yn galw ar y Llywodraeth ei thynnu'n ôl yn ddioed, ac (c) yn condemnio ymddygiad Cyngor Coleg Abertawe tuagat Mr. Saunders Lewis. Nid oedd (c) ar raglen y cyfarfod, codi o eiddigedd y gynulleidfa dros un o feibion mwyaf Cymru a wnaeth. Gwnaed casgliad o £66, gwerthwyd gwerth £40 o lenyddiaeth, ac ymunodd 500 o aelodau newydd â'r Blaid.

Source: Y Ddraig Goch, October, 1937.

On their release the men were greeted as heroes by an enormous meeting in Caernarfon.

Source 220 *(See page 109)*

Source 217

Dramatic End to Nationalists' Trial

SCENES AT THE OLD BAILEY

Accused Refuse to Call Witnesses

"NO DEFENCE OF ANY SORT" SAYS JUDGE

DEMONSTRATION IN HYDE PARK

(Special Press Association Report).

LONDON, Tuesday.

Three Welsh Nationalists appeared before Mr. Justice Charles at the Old Bailey to-day on charges arising out of a fire at the Royal Air Force base and bombing school near Pwllheli last September. They were:—

John Saunders Lewis, (42), of St. Peter's-road, Mumbles, Swansea.

The Rev. Lewis Edward Valentine, (42), of St. Andrew's-place, Llandudno;

David John Williams, (51), of High-street, Fishguard.

All the defendants are well-known figures throughout Wales. Mr. Lewis is President of the Welsh Nationalist Party and a lecturer in Welsh at Swansea University College.

The Rev. Lewis Valentine is Vice-President of the party and pastor of the Welsh Baptist Church, Llandudno.

Mr. Williams is a Welsh master at Fishguard Secondary School, and has attained some prominence as a Welsh novelist.

The trial was removed from Caernarvon Assizes where, in October, before Mr. Justice Lewis, the jury failed to agree.

The charges upon which accused were committed for trial accused them of unlawful and malicious damage to buildings, timber and other articles, the property of the King, to the extent of £2,355, and feloniously and maliciously setting fire to certain buildings, the property of the King.

Counsel for the prosecution were Mr. W. N. Stable, K.C., and Mr. Bertram Reece (Recorder of Birkenhead).

AN EARLY QUEUE.

The Old Bailey has had many queues outside its entrances for famous trials, but never one of the type that waited for hours to-day. They spoke Welsh, and comprised bankers, stockbrokers, shopkeepers, ministers, and schoolmasters. Many of them were accompanied by their wives.

The first Welsh contingent—one from North Wales—arrived promptly at eight a.m. They had reached London about three hours previously and after breakfast marched to the Old Bailey. They were the "advance guard" of about seven hundred Welsh men and women coming to London.

Among the places represented in the queue shortly after nine a.m. were: Caernarvon, Llanberis, Penygroes, Menai Bridge, Conway, Llandudno, and Colwyn Bay. The wife, sister, and sister-in-law of Mr. Valentine, one of the defendants, were in the front of the queue. They had a letter from the Chief Constable of Caernarvon asking the police to give them every facility in order to hear the case.

It was only after much persuasion that any of the Welsh people consented to speak in English to a Press Association reporter.

... out a special ticket was allowed to enter the well of the court. Among those left outside were many prominent public men in Wales, religious leaders, and "Bards."

Nevertheless, the floor of the court was filled to its utmost capacity when the three accused were called upon to surrender to their bail. They came from the lobby into the court and passed through the dock to the rooms below, and there waited until the jury, which had been engaged in the part-heard case, had been dismissed.

THE TRIAL BEGINS.

Then the three men walked to their places in the dock. Valentine stood in the centre, and was an impressive and commanding figure. Lewis, had his hair brushed smartly back, revealing a high forehead, with eyes which took a deep interest in everything round him.

Williams, stout, with ruddy complexion, and wore thick horned spectacles.

ONE WOMAN ON JURY.

There was one woman on the jury.

Mrs. Valentine did not enter the court but remained seated outside with a friend.

None of the prisoners was legally represented.

THE CHARGES.

The charge against them was of maliciously setting fire to certain buildings belonging to His Majesty the King on September 8, 1936.

On a second count they were charged with maliciously committing damage to buildings, stacks and other articles, the property of the King, to the amount of £2,355, in the night, between September 7 and 8, 1936.

The prisoners pleaded not guilty, and the judge allowed them to be seated.

PROSECUTION'S CASE.

Mr. Stable, opening for the prosecution, said that the indictment against the three defendants contained two counts, but the occurrence, the facts in relation to which they were charged, all related to one occurrence and one occasion. Those facts lay in the smallest possible compass. In the summer of last year the Government, having bought the ground, was in course of constructing a camp for the R.A.F. near Pwllheli. On the night of September 7–8 the night watchman who was employed at the camp was making his rounds, and up to a point he found that everything was in order. Some time after midnight he was set on from behind by two men. He was thrown to the ground, and was held there. While he was on the ground he saw another person quite close moving about this partially constructed camp, and then he saw flames beginning to spring up in one or two places. He did not suggest that he was struck, or that he was ...

... tion to build a bombing camp was first announced, we and many leaders of the public life of Wales did everything we could to get the English Government to refrain from building an institution which would endanger all the culture and traditions of one of the most Welsh regions in Wales. But in spite of all our pleas, in spite of letters of protest that we have had from hundreds of religious and lay societies throughout the whole of Wales, and though thousands of the electors at Pwllheli itself sent a petition imploring the prevention of the atrocity, yet the English Government refused even to receive a deputation from Wales to talk over the matter. Lawful and peaceful methods failed to secure for Wales even common courtesy at the hands of the Governmet of England. Therefore, in order to compel attention to this immoral violation of the sure and natural rights of the Welsh nation, we have taken this method, the only method left to us by a Government which is contemptuous of the Welsh nation."

The statement was signed by the three accused. The Chief Constable pointed out to them that they had admitted doing a very serious thing, and asked them if they understood the position. Each answered, again speaking in Welsh, that they did understand.

The Superintendent asked them how they set the place on fire. Lewis answered first, saying that everything was in the letter, that it was all explained there. That was not quite what the Superintendent meant and he asked them again how they set it alight. Saunders Lewis, looking at the other two, answered, "With petrol and a syringe."

"It is a commonplace of British justice that the prosecution have got to prove a criminal charge before anyone can be convicted. If there be any reasonable doubt in the matter then it is the duty of the jury to acquit. But in this case there is no room for doubt of any sort, kind or description. To set fire to a camp of this kind, is, of course, a criminal act. These men have admitted in the clearest possible way that it was they who set fire to the camp, that they did it deliberately and intentionally with the object of calling attention to a grievance

"They felt that this particular part of the United Kingdom had suffered by having an Air Force camp erected there. It is clear from the statement by the accused that what they did, they did deliberately, knowing that they were breaking the law and that they would in consequence have to stand their trial on a criminal charge. Indeed, they did it with that very object. In pleading not guilty to that charge they are presumably inviting you to return a verdict in their favour of not guilty, notwithstanding their admission of their direct responsibility for what was done."

"It is no part of my duty" (added Counsel) "in presenting the case for the Crown, to suggest that these three men were not honestly opposed to the erection of this Air Force camp on that site. I do not suggest for a moment that their opposition to the camp was not a perfectly honest opposition. But neither is it part of the duty of those on whom falls the responsibility of saying by their verdict whether the defendants did what the prosecution alleges they did, and which, incidentally, is admitted by the defendants themselves, to decide or even to consider whether the opposition of these men to this camp was well or ill-founded.

"In this country there are other places and other occasions for the discussion of the different points of view on these and similar matters, which may be the subject of perfectly honest controversy between honest men.

"This is a court of justice, and here, the administration of justice in this country, no political or other outside consideration is allowed on one side or the other to deflect us for a moment or by a hair's breadth from the discharge of our duty which is to administer the law of the country as we find it."

Mr Stable said that the defendants in asking the jury to return a verdict of not guilty—the three defendants on their own admission having broken the law—were inviting the jury to return a verdict which was in flat contradiction to the whole of the evidence, and which must involve a violation by each of them of the oath which they had taken.

"I invite you to return a true verdict and ...

Mr. Justice Charles: Of your own knowledge can he speak English?—He can, my lord.

Have you heard him speak English?—I have my lord.

Now regarding Williams: Of your own knowledge can he speak English?—I have never heard him speak English, my lord.

You can only deal with the other two?—Yes.

Supt. Hughes then left the box and Davies returned.

"ENGLISH OR NOT AT ALL."

Addressing the accused, Mr. Justice Charles said: "John Saunders Lewis, do you wish to ask the witness any question, because if you do you will ask it in English or not at all?"

Lewis made no reply.

Mr. Justice Charles then put the same question to Valentine, who replied to him in Welsh, and his Lordship said, "I have said if you want to ask a question, you must do so in English or not at all."

Valentine replied again in Welsh and was told to sit down.

When there was some talking in the public gallery the judge said, "I must have no talking in court. If people wish to talk let them talk outside and not inside."

The Judge added that the police inspector had told him that he had never heard David John Williams speak English. Williams must have an interpreter.

An interpreter was sworn and asked Williams if he had any questions to ask. Williams, through the interpreter, replied that he did not wish to ask any questions.

The judge: Ask him whether he has understood the evidence which has been given by this witness.

Williams, through the interpreter, replied that he did.

TIMEKEEPER'S EVIDENCE.

John Mackie Abbott, of Dundee, who is employed as a timekeeper at the aerodrome, stated that about ten minutes to three on the morning of September 8 he went to the aerodrome. Stacks of cedar wood and sections of huts were ablaze. His own office was burned to the ground and all the men's health and unemployment insurance cards and the office records and letters were burned. After the fire was extinguished he found that a number of buildings had been burned, including the office, a big tool shed and two huts.

Counsel: After the fire did you find anything about the place?—Yes, I went back to where my office stood to see if I could find several of my own belongings and just in front of where the door had been I found a syringe.

A brass syringe about two feet long was produced and Mr. Abbott said that it was the one that he had found.

Counsel: So far as you know is that the sort of thing kept at the aerodrome?—I have never seen one at the aerodrome.

Three petrol tins, two painted green and one blackened as if by fire, were produced.

Counsel: Have you ever seen those at the aerodrome?—No, not until just after the fire.

Two more brass syringes were shown to the witness who said that he had never seen them at the aerodrome.

The Judge asked Lewis and Valentine whether they wished to put any questions in English. Lewis shook his head and Valentine replied "No" in Welsh.

The Judge then called the interpreter to put the same question to Williams.

Williams uttered a few sentences in Welsh.

The Judge: What does he say?

"He says," the interpreter replied, "that he will not ask any questions in this court since he refuses to recognise the jurisdiction of the court and asks for the trial to be removed to his own country."

The Judge: Very well, he may sit down.

Andrew Ferris, of Baker Street, Glasgow, said that he was employed as foreman-bricklayer at the aerodrome. On the night of the fire he was roused and went to the aerodrome with Mr. Abbott, arriving about ten to three in the morning. Before the fire was put out he found a petrol tin beside a stack of bricks about thirty yards from the buildings which were burning. The tin, when he found it, was half full of petrol, and the stopper was off. The fire was blazing pretty fiercely.

asked if it were important, and Va
plied that the aerodrome was on
Superintendent got up and came
office, where Lewis handed him a

Preston said that he subsequen
pamed the Superintendent to the
and later in the day cautioned an
the three defendants. They we
charged on September 16, but mad

Superintendent W. M. Hughes, o
said that he was called by Constab
and saw the three defendants in th
the police station. Lewis handed
statement which had been written
The Superintendent said that he
statement and then told defend
they admitted having done a ve
thing. He asked them how they h
place on fire, and Lewis replied, "I
is in the letter." He again asked
had set the aerodrome on fire. Le
at the other two defendants and
plied, "With a syringe and petro

Answering Mr. Justice Charles,
tendent Hughes said that the doc
signed by the three defendants
joint statement.

He visited the aerodrome and
stacks of timber all ablaze. The
north-westerly gale blowing.

Thomas William Jones, a solicito
clerk, of Pwllheli, who had acted
preter in the court, was the next w
said that he had prepared a tra
the statement that had been referre
other witnesses. This was the
dressed to the Chief Constable o
von, and dated September 7. It w
and accurate translation.

ACCUSED'S LETTER TO PC

The Clerk of the Court was th
the two pages of foolscap which
witnesses had identified as the stat
tained in the letter to the Chief
He read it as follows:

"Sir, we who sign this letter ac
our responsibility for the dam
was done to the buildings of th
camp this evening. Ever since th
to build a Lleyn bombing cam
announced we, and many of the
the public life of Wales, did eve
could to get the English Govern
frain from placing in Lleyn an
which would endanger all the c
traditions of one of the most
gions in Wales. But in spite of
ings, in spite of the letters ar
forwarded from hundreds of re
lay societies throughout the
Wales, and although thousan
electors of Lleyn itself signed
imploring prevention of the at
the English Government refus
receive a deputation from Wa
over the matter. Lawful an
methods failed to secure for V
common courtesy at the hands c
ernment of England. Therefor
to compel attention to this imn
tion of the sure and natural rig
Welsh nation, we have taken th
the only method left to us by
ment which is contemptuous of
nation.

"Yours in the bonds of Wale

The letter was signed by the
fendants.

Mr. Stable said that at the Assi
fendants had said, "We do not v
anything, we do not wish to ca
nesses."

This was the case for the Cro

ACCUSED DECLINE TO EVIDENCE.

Lewis and Valentine both dec
Justice Charles' offer to go into t
box or address the jury, and whe
was asked by the interpreter if
to say anything, he replied in Wel
going to say one word, my Lord

Addressing the jury in Welsh,
translated by the interpreter, wil
"I am not going to plead my case
consider, with every respect to the
jurymen, that they can do just
cause, and that no one can do jus
cause except jurors from our ov
nation."

JUDGE'S SUMMING U

Source: Document 3, produced in association with the HTV series The Dragon has Two Tongues.

This support did not last. There was no long term increase in membership of the Party. There were no successes of the Party's candidates in the County Council elections. It was still not clear what exactly the Welsh Nationalist Party stood for and particularly how it achieved its aims. Its leaders, Saunders Lewis certainly, believed that the Party would not succeed if it just relied on fighting elections. He was convinced, and always remained so, that the government would not listen to reason and that the only way to achieve full recognition for the Welsh language and independence was by civil disobedience. In 1939 Saunders Lewis resigned as President of the Party which he had helped to establish.

Source 220

Some of the thousands who packed the Caernarfon Pavilion in 1937 to welcome Saunders Lewis, D. J. Williams and the Revd. Lewis Valentine following their release from prison. It was an euphoric occasion.

Further work on the evidence

Source 206: This obituary to E. T. John, former Liberal M.P., later a member of the Labour party, written in the newspaper of the Welsh Nationalist party, is very flattering. Does this strike you as strange? Can you think of any reasons for it?

Source 207: Can you see any evidence of bias in this document?

Sources 208-211: Do these sources agree on policy?

Source 213: *Y Ddraig Goch* was the Welsh nationalist's party's newspaper. What *other* information would you like to have about articles written in the newspaper before deciding how reliable the information was?

Source 215 Do you think this photograph was taken at the time of the incident at the bombing school? Why?

Source 220: What use is this photograph as historical evidence?

Electoral Successes in the 1960s and 1970s.
Cymdeithas yr Iaith and the Language Question

The Welsh Nationalist Party was not popular during World War Two. There was a strong belief among many in the Party in pacifism, that on moral grounds force should never be used as a political weapon, either of attack or defence. There was also a strong belief in the party that this was not Wales' war, but England's. According to this view England had no right to enlist Welsh people for the war effort. The result was that some Welsh nationalists were conscientious objectors, and these are always extremely unpopular in war-time.

In the election of 1945 the Labour Party swept to power with a majority over all other parties for the first time. *Plaid Cymru*, the Welsh Nationalist party, did no better than in previous elections.

Source 221

Plaid Genedlaethol Cymru: Performance in Parliamentary Elections 1925–1945

Year of election	Type of election	Seat fought	Total vote	% of electorate voting for *Plaid*	No. of candidates contesting seat	*Plaid* candidate	M.P. elected and Party
1929	g.e.	Caernarfonshire	609	1·1	4	Revd. L. E. Valentine	G. Owen (Lib.)
1931	g.e.	Caernarfonshire	1,136	2·2	4	Prof. J. E. Daniel	G. Owen (Ind. Lib.)
		Univ. of Wales	914	17·9	2	S. Lewis	E. Evans (Lib.)
1935	g.e.	Caernarfonshire	2,534	5·7	3	Prof. J. E. Daniel	Sir G. Owen (Ind. Lib.)
1943 (Jan.)	by.	Univ. of Wales	1,330	n.a.	5	S. Lewis	Prof. W. Gruffydd (Lib.)
1945 (Apr.)	by.	Caernarfon Boroughs	6,844	n.a.	2	Prof. J. E. Daniel	Seaborne Davies (Lib.)
1945 (May)	by.	Neath	6,290	n.a.	3	Wynne Samuel	D. J. Williams (Lab.)
1945	g.e.	Caernarfon Boroughs	1,560	3·2	4	Prof. J. E. Daniel	D. Pryce-White (Con.)
		Caernarfonshire	2,152	4·1	3	Ambrose Bebb	G. O. Roberts (Lab.)
		Neath	3,659	5·3	3	Wynne Samuel	D. J. Williams (Lab.)
		Univ. of Wales	1,696	14·4	2	Dr. Gwenan Jones	Prof. W. Gruffydd (Lib.)

Note. Results for the 1945 general election are not complete. The information concerning the four contests mentioned is for the purpose of comparison.

Abbreviations. g.e.—general election; by.—by-election; n.a.—not available; Lib.—Liberal; Lab.—Labour; Ind.—Independent; Con.—Conservative.

Source: Alan Butt Philip, *The Welsh Question*, Cardiff, 1975, p. 19.

From this list can you make any statement about the kind of candidates who were standing for *Plaid Cymru*?

In the twenty years after the war, parts of Wales were to change dramatically, and in some ways this increased support for the Welsh Nationalist Party. There were two main changes. The economic change was that after the war, Wales was much more prosperous. Instead of the terrible years of the Depression there was now almost full employment and far greater prosperity. The political change was that Wales was, on the whole, a country which voted Labour. Many individual Welshmen became important government politicians because Labour was in power from 1945-1951 and from 1964-1970. The Labour party's attitude to Welsh nationalism, of the cultural or the political sort, has normally been luke-warm and often hostile. However, many individual Welsh Labour M.P.s, from the west and north of Wales, were very sympathetic to the Welsh language and culture and, when in Government, were prepared to support giving the Welsh more control over their own affairs. Two such men, James Griffiths and Cledwyn Hughes became the first and second persons to be Secretary of State for Wales. It is against this changed background that we need to see changes in Welsh nationalism in the post war period. In 1949 there was a campaign for a parliament for Wales, for which there was some support from all the political parties. Once again there was not much popular support so the movement broke up. *Plaid Cymru* itself made some headway, at least compared with its pre-war situation. In the 1959 General Election the party put up twenty candidates, a good proportion of the thirty six Welsh constituencies. These candidates managed to get over 10% of the votes cast in the constituencies fought in Wales though all but three of them lost their deposits.

Even this level of support was perhaps disappointing after an event which proved as emotional in Wales as the pre-war action of Saunders Lewis and his colleagues at the proposed R.A.F. bombing school at Penyberth. In the late 1950s the Liverpool City Council wanted more water for its population. One of the main natural resources in Wales is water especially in the upland areas where dams can easily be constructed to store it. All Liverpool Council had to do to build a dam in the Tryweryn Valley in Merioneth was to get a private bill through Parliament.

Source 222
Penderfynu tynged Tryweryn ar ddiwrnod Ffwl Ebrill

Mwyafrif y genedl yn derbyn arweiniad y blaid

GAN EIN GOHEBYDD GWLEIDYDDOL

AR y dydd cyntaf o Ebrill fe ddaw Mesur Corfforaeth Lerpwl i foddi Cwm Tryweryn o flaen Ty'r Arglwyddi am y Trydydd Darlleniad. A gwyddom ymlaen llaw mai Cymru fydd yn chwarae rhan y ffŵl yn Nhy'r Arglwyddi y diwrnod hwnnw . . .

Fe wneir esgus, fe wyddom, o roi chwarae teg i bob ochr yn y ddadl. Ond bydd y dyfarniad wedi'i benderfynu ymlaen llaw. Am nad oes gan yr Arglwyddi, ac ni fu ganddynt erioed, y syniad lleiaf o genedligrwydd y Cymry. Ac fe rydd yr Arglwydd Woolton fendith y Llywodraeth ar y Cynllun. Yn yr un modd, y rhan fwyaf o'r Arglwyddi Sosialaidd. Ni bydd safiad dewr yr Arglwydd Ogmore a Gwaunysgor yn tycio dim.

Ac am Ebrill arall fe gaiff Cymru ei thwyllo. Ac fe ddeil y Cymry i ddal i gredu y gallant gael cyfiawnder i'w hiawnderau cenedlaethol o flaen cynulleidfa o Saeson.

O FLAEN TY'R CYFFREDIN

Yn nes ymlaen wedyn, wrth gwrs, fe ddaw'r Mesur (wedi'i basio'n ddiau) o flaen Ty'r Cyffredin. Dim ond rhyw ddeg ar hugain o Aelodau Cymreig a fydd yno yn erbyn chwe chant o Saeson.

A chawn weld faint o awdurdod (ac o gydymdeimlad at Gymru) a fydd gan Mr. Henry Brooke. Faint hefyd o ddylanwad a fydd y Fonesig Megan wedi'i gael ar y Blaid Lafur. Tybed a wrthwynebai'r Blaid honno'r Mesur yn swyddogol? Mae digon o Aelodau Cymreig tanbaid yn honno bellach iddynt allu cario eu plaid gyda hwy. Byddwn yn disgwyl yn hyderus.

Eithr y mae un ffaith ddiymwad yn wynebu unrhyw un sy'n ceisio sylwi'n ddiduedd ar y sefyllfa boliticaidd Gymreig.

A hynny yw: Bod Cymru'n gyffredinol wedi derbyn arweiniad Plaid Cymru ar bwnc Tryweryn. A bod yr Aelodau

Seneddol Cymreig, ar ol eistedd yn hir ar y clawdd, wedi gorfod arddel yr arweiniad hwnnw o'r diwedd, a'i briodoli iddynt eu hunain.

Felly y bu'r stori yn gyson yng Nghymru er diwedd y Rhyfel, yn erbyn y Swyddfa Ryfel a'r Comisiwn Coedwigo etc., y Blaid yn arwain, a'r Aelodau Seneddol yn dilyn.

DIOGELU EIN TREFTADAETH

Ni ellid teyrnged uwch i'r Mudiad Cenedlaethol, na bod ein Haelodau Seneddol yn gorfod chwifio'i sloganau, ac ymladd ei frwydrau. Ni ellid dadl rymusach dros gyfrhau'r mudiad. Dyma brawf hefyd, er gwaethaf rhif y pleidleisiau mewn etholiad, sy'n dangos fod y mudiad yn deffro'r genedl.

Safed Cymru'n unol y tu ol i'n Haelodau Seneddol ar bwnc Tryweryn. Canys os byddant hwy'n unol, ni fedr Senedd gyfan o Saeson, hyd yn oed, yn hawdd eu diystyrru.

Nid yw o bwys pwy sy'n arwain. Y peth pwysig yw fod Cymru'n cael ei gwarchod, a'n treftadaeth yn cael ei diogelu.

Source: Y Ddraig Goch, April, 1957.

Although nearly every Member of Parliament for a Welsh constituency opposed this measure there was nothing that anyone in Wales could do to stop Liverpool Council drowning the valley and, what was important, a community—chapel, shop, farms, houses.

The Parliament at Westminster seemed to be treating Wales with contempt. More evidence of this came when Lord Brecon was made Minister of State with responsibility for Wales in the same year.

Source 224

'The fun Labour has had with last week's announcement lies in the peculiarity of politics, not in rudeness about personalities. How an obscure Brecon county councillor, visiting London (in his tweed suit) for the University Rugger match, was called to Downing Street to be made a baron and a Minister of State, represents one of the most curious political appointments since Caligula made his horse a consul.'

Source: The Economist, 21 December, 1957, p. 1034. Quoted in Davis, *The Welsh Nationalist Party*, p. 298.

Then in 1962, came another event of great significance in the recent history of Wales. As we have seen, Saunders Lewis had helped to found the Welsh Nationalist Party. Then he had been one of the three involved in the token setting fire to the Llŷn Bombing School. After the second world war Saunders Lewis did not

Source 223

Source: Document Pack 3 associated with H.T.V. Series, The Dragon Has Two Tongues.

Source 225

PROFILE—SAUNDERS LEWIS

BY washing his hands of the National Eisteddfod, Saunders Lewis, one of the most distinguished Welshmen of the century—in the Nationalist view the greatest Welshman since Owain Glyndwr—has made the last possible gesture of disassociation from organised Welshness.

That the best and most famous Welsh poet, playwright and scholar should have nothing more to do with what is popularly thought of as the power behind poetry and drama, if not scholarship, in Wales is a restatement of Lewis's paradoxical position in Welsh life, of the almost fanatical idealism which has characterised his career.

He has been the Roman Catholic leader of a predominantly Nonconformist political party; the ex-Army officer at the head of a band of pacifists; the most brilliant Welsh teacher of his generation who in his own country could not find a place to teach in; the Welshman who went to an English gaol because of his Nationalism and had his job taken away from him by Welshmen; a man of all the talents but that for compromise, who began his career as a lecturer at a Welsh University College and is ending it lecturing at a Welsh University College.

❖   ❖

JOHN SAUNDERS LEWIS was born in 1893 in Liverpool. His father was a Calvinistic Methodist minister; his maternal grandfather one of Wales's most famous biographers. At Liverpool University he took a first under Lascelles Abercrombie, immediately volunteered for the Army, was commissioned in the South Wales Borderers, wounded in France and, towards the end of the war, served in Greece under that uncrowned King of Scotland, Sir Compton Mackenzie.

He returned to the University, until in 1923 he became a lecturer in Welsh at the new University College of Swansea. Three years later, after establishing a reputation as teacher, poet, scholar and orator, he founded the Plaid Cymru (Welsh Nationalist Party) and became its first president. The philosopher had come down into the market place.

Lewis's vision was of a Wales that no longer existed. His Wales—he has re-created it movingly in his plays—was a gentle and civilised country, its culture homogeneous, its literature the oldest and among the greatest of the European literatures. It was also a Roman Catholic Wales.

A man with this vision could not help but find the contrast between the golden days of Wales and the impoverished Wales of the nineteen-twenties intolerable. Everywhere, it seemed to Lewis and others, the interests of Wales were being subordinated to foreign wishes; the major political parties were obsessed with their doctrinaire squabbles when an historic European culture was dying. Lewis's new party demanded " . . . not independence but freedom. And the meaning of freedom in this matter is responsibility. We who are Welsh people claim that we are responsible for the civilisation and the ways of social life in our part of Europe."

❖   ❖

MANY notable Welshmen supported their articulate young compatriot. Many more were sympathetic to the Plaid's cultural arguments but found the party's economic programme absurd, considering economic devolution anachronistic and unreasonable. It has never won a seat in the British Parliament.

What its supporters have done, by persisting in their extreme and rather impractical nationalism, is to create a situation in which a watered-down version of their policy, like Lady Megan Lloyd-George's present campaign for a Parliament for Wales, can gain public support and cause the Labour Party machine

JANE BOWN

much trouble. By functioning as a revolutionary cadre, but without arms, and, as they claim, infiltrating influential places, schools, university, pulpit, the stage, journalism, they have done a great deal, if by no means all, to bring about the revival of interest in Welsh language and culture within Wales and in Welsh affairs outside, which has been so marked a post-war development.

❖   ❖

IT has been known for Nonconformist ministers in Wales to speak of Roman Catholicism as if it were the work of the Devil. Therefore, when the leader of the mainly Nonconformist Plaid became a convert to Roman Catholicism there was widespread uneasiness; the conversion emphasised the difference between Lewis and his followers. His Wales was not their Wales; his life even was quite unlike theirs.

He had a highly cultivated taste in wine; among wine merchants in South Wales he is regarded as a connoisseur. Yet total abstinence was the traditional doctrine of the chapels from which the Plaid drew its support. Lewis liked cigars—in the context a curiously aristocratic trait. He was passionately concerned to raise standards in Welsh literature and always considered it from the highest standards of European criticism. Inevitably he found much in Welsh writing wanting and never minced his words in saying so. The more parochial of his followers, for whom it was enough that a work was Welsh for it to be perfect, were baffled or angry at his intellectual honesty.

In time, the pressure of these incompatibilities became intolerable, and in the early years of the war Lewis resigned his presidency of the Plaid. The simple reason given was that he considered his Roman Catholicism hindered the progress of the party. This, however, was not the first time that the people to whom he had devoted himself had behaved curiously towards him.

In 1936 Saunders Lewis and two Nationalist colleagues, the Rev. Lewis Valentine and the Welsh short-story writer, Mr. D. J. Williams, tried to set on fire a bombing school which the

Air Ministry had begun to build in the Lleyn Peninsula. Although the men admitted their offence, the jury at Caernarvon failed to agree on a verdict; throughout the trial there were large Nationalist crowds outside the courthouse. The trial was then removed to the Old Bailey, where the Welshmen refused to plead and were sentenced to a year's imprisonment.

Lewis's speech in his own defence at Caernarvon was characteristic of him, lucid, reasonable and persuasive. He drew the court's attention to the other proposed bombing schools, at Abbotsbury and Holy Island, which the Air Ministry had *not* built after highly-publicised protests:—

> Will you try to understand our feelings when we saw the foremost scholars and literary men of England talking of the " sacredness " of ducks and swans, and succeeding on that argument in compelling the Air Ministry to withdraw the bombing range, while here in Wales, at the very same time, we were organising a nation-wide protest on behalf of the truly sacred things in Creation—a Nation, its language, its literature, its separate traditions and immemorial ways of Christian life—and we could not get the Government even to receive a deputation to discuss the matter with us? The irony of the contrast is the irony of blasphemy.

When the conspirators were released from prison the Rev. Lewis Valentine resumed his pulpit; Mr. Williams, who had been English master at Fishguard Grammar School, became the Welsh master there—and Saunders Lewis was dismissed from his post at University College, Swansea.

This extraordinary behaviour had serious results for Lewis. For fourteen years he found nowhere to teach, and supported himself and his family by his Welsh-language journalism and his plays, neither of which earned him much money. His journalism during this time is regarded by many Welshmen as having been the finest in the language, as his verse and plays are recognised as being in the highest tradition.

But even during the lean years he would not write in English and still does not. He reads as little English as possible; the influence of the English language in Wales being so great, he believes it has to be resisted positively; and so mostly he reads Italian and French.

❖   ❖

SINCE 1943, when he stood unsuccessfully as a Welsh Nationalist candidate in a University of Wales Parliamentary by-election, he has cut himself free from politics, although he still believes in the Plaid Cymru policy and is willing to comment, usually scathingly, always with great humour, on movements such as the " Parliament of Wales Campaign." He regards his excursion into politics as a necessary duty which has now been performed; he has finally returned to his scholarship, which has won him a European reputation if little recognition in England.

In 1951 he was appointed senior lecturer in Welsh at University College, Cardiff. He lives now in Penarth, on the outskirts of Cardiff, among the decaying Gothic Palaces, the Rhine Castles and the Chateaux of the long-dead coal millionaires—a lonely eminence in Welsh life, respected as incorruptible, as the supreme idealist, the genius of modern Welsh literature, the man whose life with its promise and tragedies is the solitary exemplar of his argument that Wales is a European nation, and of the predicament of small cultures.

Saunders Lewis, a frail, small man, persuasively eloquent, even *tête à tête*, is, in the words of a friend, " an omniscient sort of joker."—*Copyright.*

The Observer, 8 August 1954.

get involved in politics any more. In 1951 he began to work once more as a teacher in the University of Wales. He now had a national and international reputation as a scholar and writer.

Source 225 *(See page 112)*

In 1962 Saunders Lewis emerged again into the public eye. He gave a radio lecture. In it he argued that the first priority in Wales was not self-government but saving the Welsh language. There must be an organised movement to make sure that Welsh, at least in the Welsh-speaking parts of Wales, was the language of the day-to-day government of the country. Welsh must be made an official language.

Source 226

'Welsh can be saved, Welsh-speaking Wales is still an extensive area of the country, and the minority is not wholly unimportant . . . It should be made immediately impossible for the business of local and central government to continue without using Welsh. Tax forms in Welsh or in English and Welsh must be demanded. The Postmaster-General must be warned that annual licences will not be paid unless they are obtainable in Welsh. This is not a policy for individuals, here and there. It would demand organizing and moving step by step, giving warnings and allowing time for changes. It is a policy for a movement, a movement in the areas where Welsh is in daily use. Every election form and every official form to do with elections must be in Welsh. Welsh must be the chief administrative matter in the district and the county.

Perhaps you will say that this can never be done, that not enough Welshmen could be found to agree and to arrange it as a campaign of importance and strength. Perhaps you are right. All I maintain is that this is the only political matter which it is worth a Welshman's while to trouble himself about today.'

Source: Saunders Lewis, Radio Lecture 1962. Quoted in Philip, *The Welsh Question*, p. 89.

As a direct result of Saunders Lewis' lecture *Cymdeithas Yr Iaith Cymraeg* (the Welsh Language Society) was set up. Its foundation came at a time when it was obvious that the number of people able to speak Welsh was going down all the time—only about a quarter could now speak the language. There had been some progress in education, especially in the setting up of Welsh language schools, but the situation was serious.

After the two events of Tryweryn and the establishment of *Cymdeithas yr Iaith*

Cymraeg, there followed a programme of direct action. This was supported by some Welsh Nationalists though by no means all. On the Tryweryn site there was an attempt to put the power supply out of action in 1962 and in 1963 an electricity transformer was damaged there, and the nearby electricity pylon damaged. Also in 1963 *Cymdeithas Yr Iaith* started on a campaign to get the language issue taken seriously in Wales. They wanted official forms to be available in Welsh and road signs to be bi-lingual. In 1967 an Act of Parliament went some way towards giving Welsh official status.

Source 227

Welsh Language Act 1967

ELIZABETH II

1967 CHAPTER 66

An Act to make further provision with respect to the Welsh language and references in Acts of Parliament to Wales.   [27th July 1967]

WHEREAS it is proper that the Welsh language should be freely used by those who so desire in the hearing of legal proceedings in Wales and Monmouthshire; that further provision should be made for the use of that language, with the like effect as English, in the conduct of other official or public business there; and that Wales should be distinguished from England in the interpretation of future Acts of Parliament:

Be it therefore enacted by the Queen's most Excellent Majesty, by and with the advice and consent of the Lords Spiritual and Temporal, and Commons, in this present Parliament assembled, and by the authority of the same, as follows:—

1.—(1) In any legal proceeding in Wales or Monmouthshire   Use of Welsh the Welsh language may be spoken by any party, witness or   in legal other person who desires to use it, subject in the case of proceedings   proceedings. in a court other than a magistrates' court to such prior notice as may be required by rules of court; and any necessary provision for interpretation shall be made accordingly.

(2) Section 1 of the Welsh Courts Act 1942, and in paragraph 7   1942 c. 40. of the Schedule to the Pensions Appeal Tribunals Act 1943 the   1943 c. 39. words from the beginning to " language and ", are hereby repealed.

2.—(1) Where any enactment passed either before or after this   Welsh Act specifies the form of any document or any form of words   versions of which is to be or may be used for an official or public purpose,   statutory the appropriate Minister may by order prescribe a version of   forms etc.

Source: Reproduced in Pack 3 of H.T.V. Documents produced in association with the series The Dragon Has Two Tongues.

Government and Local Authorities and public bodies still had a lot of discretion as to how far they would go in their bi-lingual policy. The result was that the Welsh Language Society carried on with its campaign of direct action. The best known, and probably the one which affected the public most, was that of painting over road signs in green paint if they were in English only. The direct action had some interesting results. Generally, people in Wales, certainly those who spoke English only, were against it. The Welsh Nationalist Party, *Plaid Cymru*, was in a difficult position. It supported the aims of the direct action but knew that the action would be unpopular with electors. *Plaid Cymru* blamed the sign-daubing campaign for the party's poor results in the local elections of 1969. On the other hand the language campaign did prove to be remarkably successful. Local authorities began replacing old road signs with bi-lingual ones. There have been other successes, too, sometimes connected with direct action, sometimes not. Increasingly, bi-lingual official forms have been made available.

Source 228 *(See opposite column)*

While *Cymdeithas Yr Iaith* has often captured the headlines, enormously important changes have taken place without very much publicity. Probably the most important in the years since World War Two have been in education. The first school to be conducted in the Welsh language opened in Aberystwyth in

Source 228

Rhestr o Ffurflenni Cymraeg a dwyieithog a gyhoeddwyd gan Lywodraeth Ei Mawrhydi.

A list of Welsh and bi-lingual forms issued by Her Majesty's Government.

1939. There are now over four hundred Welsh-language nursery schools, and pupils can go on to Welsh-language primary schools and secondary schools.

Source 231 *(See page 115)*

The Welsh Language Nursery School Movement gets money from the Welsh Office, as do many other bodies which provide some kind of educational or cultural service in the Welsh language.

Source 229

(✗ Bi-lingual)

Title of Form	Statutory Instrument No (where applicable)
WELSH EDUCATION OFFICE (cont'd)	
14 PEN Application for a Pension	
121 UP Request to Student for Statement of Finance	
133 UP) Letters to Students announcing the	
138 UB) value and tenure of awards	
194 PEN) Teachers pensions	
207A PEN)	
101A (Schools) Independent Schools	
AE5	
AE6 Register for Adult Education	
AE7 Register for Adult Education	
28RQ Medical Report on Candidate for Employment as a Teacher	
POST OFFICE	
Broadcasting Receiving Licence	
✗(a) Radio	
✗(b) Monochrome Television and Sound Radio	
✗(c) Colour Television (including monochrome television and sound)	
INLAND REVENUE	
Tax Return	
Tax Return Guide	
PRIVY COUNCIL OFFICE	
Declaration of Sheriff	1969 No 1276

Source 230

(✗ Dwyieithog)

Teitl y Ffurflen	
SWYDDFA ADDYSG CYMRU (parhad)	
14 PEN Cais am bensiwn	
121 UP Cais i fyfyriwr am Adroddiad Ariannol	
133 UP) Llythyrau at Fyfyrwyr yn cyhoeddi	
138 UB) gwerth a daliadaeth dyfarniadau	
194 PEN) Pensiynau athrawon	
207A PEN)	
101A (Ysgolion) Ysgolion Annibynnol	
AE5	
AE6 Cofrestr ar gyfer Addysg Oedolion	
AE7 Cofrestr ar gyfer Addysg Oedolion	
28RQ Adroddiad meddygol ar Ymgeisydd i'w gyflogi fel Athro.	
SWYDDFA'R POST	
Trwydded derbyn darllediadau	
✗a) Radio	
b) Teledu monocrom a radio sain	
✗c) Teledu Lliw/ (gan gynnwys teledu monocrom a radio sain)	
CYLLID Y WLAD	
Ffurflen y Dreth Incwm	
Cyfarwyddyd i'r Ffurflen Dreth	
SWYDDFA'R CYFRIN GYNGOR	
Datganiad y Siryf	

Source 231

Would you like your child to speak Welsh? Yes? Then join a Welsh medium playgroup toddler group.

Source 232

Language grants up to £1m

GRANTS totalling almost £1m to help the Welsh language are announced today by Mr Wyn Roberts, Under-Secretary for Wales.

The grants, to non-local government organisations, have increased in line with inflation.

Among those receiving cash are the National Eisteddfod to help build a new theatre, and Yr Academi Gymreig, to speed publication of a much-needed high standard English to Welsh dictionary.

The grants total £996,000 compared with £951,000 last year. They are additional to the £920,000 for local authorities announced early last month.

Grants include: Mudiad Ysgolion Meithrin, for the development of Welsh language nursery groups throughout Wales, £190,000.

National Eisteddfod, for capital spending on a new theatre, literary pavilion and general development work, £180,000.

Welsh Books Council, for the Welsh books grant, £320,000, plus the development of books clubs in schools, £22,000.

Welsh National Centre for Children's Literature, Aberystwyth, for continuing development work, £13,000.

Yr Academi Gymreig, for the dictionary, £22,000.

YFCs, £3,300 and Papurau bro to be distributed between these monthly community papers by the regional arts associations, £18,000.

The balance will be distributed later. Some will go for further development at the Glanllyn, Bala, camp of Urdd Gobaith Cymru.

One of the Welsh Language Society's main campaigns was to get the B.B.C. to provide far more broadcasting in the Welsh language, especially on television. There were some Welsh programmes but they were sandwiched in between English ones. It made good sense for the Society to take a strong line on this. The effect of broadcasting, first radio, then—and especially—television, has been immense. From the 1950s when television reception became available in most parts of Wales, television became the main leisure-time activity of the population, young and old. It largely replaced those spare-time activities which had once centred around the chapels or the miners' institutes. It soon began to replace the cinema and watching sport. Television set standards, and the previous night's programmes became one of the main topics of conversation at home and at school. There were problems here which were not only of concern to Welsh-speaking Wales, because television was—and is—planned by a small number of people who tend to have a similar kind of educational background and outlook. It is the London view of the world which often comes across on television. On top of this much of our television comes from America. This is not a threat to the English language because the Americans speak a version of English, but it may be a strong influence on our ideas. For the Welsh language and Welshness, a broadcasting service dominated by English is a grave threat. There was a strong campaign, therefore, for a television channel in the Welsh language for Wales. Increasing pressure on governments had some effect. In the Conservative Party election manifesto of 1979 there was a promise to make the fourth channel in Wales a mainly Welsh-language one. Three months after it was elected, the Conservative Government went back on its election promise in September 1979. There was a real sense of outrage in Wales, certainly among Nationalists, not only because a vitally important Welsh-language cause looked doomed but also because there seemed to them something immoral and fundamentally unjust about a Government changing its manifesto promise.

Once more the Welsh Nationalist cause found a martyr—or at least a possible one. The most senior and respected person in the party, its former President, Gwynfor Evans, said that if the Government refused to set up the Welsh T.V. Channel and went back on its election promise, he would go on hunger strike. Since no one had ever doubted his word, or his courage, this threat was taken very seriously indeed. Gwynfor Evans received a lot of support from people with influence in Wales, including religious leaders like the Archbishop of Wales. They persuaded William Whitelaw, then Home Secretary, to change direction once again. In 1982 *Sianel Pedwar Cymru*, S4C, started its transmission, mainly in the Welsh language.

Source 233

It will be many years before it will be possible to judge its effect on the Welsh language, and whether it has helped in any way to stop a steady decline in the number of Welsh speakers.

Source 234

Table 4   POPULATION PRESENT ON CENSUS NIGHT AGED 3 AND OVER 1921–81: proportion of population speaking Welsh

Area	Percentage of all persons speaking Welsh					
	1921	1931	1951	1961	1971	1981
a	b	c	d	e	f	g
WALES	37.1	36.8	28.9	26.0	20.8	18.9
Counties						
Clwyd	41.7	41.3	30.2	27.3	21.4	18.7
Dyfed	67.8	69.1	63.3	60.1	52.5	46.3
Gwent	5.0	4.7	2.8	2.9	1.9	2.5
Gwynedd	78.7	82.5	74.2	71.4	64.7	61.2
Mid Glamorgan	38.4	37.1	22.8	18.5	10.5	8.4
Powys	35.1	34.6	29.6	27.8	23.7	20.2
South Glamorgan	6.3	6.1	4.7	5.2	5.0	5.8
West Glamorgan	41.3	40.5	31.6	27.5	20.3	16.4

Table 5   POPULATION PRESENT ON CENSUS NIGHT AGED 3 AND OVER 1921–81: proportion of population speaking Welsh by age

Age last birthday	Percentage of all persons speaking Welsh					
	1921	1931	1951	1961	1971	1981
a	b	c	d	e	f	g
All ages 3 and over	37.1	36.8	28.9	26.0	20.8	18.9
3–4	26.7	22.1	14.5	13.1	11.3	13.3
5–9	29.4	26.6	20.1	16.8	14.5	17.8
10–14	32.2	30.4	22.2	19.5	17.0	18.5
15–24	34.5	33.4	22.8	20.8	15.9	14.9
25–44	36.9	37.4	27.4	23.2	16.3	15.5
45–64	44.9	44.1	35.4	32.6	24.8	20.7
65 and over	51.9	49.9	40.7	37.2	31.0	27.4

Further work on the evidence

Source 221: Did *Plaid Cymru*'s performance in elections improve or get worse between 1929 and 1945?

Source 222: What do you think *Y Ddraig Goch*'s attitude to the drowning of Tryweryn valley might be?

Source 225: Do you think the writer is in a good position to comment on Saunders Lewis? What would you need to know before answering this question?

Sources 228–230: Do you think this is evidence that the Welsh language now has equal status with the English language?

Source 232: What does this source tell you about the Government's attitude to the Welsh language?

Source 234: What do these figures tell you about the history of the Welsh language between 1921 and 1981?

Devolution

What exactly does devolution mean? Strictly, we might apply it to any moves made by governments in London to set up departments of government which allowed the Welsh to take decisions for themselves in matters which affected them. We have seen that for over four hundred years after the Acts of Union there was no indication in law or Acts of Parliament that Wales existed as a separate nation. This changed in the second half of the nineteenth century. For example, after 1889 a system of secondary schools was set up in Wales which was different from that in England, as we have seen. In 1907 a Welsh Department of the Board of Education was set up. There was nothing more than this kind of recognition of Welsh separateness until after World War Two. After that war, with the Labour Party dominating Wales, there was increasing pressure from some Labour M.P.s for a Secretary of State for Wales and a Welsh Office. These demands were opposed by Prime Minister Attlee after 1945 and the Cabinet generally. Even so, there were some small changes. An Advisory Council for Wales was set up in 1948. In 1951 the new Conservative Government set up a Ministry of Welsh Affairs. How seriously the Conservatives took it is summed up by the fact that the first Minister was a Scotsman, Sir David Maxwell-Fyfe, known as 'Dai Bananas' by the Welsh. The politicians who followed him in this office were not taken much more seriously. Usually their interest in Wales was not particularly obvious. It seemed that the 'Parliament for Wales' group in the 1950s and 1960s, with representatives from all parties, would get nowhere with its demands.

Source 235

'Parliament only allocated one day to consider Welsh problems. If Parliament was to work effectively it had to shed its load. Wales was going to ask Parliament for justice . . . Our action is 400 years overdue . . .'

Source: Megan Lloyd George, Llandrindod, 1950, quoted in Document Pack 3, connected with the HTV Series, The Dragon has Two Tongues.

Source 236

At the same time, *Plaid Cymru* was making slow progress with the electors. The Welsh Language Society was getting a lot of publicity, though it was not by any means all favourable.

In 1964 the Labour Party came back into

Government after thirteen years, after an election in which *Plaid Cymru* did not do very well. However, the Labour Government gave Wales its own Secretary of State for the first time, though his powers were very limited.

Source 237

WALES AND WESTMINSTER

WESTERN MAIL, TUESDAY, DECEMBER 1, 1964

How will the changes in the structure of Welsh government affect us? How much power will the new Secretary of State be able to exercise? How does the new system compare with that of Scotland? These questions are answered today in this special Focus.

In this exclusive interview the Rt. Hon. JAMES GRIFFITHS, M.P., Secretary of State for Wales, discusses the implications of his appointment with the Western Mail's Political Correspondent, DAVID G. ROSSER.

A seat in the Cabinet

Source: Reproduced in Document Pack 3 associated with H.T.V. series The Dragon has Two Tongues.

Plaid Cymru did not do well in the 1966 election either. Actual membership in the Party was small. Here are the figures for one town in west Glamorgan.

Source 238

Members 1962–3: 16 men and 13 women. 21 of the members were known to be Welsh-speaking. No new or Youth members.

1 Student (M)	1 Coal merchant and wife	
1 Pensioner (M)	4 Steelworkers	
1 Pensioner and wife	1 Foreman	
2 Shopkeepers	1 Gipsy and wife	
1 Shopkeeper's wife	1 Railwayman	
1 Typist (F)	1 Stationmaster and wife	
3 Housewives	1 Retired man	
1 Schoolmaster	2 Women (occupation un-	
2 Schoolmistresses	known)	

Members 1967–8: 33 men and 24 women. 29 of the members were known to be Welsh-speaking, 29 Youth members, 23 new members.

* † 1 Girl, aged 18
* (1 Housewife
  (1 Housewife's daughter
* 1 Schoolmistress
* 1 Retired man
* † (1 Minister
  (1 Minister's son, aged 12
† 1 Boy, aged 16

† 1 Schoolgirl, aged 15
* † 1 Schoolgirl, aged 15
* 1 Schools organizer
* † 1 Student (M)
† 1 Student (F), aged 16
† 1 Student (M)
(1 Doctor
† (1 Doctor's son, aged 15

1 Secretary (F)
1 Single woman
† 2 Girls, aged 17
† 1 Girl, aged 16
* 1 Housewife
* (1 Minister's son, aged 15
* † (1 Minister's daughter, aged 12
* † (1 Minister's daughter
* 1 Railway official
† 1 Railway fireman
1 Fitter
* 1 Tramguard
2 Engine drivers
1 Engine Driver's wife
† 1 Schoolgirl, aged 13
* † 1 Schoolgirl, aged 16

* 1 married woman
* 1 Forester
2 Single women
* 1 Schoolboy, aged 14
† 1 Schoolboy, aged 13
* 1 Schoolboy, aged 12
* † 1 Schoolboy, aged 12
2 Schoolboys, aged 10
* † 1 Schoolboy, aged 7
† 1 Schoolboy, aged 12
2 Schoolgirls
† 1 Schoolboy
† 1 Man
* † 1 Man
6 Men (occupation un-
known)

Key: † = Known new member
* = Known Welsh-speaker
M = Male
F = Female

Source: Butt Philip, *The Welsh Question*, pp. 340, 344.

Yet a few months afterwards there was an unexpected and quite remarkable political event in Wales. There are people all over Wales who can remember exactly where and how they heard of the election of Gwynfor Evans, Plaid Cymru's President, as M.P. in the Carmarthen by-election in 1966. One reason was that he had appealed to people's idealism.

Source 239

Wales has a duty to serve humanity. What is the use of all our sentimental talk about universal brotherhood if so much more of the Welsh taxpayer's money goes to support military bases in the Far East than to help the famine-stricken countries of Asia? With world food shortages imminent, where is the morality and the sense of Labour's agricultural policy of putting the family farmer of Wales out of business?

Charity of course begins at home. There must be work for our young people in their own communities. New jobs must be available for our miners before the mines close. Motorways and dual carriageways must be built and railways modernised. A more just tax system must be created. The great water resources of Wales must be protected and developed to help her poorer areas.

We have no right to preach to the world without first making Wales a country that commands admiration and respect.

There is a great reservoir of untapped ability and idealism in the people of Wales, a pride which could not only transform Wales herself but make her one of the best citizens of the world community as well. Will you help us to make every Welshman prouder, more responsible and truer to himself by voting for a *cause* this time?

Yours sincerely,

GWYNFOR EVANS

Source: Reproduced in document pack 3 associated with H.T.V. series The Dragon has Two Tongues.

He was an immensely popular figure in Wales and his supporters, especially the younger ones, sang and danced in the streets of Carmarthen to celebrate not only a famous victory but also, perhaps, a break-through for *Plaid Cymru.*

Source 240 *(See opposite column)*

Source 241 *(See opposite column)*

In two other by-elections, in 1967 and 1968, it seemed that great things were possible for the party. In Rhondda West and then in Caerphilly, in the industrial part of Wales which seemed least likely to support *Plaid Cymru,* the party came close to providing the biggest political upset ever seen in Wales.

Source 240

Plaid soar to great win

EVANS DOUBLES VOTE

THE Carmarthenshire by-election produced a major political sensation when the Welsh Nationalists gained their first-ever seat in Parliament early this morning.

President of the party, Mr. Gwynfor Evans, aged 54, ended the nine-year Labour dominance with a win over Labour's Gwilym Prys Davies, a Pontypridd solicitor.

Plaid Cymru turned a 9,000 Labour majority into a 2,436-vote victory with the Liberal Hywel Davies polling 8,615 votes, and Simon Day, the Tory, 2,934. The Tory candidate loses his deposit.

Outside the hall, the result —announced shortly after 1.05 a.m.—was greeted with a tremendous roar from Welsh Nationalist supporters singing Welsh songs

The shock result

Gwynfor Evans (Plaid Cymru)		16,179
Gwilym Prys Davies (Lab.)		13,743
Hywel Davies (Lib.)		8,650
Simon Day (Con.)		2,934
Majority		2,436

Plaid Cymru gain from Labour.

General election: Lady Megan Lloyd George (Lab.), 21,221; H. Davies (Lib.), 11,988; G. Evans (Plaid Cymru), 7,416; S. Day (Con.), 5,338. Labour majority, 9,233.

Percentage of poll: 75 per cent. (82.6 per cent. at the general election).

Third attempt

In the packed audience at the Shire Hall to hear the declaration by the clerk of the county council, Mr. W. S. Thomas, were Mr. Evans's wife and seven children, aged between 10 and 24.

One of the first to congratulate Mr. Evans was the beaten Mr. Day.

It was the third time that the Plaid president had contested Carmarthen. Since 1959 he has turned a 2,000-vote into a sensational victory.

It was Black Friday for the Liberals and a Golden Day for Plaid Cymru. Ten years ago Carmarthen was recognised as one of the bastions of the famous Celtic fringe of Liberalism.

Personal appeal

Many observers believe this latest blow might well sound the death knell of the Liberal Party in West Wales, particularly with the loss of Cardiganshire in the general election.

Immediate reaction after declaration of the poll was whether this was the vital breakthrough for the "Cinderella" party in Wales.

Main reason for Mr. Evans's success was his personal appeal to the electorate. He undoubtedly proved to be the outstanding personality of the election, and it was an attractive proposition for the electorate to have an independent voice speaking for Wales in the House of Commons.

MR. GWYNFOR EVANS
He makes history

especially when the fate of the Government was not at stake.

An analysis of the figures show that Plaid have taken votes from Liberals, Labour and Tory. It is arguable whether the handling of the

seamen s strike by Mr. Wilson has alienated the feeling of workers' solidarity so traditional among the miners of the Gwendraeth and Amman valleys who form the bulk of Labour Party support in the constituency.

Liberal Party chiefs were discussing this morning at party headquarters what went wrong with their campaign. They had in a local man, Mr. Hywel Davies, a personable candidate, a fine platform performer, and an energetic worker.

Breakthrough

Afterwards, Mr. Prys Davies said, "I think this has been a protest vote and not a positive vote.

"Carmarthen will return to Labour in the next general election."

Mr. Hywel Davies said, "This is clearly a protest vote. The issues affecting the neglect of Wales have been prominently brought forward, and obviously the electors of Carmarthen have decided that the most effective way of making a protest was by electing a Welsh Nationalist member."

Mr. Evans said, "No one can mistake this sign of great national awakening. A Parliament for Wales cannot long be delayed after this result.

"Now that we have broken through the rest of Wales will follow at once. It is all the more heartening because the work is mainly that of the younger generation."

Figures at the last election were: Lady Megan Lloyd George (Lab.) 21,221, Hywel Davies (Lib.) 11,988; Gwynfor Evans (Plaid Cymru) 7,416; Simon Day (Con.) 5,338. Majority 9,233.

Source: Western Mail; 15.7.1966.

Source 241

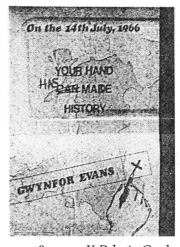

On the 14th July, 1966

YOUR HAND HAS MADE HISTORY

GWYNFOR EVANS

Source: Y Ddraig Goch, August, 1966.

Source 242

PLAID PIPPED
Labour's iron grip cut by 14,582

Western Mail Reporter FRIDAY

LABOUR scraped home in the Rhondda West by-election last night-but Plaid Cymru slashed the Socialist general election majority from 16,888 to a mere 2,306.

Welsh Nationalist Mr. Vic Davies increased his share of the poll from 2,172 to 10,067 and came within a hair's breadth of pulling off Plaid Cymru's second major election sensation within a year.

Jubilant barracking from hundreds of Plaid Cymru supporters drowned the Labour winner. Mr. Alec Jones, as he made his victory speech outside the Rhondda College of Further Education at Llwynypia.

Mr. Jones polled 12,373 votes —his majority dropping from 16,888 to a shock 2,306.

Both the Conservative and Communist candidates lost their deposits.

Chanting

Tory Mr Gareth Neale came bottom of the pool with almost 50 per cent. fewer votes than his party polled at the general election.

The 82.3 per cent. turnout was higher than at the last two general elections.

The Communist, Mr. Arthur True, a Rhondda-born electrician, also polled fewer votes than at the general election.

Wild scenes took place outside the school where the count took place. Several hundred people, standing in the rain, kept chanting "Victor" for Plaid's Mr. Davies.

The acting returning officer, Mr. Noel Thomas, could not be heard by all the crowd as he shouted the figures.

Threat

It took 10 minutes before the candidates were able to come forward to make their speeches and half of what they said was drowned in the continual noise.

Welsh flags were waved in the air and the crowd sang, Land of my Fathers.

Mr. Jones described the demonstration as "the worst manifestation of Rhondda politics

RHONDDA WEST (30,692)

A. Jones (Lab.)	12,373
H. V. Davies (Plaid Cymru)	10,067
A. C. True (Comm.)	1,723
G. Neale (C.)	1,075

FRIDAY 10 MAR 1967 Majority **2,306**

No change. Percentage of poll—82.3.

1966 general election: L. Thomas (Lab.), 19,060; H. V. Davies (Plaid Cymru), 2,172; B. S. Hill (C.), 1,955; A. C. True (Comm.), 1,853. Labour majority—6,888. Electorate—31,189. Conservative and Communist candidates lost deposits. Percentage of poll two per cent. higher than at the last two general elections.

NUNEATON (65,564)

L. Huckfield (Lab.)	18,239
D. Knox (C.)	14,185
A. Meredith (Lib.)	7,644
J. Creasey (All Party Alliance)	2,755
Air Vice-marshal D. Bennett (Nat. Party)	517

Majority **4,054**

No change. Percentage of poll—66.1.

1966 general election: F. Cousins (Lab.), 27,452; D. S. Marland (C.), 10,049; A. Meredith (Lib.), 7,356. Labour majority—11,403. Electorate—63,826.

POLLOK, GLASGOW (51,079)

Prof. E. Wright (C.)	14,270
R. Douglas (Lab.)	12,069
G. A. Leslie (Scottish Nat.)	10,884
I. D. Miller (Lib.)	735
A. C. Murray (Comm.)	694

FRIDAY 10 MAR 1967 Majority **2,201**

Conservative gain. Percentage of poll—75.7

1966 general election: A. Garrow (Lab.), 21,257; P. T. Smollett (Con.), 19,282. Labour majority, 1,975. Electorate, 51,301.

for many years and a threat to democracy."

Commenting on his success, he added, "I never set out in life to become an M.P.

"I have strong feelings towards the needs of Rhondda. I acknowledge the difficult position of the Rhondda and

I consider this will be my lifetime's work."

Mrs. Irene Davies, wife of the Plaid Cymru candidate who polled 10,067, said, "It is a pity if youngsters got out of hand. I see this tremendous vote for my husband as a positive, rather than a protest vote.

"The Rhondda will never be a safe Labour seat again."

Mr. Davies, whose vote had increased from a meagre 2,172 at the last election, was chaired shoulder-high around the college forecourt by his supporters.

After the candidates returned into the school the crowd continued to chant and sing. A triumphant Mr. Jones was booed.

Welsh Nationalist Mr. Davies

said. "Our success was a victory for Rhondda and Wales, more than Plaid Cymru.

"They can't kick us around any more with impunity. We have shaken the safest seat in the three countries of Britain to its foundation.

"The result is a powerful challenge to the London establishment to do right by Rhondda and Wales."

Wales and the Rhondda have been kicked about far too long.

"We are going to stop it. The message goes out tonight that Wales is marching on in her campaign for what is good and right for every nation — self-government.

"This tremendous reduction in the Labour majority should impress upon Mr. Wilson and the Labour Government that the people of Wales and the Rhondda are not going to take things lying down.

Signal

"It was more than a protest vote. It is a tremendous step forward and I have no doubt the support given to me by the Rhondda people will set all Wales on fire.

"After the victory at Carmarthen, this comes as a clear signal for the future."

Mr. Emrys Jones, Labour Party organiser for Wales and Labour election agent during the by-election, said "I congratulate Mr. Alec Jones on being a first-class candidate and I know he will make a first-class Member of Parliament and Rhondda will grow to be proud of him.

"The Nationalist Party can only make headway when other parties are struggling with difficult problems and forced to take unpopular decisions."

● The Welsh Nationalist gain in Rhondda West was even greater than the shock victory of Gwynfor Evans in the Carmarthenshire by-election last July.

In Carmarthen, they increased their share of the vote from 7,416 to 16,179, while in Rhondda the Nationalist candidate increased his poll five-fold.

The Labour share of the poll in Rhondda West dropped dramatically from 76.1 per cent. in 1966 to 49 per cent., while the Welsh Nationalist share soared from 8.7 per cent. to 39.9 per cent.

The Tory polled 4.3 per cent. (7.8 per cent. in 1966) and the Communist 6.8 per cent. as compared with 7.4 per cent.

THE VALLEY THAT SHOCKED ITSELF — PAGE 3.

Source: Western Mail, 10.3.1967.

Source 243

CHURCH BACKS HOME RULE

Western Mail Reporter

A religious body yesterday declared itself on the side of Home Rule for Wales because—its spokesman said — the time has come for the country to demand full recognition of its nationhood.

The council of the Union of Welsh Independents made the declaration at a conference at Swansea.

The union's secretary, Mr. Trevor Lloyd-Evans, said in his resolution at the meeting. "The tide is turning in Wales. It is time to demand full recognition to our nationhood — and full control over our affairs and our destiny."

Essential

He said that those who made this demand were not moved by a spirit of narrow nationalism, but by the conviction that it was only by self-government that the needs of Wales could be adequately met and her interests better advanced.

"Freedom is essential to the restoration of a sense of confidence in her future," said Mr. Lloyd-Evans.

It was now recognised by the Press in Wales and England, and by radio and television, that any relevant treatment of the political scene in contemporary Wales must include a reference to Home Rule.

The Union of Welsh Independents believed that this development was not a passing phase, which could be lifted by measures of devolution, or dispelled by an improvement in economic conditions.

The resolution was accepted.

Source: The Western Mail, 25.9.1968.

Source 244

O FEWN Y DIM I GIPIO CAERFFILI

BYDDAI WYTHNOS ARALL WEDI TROI 'R FANTOL

YN wyneb ymosodiadau unol a phenderfynol y tair plaid Seisnig, Llafur, y Rhyddfrydwyr a'r Toriaid, daeth Plaid Cymru o fewn trwch blewyn i gipio sedd Caerffili. Torrwyd mwyafrif Llafur i lawr bron ugain mil ac roedd y swing at Blaid Cymru, 28.9 y cant, yr uchaf mewn unrhyw is-etholiad ym Mhrydain—ar wahan i Hamilton —ers dros ugain mlynedd.

Ymladdodd y pleidiau eraill yn fudr ac yn gelwyddog. Y funud olaf rhannodd Lafur daflen liwgar yn cyhuddo Plaid Cymru o fod yn Ffasgaidd. Ychydig ddyddiau ynghynt cyhuddodd y Toriaid ni o fod yn "ffrwydrwyr argaeau." A'r Sul cynt ceisiodd Mr. Emlyn Hooson ledaenu'r si cwbl ddi-sail bod Pleidiau Cymru a'r Alban wedi derbyn rhoddion o £37,000 o'r Unol Daleithiau.

Eto, ni thyciodd hyn oll ddim. Ar ddydd yr is-etholiad aeth pleidlais o 3,949 gan Blaid Cymru yn Etholiad Cyffredinol 1966 i fyny i 14,274. Collodd y tair plaid arall yn druenus. Aeth, mwyafrif Llafur i lawr o 21,148 i 1,874. Pleidlais y Toriaid o 5,182 i 3,949. Ac ni chafydd y Rhyddfrydwyr ond 1,257. Collodd y ddau olaf eu hernes.

Dangosodd Caerffili yn gwbl glir bod y swing tuag at Blaid Cymru 'n parhau'n rymus hyd yn oed mewn etholaeth ddiwydiannol o di-Gymraeg. Grymusodd y swing tuag at Blaid Cymru o 17 y cant yng Nghaerfyrddin a 26 y cant yn y Rhondda i 28.9 y cant yng Nghaerffili. Roedd ar y Blaid angen swing o 31.6 y cant i gipio'r sedd.

Wedi Caerffili mae'n gwbl amlwg bod Plaid Cymru yn her gredadwy a difrifol i Lafur yn · holl etholaethau'r De, ac nad oes bellach un sedd yng Nghymru yn ddiogel rhag ein hymosodiad. Dangoswyd hefyd na thry Cymru at na Thoriaeth na'r Rhyddfrydwyr am ymwared.

Ond yr hyn sydd debycaf o greu'r arswyd pennaf yn rhengau Llafur yw'r ffaith bod pobl ifanc a phobl i fyny i ddeugain oed yng Nghaerffili wedi troi'n solet at Blaid Cymru. Dim ond yr henoed na fedrent ymddihatru o'u hen ffyddlondeb i Lafur a bleidleisiodd iddi hi.

Roedd yn amlwg pe bai'r bleidlais gan yr ifanc o 18 i fyny, y buasai Plaid Cymru wedi cipio'r sedd yn hawdd. A gyda rhyw 2,000 o'r rhai ifanc hyn yn cael y bleidlais yn flynyddol y mae'n amlwg y gall Plaid Cymru gipio'r sedd yn 1970.

Gwnaeth y Dr. Phil Williams ar flaen ymgyrch Plaid Cymru argraff ddofn ar yr etholaeth—hyd yn oed ar y rhai a barhaodd i bleidleisio i Lafur. Roedd canlyniad yr is-etholiad yn gryn sioc iddynt hwy'n arbenning.

Wynebodd Plaid Cymru bobl Caerffili am noson ar ôl noson a dydd ar ôl dydd am dair wythos â dadleuon sylweddol a dylid dwyn rheolaeth ar fywyd y genedl Gymreig o Lundain i Gaerdydd; bod raid inni gymryd y cyfrifoldeb tros

weithio allan ein hiachawdwriaeth ein hunain. Daliwyd gwledydd bychain Llychlyn fel delfryd yn gyson o flaen yr etholaeth. Pwysleisiwyd mai gwan a fyddai'r Wladwriaeth Gymreig ac mai lles yr unigolyn a'i gymdeithas a ddeuai'n gyntaf ac yn olaf.

Yn wir, disgrifiwyd yr holl ymgyrch gan ohebyddion o Loegr fel 'un 'teach-in'anferth ar genedlaetholdeb. Tyrrodd pobl Cwm Rhymni i'n cyfarfodydd ah olasant gwestiynau call a synhwyrol. Cipiwyd calon a meddwl pobl feddylgar a phobl ifanc y dyffryn. Dim ond traddodiad henaint, ynghyd â byrder bwriadol yr ymgyrch a gadwodd y sedd i Lafur.

Gofynnais i Dr. Phil Williams faint o effaith a gafodd y ffrwydradau ac ati ar yr etholiad. Meddai: "Bydd y dulliau a ddefnyddiwyd yn ein herbyn yn yr is-etholiad hwn yn sicr o ladd ein gwrthwynebwyr eu hunain yn y diwedd." Nid ymddengys i'r cy-

huddiadau di-sail gael fawr o effaith.

Ond pan na chipiwyd y sedd? Yn ôl Dr. Phil Williams y prif reswm oedd bod yr ymgyrch wedi bod mor fyr. "Mae'n amlwg pam y bu i'r Blaid Lafur roi inni cyn lleied o amser i ymgyrchu. Oherwydd dangosai ein tair canfas bod y swing tuag atom yn cynyddu bob tro. A beth fyddai canlyniad wythnos arall o ymgyrchu?"

Bu Plaid Cymru'n ffodus yn ein hymgeisydd. Telid teyrnged iddo ar bob llaw. Ni fedrai hyn yn oed Llafur ei bardduo ef. Yn wir, ar y radio trannoeth yr etholiad, gwahoddodd Michael Foot ef i ymuno â'r Blaid Lafur!

Ni ellid tanlinellu'n gliriach na hynyna ofn Llafur y bydd i Phil Williams a'i genhedlaeth ifanc gipio Caerffili yn 1970 — neu gynt. Gosododd yr is-etholiad faner Cymru'n beryglus-gadarn reit ar gwr y brifddinas, libart Callaghan a George Thomas hyd yn hyn.

FFIGURAU CAERFFILI

Fred Evans (Llafur)	16,148
PHIL WILLIAMS (PLAID CYMRU)	14,274
Robert Williams (Ceidwadwr)	3,687
Peter Sadler (Rhyddfrydwr)	1,257
Mwyafrif Llafur	1,874

Yn etholiad Cyffredinol 1966

Llafur (y diweddar Ness Edwards): 26,330; Tori: 5,182; Plaid Cymru (John Howell): 3,949.,

Y Gogwydd at Blaid Cymru

Yng Nghaerfyrddin	17 y cant
Yn y Rhondda	26 y cant
Yng Nghaerffili	28.9 y cant

Source: Y Ddraig Goch, August 1968.

Ideas of giving greater powers to Wales to look after its own affairs were not by any means confined to *Plaid Cymru*. It seemed as if public opinion was all in favour.

Some senior Labour politicians had worked to the same end. After 1966 Cledwyn Hughes put pressure on for an elected Welsh Council which would have some powers to make laws for Wales.

Other Welsh M.P.s, like George Thomas, strongly opposed such ideas. However, the government of the day felt it needed to do something to meet the growing indications from both Wales and Scotland that people wanted more say in the government of their countries. In 1968, for example, the Scottish Nationalist Party had won an amazing by-election victory in Hamilton.

Source 245

Wilson orders probe into Welsh Home Rule

THE BIG CHANGES

The main changes in legislation planned for the next session of Parliament were outlined by the Queen in her Speech yesterday. These are:

- Votes at 18, in time for the next election.
- Reform of the House of Lords.
- The appointment of a Commission on the constitution.
- Home improvement grants.
- New National Insurance scheme.

Other plans include: Further protection for immigrants, reducing the age of majority to 18, and the transfer of London Transport to the Greater London Council.

TALKS WITH PARTIES SOON

By David G. Rosser,

Our Political Correspondent

A Government commission is being set up to look at the desirability of a mini-parliament for Wales.

But the precise form the inquiry will take is somewhat confused.

And the big question at Westminster last night was whether the proposal will amount to nothing more than long talks. The Prime Minister, announcing the proposal, was careful not to be committed to any timetable, though some Government circles insist that this is a matter of special priority.

Rejected

The commission will also look at devolution in Scotland, together with regions of England, and will examine the relationships with the Channel Islands and the Isle of Man.

They say consultations with the other parties about the form of the commission will be held as speedily as possible, so that the actual inquiry can be got underway early in the New Year.

It will also inquire into the existing system of the Northern Ireland Government.

Since the war there has been a Royal Commission on Scottish affairs, but there has been no comparable inquiry on Welsh affairs.

The Scottish commission, which reported in 1954, made recommendations, principally on administrative matters. But it put forward no radical proposals.

It rejected home rule on the Northern Ireland model.

The Conservative Shadow Cabinet said last night the commission would take years, and that this was the Government's intention.

Cautious

The Secretary of State for Wales, Mr. George Thomas, welcomed the proposal, because he did not think that a constitution which had endured for centuries ought to be changed, either in a panic or as a result of sloganising.

"This is a matter for cold examination of the facts," he said.

Mr. Gwynfor Evans, Welsh Nationalist Party leader, gave a cautious reception.

"The decision is the most important one taken by the Government in this field, but although the Government has been compelled to take this step, it is not bound to take further actions," he said.

"The matter is one of urgency because of the extent of depopulation, emigration and unemployment in Wales.

"One fears the commission could prove to be a time-waster."

Sir Douglas Glover (Con, Ormskirk), speaking of devolution, said that what was exemplified by the Scottish and Welsh Nationalists was strongly held in other parts of Britain.

"Very often one meets people who say they would like to re-establish all the old ancient kingdoms," he said. "I would like the great nations of Northumbria, Merica and Wessex to be re-established."

Suggestions that the proposal is no more than a marking time operation by the Government were stoutly denied last night.

Mr. Wilson, however, has set out only provisional terms of reference for the inquiry.

He called attention to the strong feelings in Wales and Scotland about the need for participation in decision making in places nearer where the people lived.

And he warned against discounting the extremists' feelings on this issue, though their demands were highly prejudicial to both countries.

The exact form of the commission will have to await the consultations promised by Mr. Wilson — and these include consideration of the survey already being made by the Labour Party's national executive.

Many M.P.s inferred from Mr. Wilson's remarks that what eventually would emerge would not be a Royal Commission. One reason for this possibly is that the term "Royal Commission" suggests the matter is being indefinitely deferred.

Panels

But Mr. Wilson suggested that the Government would not be inhibited in taking any action considered desirable, even while the commission was continuing with its inquiries.

Ministers are agreed on one aspect of inquiry. Since it will cover such a wide field, there ought to be separate panels, each one with specific responsibility for various areas.

In the event the possibility is that Wales and Scotland would have their own panels of the commission.

It was clear last night, however, that no clear cut approach has been settled, and that the statement of intent will require a lot more consideration before the actual processes get underway.

Editorial comment—Page 8, Full reports—Page 4.

Source: The Western Mail, 31.10.1968.

Source 246

Home Rule for Wales probe to take 3 years

By DAVID G. ROSSER, Our Political Correspondent

Any hope Wales and Scotland may have had about separate parliaments before the next general election were ruled out last night when it was announced the report on the Government commission would take two or three years to compile.

Lord Crowther, chairman of the 16-man Commission on the Constitution, said this would also apply to further devolution for other parts of Britain.

He made the statement after the first meeting of the commission in London.

The commission's job would be to see how the functions now performed by the Government could be transferred to administration, government, or even parliaments set up in other parts of Britain, he said.

He invited anyone to give evidence to the commission and said selections would be made so that it could be taken at open meetings in Cardiff, Belfast, Edinburgh, London and other centres.

The commission has decided that all written evidence must be submitted wherever possible by the end of July.

Source: Western Mail, 30.4.1969.

Then the issue of Welsh devolution was combined with a wider discussion of how Britain should be governed at local and at national levels. In 1969 a Royal Commission was set up to consider the constitution and how much independence should be given to Wales and to Scotland, but it was going to be a long process.

The first Chairman of the Commission was Lord Crowther. When he died he was replaced

Source 247

Wales must not let this issue die

WESTERN MAIL

Thomson House, Cardiff. Tel. 23022.

AT LAST. Five years and one day since the Labour Government announced it was going to set up a Commission on the Constitution, that commission has reported. As a milestone in the devolution debate it can have no equal, though only the Government can make it a milestone in the history of devolution itself. Yet already it has performed a valuable function. It has elevated the whole argument. The very existence of the commission has forced the political parties, public and private bodies and individuals to think through their own ideas as never before. The report itself will, hopefully, develop that debate still further.

The scope and scale of the commission's investigations have uncovered once and for all the jungle of implications behind every easy political slogan and, with the impartiality expected of it, it has done the same for both sides of the argument. It has dealt with the nationalist case sympathetically, but provided solid ground for rejecting it. It has recognised the strengths of the status quo and enumerated its many weaknesses. It has described the potential of devolution and its limitations. Despite all this, perhaps because of all this, there will be no shortage of critics. There will still be complaints about bias, as there are in the minority report, complaints about "the approach," and about the presentation of subjective opinion as objective fact. In reply one can only say that the commission appears to have done its work honestly. The task was inherently difficult for reasons foreseen by the commission itself. It says that "all the issues raised by our terms of reference are of a kind which ultimately call for political decisions. They cannot be determined in an academic way by the collection and assessment of evidence of a technical nature." This is the very reason why, in the wake of this report, more than in the wake of any other Royal Commission, it is right and proper that the Government should allow time for the public voice to be heard. What is done in Scotland will depend upon the Scottish people. What is done in Wales will depend upon the Welsh nation.

The essentially political nature of judgments on these issues does much to explain the apparent division between members of the commission. They are divisions which were seized upon in the Commons yesterday in an attempt to diminish the value of the report. Are those disagreements really comparable in importance with the recommendation upon which the commissioners are all agreed? How many times in the coming months, perhaps years, is one going to have to stress that the whole commission, yes, even the authors of the grievously mistitled Memorandum of Dissent, is completely united in demanding for Wales and Scotland democratically elected assemblies to represent those countries' interests? That fact deserves to, and must be made to, stand head and shoulders above all else. Without the acceptance of that one step, by whichever Government is in power, British democracy will not be able to evolve effectively to cope with the pressures that the commission has listed and which grow daily heavier.

The argument for a substantial measure of devolution has never and does not now rest solely on the moral case for greater self-determination for the Welsh and Scottish peoples. There are equally pressing functional arguments for taking steps to lighten the load on the central government and legislature. Even an unenthusiastic Mr. Heath was obliged to say yesterday that the present situation could not be allowed to persist. Those M.P.s who greeted the report with a barrage of cynicism must be made to see that their complacency in the face of the yawning gulf between the Government and the governed is a grave threat to the peaceful democracy they purpo defend.

As to the alternatives which the commissio forward, the *Western Mail* accepts the argumer those who advocate a scheme of legislative devol We accept such a scheme as an ultimate objectiv not as a first step. The sort of conventions would be essential to the working relationship be the national and regional governments cann established overnight. The acclimatisation to constitutional relationships by means of an mediate stage of devolution, such as is outlined scheme of executive devolution, will be as nec for central government as it will be for new in tions in Cardiff or Edinburgh. On the other ha look with the utmost disfavour on the propos three commissioners for an elected Welsh ad council. The people of Wales have had a surf advisory bodies. To create an elected advisory c which would debate matters in an atmos unconstrained by the responsibilities of power best an insulting waste of the nation's time a worst positively dangerous.

It is already clear that the opposition to action on the lines proposed will be fierce. The of the reformers will no longer have the sta themselves. But in the interests of justice, demo and its better government, Wales must not le issue lie down.

Source: *Western Mail*, 1.11.1973.

by Lord Kilbrandon. The report of the Kilbrandon Commission was published in 1973.

It recommended devolution for Wales. The majority recommended an elected assembly, though without the power to make separate laws. Nearly half the Commission's members wanted more, a Welsh Assembly with power to raise money by taxation.

Source 248

LENGTHY DEBATE ON KILBRANDON COULD BE JUST A COVER TO MASK INACTION

Biggest dilemma in 50 years for two parties

By DAVID G. ROSSER

KILBRANDON'S PROPOSALS for Wales and Scotland present both Labour and Conservative parties with their biggest dilemma in 50 years.

There is between them one solid piece of agreement — neither supports any devolution involving Home Rule for Wales or Scotland.

Otherwise the Tories stand opposed to elected assemblies with legislative powers and support a process of greater administrative devolution through the Secretaries of State for Wales and Scotland.

Labour is committed to an Elected Council for Wales with administrative powers and even some executive powers.

Full debate

On this, for some Labour M.P.s, there is a certain appeal in the dissenting report by the two commissioners, but this scheme involving tight Westminster controls goes much further than the Labour Party in Wales has as yet been prepared to accept.

There will be no Government action in this Parliament. And it is highly speculative whether the next Government, of whatever complexion, will be prepared to implement the commission's recommendations for Wales and Scotland.

Next step will be a full public debate on Kilbrandon. This will begin immediately and will apparently be without time limit.

It is said at Westminster that this could be the cover screen for the main parties to set aside indefinitely any decision whether and when to grapple with the issue.

Inevitably it must be a major general election issue. The other parties will see to that. But M.P.s are pointing out that it is not unusual for a Royal Commission report to drop out of sight after a reasonable time for study has elapsed.

In one important sense, both Conservative and Labour parties may find it easier to follow this line because of the current opinions within the parties.

Mr. Heath is fully aware of the strong resentment among Scottish back-benchers to any Kilbrandon-type constitutional change for Scotland because of the repercussions to the political representations at Westminster. At least 14 Scottish M.P.s would disappear.

Welsh Labour M.P.s, too, are strongly opposed to any reduction of Welsh representation at Westminster where at least five seats could disappear under the Kilbrandon proposal.

Labour's argument here is that Wales would require the maximum representation at Westminster to protect the financial end of central government policies for Wales.

Reticence

There is the strong possibility on the political side of a situation emerging in which under an elected legislative assembly Wales would probably be Labour dominated for the foreseeable future.

Naturally, this is something the Tories would find totally unacceptable, though as a worthwhile compensation the Westminster Parliament, shorn of about 19 seats, nearly all Labour, would probably be given to Conservative dominance for an equally long time, which would again be an intolerable situation for Labour aspirations.

With this background, as many M.P.s were not slow in pointing out last night, a marked reticence on the part of either party to be the first to act and take a positive stand would not only be understandable but acceptable at Westminster.

A consultative Green Paper will be issued by the Government in the spring or early summer.

Mr. Wilson has set up a study group under Deputy Leader Mr. Ted Short, and including the Shadow Secretaries for Wales and Scotland, to examine in depth the report and public reactions. This will begin work next week.

Not until these two functions have gone through their paces will there be any considered statement or restatement of party policy from either.

The Minister of State, Welsh Office, Mr. David Gibson-Watt, in the absence in America of Mr. Peter Thomas, issued a statement saying the report "deals with matters of great complexity and will need the fullest study by the Government."

Mr. George Thomas was critical of the commission last night.

"The commission has not done its work properly," he said. "It has not given a clearly defined set of recommendations. The ball is back in the court of the politicians.

Grave issue

"We must realise that at the end of the day it is what Parliament feels that Wales wants that will decide the issue."

It was also being stressed that the proposal for an elected legislative assembly for Wales was being advanced by only six out of the 13 commissioners, though they included the two Welsh memb Three preferred an elected W advisory body with no legisla powers.

Mr. Thomas said, "The comr sion seems hopelessly divided on the major issues. The Welsh posals are opposed by the majo but nonetheless we must give proposal serious study.

"Although the ultimate deci will be taken by politicians ther bound to be widespread pu debate and we who are the ele representatives of Wales have obligation to give a lead on issues that are raised.

"Clearly the abolition of office of Secretary of State wh a legislative assembly would inv is a grave issue for Wales must h its own direct representative wit the British Cabinet.

"The Labour Party submit evidence and recommended elected council with consider powers. We intend to give deta consideration to the evidence gi to the commission.

"We shall begin on the b that we are strongly opposed to weakening of Welsh representat at Westminster.

"We also have a preference a non-legislative body. Above all are resolved that the interests Wales lie in complete integra with the rest of the United Ki dom," said Mr. Thomas.

Source: *Western Mail*, 1.11.1973.

Royal Commission Reports are often conveniently forgotten.

What made the situation intriguing now was that in the year after this Report a Labour Government was once more in power, but without a majority of M.P.s over all the over parties. *Plaid Cymru* now had two seats in Government. Gwynfor Evans lost his seat in Carmarthen but Dafydd Wigley was successful in Caernarfon and Dafydd Elis Thomas in Merioneth. By the end of 1974 this number

Source 249 *(See page 124)*

became three when Gwynfor Evans won back Carmarthen.

For a Government without a majority even a Party with only three members had to be taken seriously. The Scottish Nationalist Party had to be taken even more seriously. Why do you think this might be?

In this situation and on the basis of the Kilbrandon Report, the Government brought out a White Paper which set out the basis on which they would put forward a Bill in Parliament. According to both there were to be elected assemblies for Wales and Scotland.

Now the political in-fighting really began. Even the Welsh members of the Labour Party were deeply divided, and the House of Commons as a whole certainly was.

Still the devolution bill staggered on. There were great changes as it did so. First, it became two separate devolution bills, one for Wales

Source 249

Tri Aelod Seneddol
Plaid Cymru, 1974.

Source: John Davies, (Ed.), *Cymru'n Deffro*, Y Lolfa, 1981, p. 153.

and one for Scotland. Then the Government had to give in to pressure to have a referendum, that is a vote in both countries on the actual question of devolution. In 1978 there was another important change which, in effect, meant that devolution would only be granted if at least forty per cent of the electorate—not those who voted, but all electors—voted in favour of it. This meant that in both countries there would have to be a massive amount of popular support. Still, in 1978, the devolution bills became Acts of Parliament. If Wales was now to get more self-government than it had since 1284, or had ever been offered before by the Parliament in Westminster, the people in

Wales would have to vote for it. They were supposed to be helped by the campaigns of supporters and opponents of devolution.

Sources 250/251 *(See page 125)*

The attitude of the various political parties was important because leading politicians are always able to get so much publicity in newspapers and on radio and T.V. The Conservative Party was against devolution. The Liberal Party supported it. *Plaid Cymru* felt that this amount of government for Wales by the Welsh was far less than they wanted but it was better than nothing, so they pressed people to vote "Yes" in the referendum. The Labour Party had supported the devolution movement since 1974 when it needed all the support it could get, including that of the Welsh Nationalist M.P.s. It was the Labour Government's bill and it should have been campaigning strongly for support for the Referendum. In fact official Labour support was luke-warm. Unofficial Labour opposition was very strong. In particular, Labour members Neil Kinnock and Leo Abse campaigned strongly against Devolution. In doing so they played on people's fears. They kept dropping broad hints to the people of Wales that if Devolution came about Wales would be governed by Welsh-speaking north-Walians and English speakers would be unable to get jobs. But in north Wales one of the reasons why Welsh-speaking Wales voted against Devolution was the fear that their interests would be swamped by those of the majority, English-speaking, south of Wales!

The Referendum was held on March 1st 1979. This is what the assembly would actually do:

Source 252

It will be for the Assembly itself to decide on the use of the Welsh language in its business.

What will the Assembly deal with?

The Assembly will be responsible for all the following:

Health matters, including the Health Service

Personal social services such as the care of children, the elderly, the handicapped and others in need of special help (but not pensions or other welfare cash benefits — these need to be the same throughout the United Kingdom)

Schools

Further and higher education, except the University of Wales

Housing, except control of mortgages from building societies, insurance companies and the like

Physical planning and the environment — such as the control of new development, restoring derelict land, new towns, sport and recreation, national parks, and controlling atmospheric pollution and noise

General oversight of local government, and providing money to local councils in support of the rates (but the proposals do not include any change in the structure of local government in Wales)

Much of transport policy — including providing roads, planning local transport, licensing road services, deciding on bilingual road signs, and subsidising bus and railway passenger services

The arts, including libraries, museums and galleries, all cultural matters, and the welfare of the Welsh language

Freshwater fisheries and most forestry functions

Tourism

A wide range of other matters — such as fire services, betting, Sunday observance, shop hours, registration of births, marriages and deaths, and licensing taxis, liquor and places of entertainment.

Source 250

Source: D. Foulkes, J. Barry
Jones & R. A. Wilford, *The
Welsh Veto*, Cardiff 1983,
p.181, Reproduction.

Source 251

For those people who wanted political recognition for Wales in the form of limited self-government it was a sad day. Here are the results.

Source 253

COUNTY - those entitled to vote	Votes Cast	% Turnout	Yes (%)	No (%)	No Majority
GWYNEDD 165,318	103,834	65.40	37,363(34)	71,157(65)	33,784
POWYS 80,027	53,520	65.87	9,834(18)	43,502(82)	33,653
W. GLAM 273,260	159,084	58.22	28,653(19)	128,834(81)	99,171
S. GLAM 288,610	165,912	59,48	21,830(13)	144,186(84)	122,355
DYFED 245,071	180,359	85.43	44,849(28)	114,947(72)	70,088
CLWYD 282,273	145,780	51.62	31,384(22)	114,119(78)	82.735
M. GLAM 388,587	232,026	59.40	46,747(20)	184,186(80)	137,440
GWENT 316,931	176,947	55.83	21,389(12)	155,388(88)	134,020
WALES 2,038,049	1,203,422	59,04	243,048(20)	956,380(80)	713,282

Results of Referendum on Devolution in Wales

You will see that in no Welsh county was there a majority vote for Devolution. There was to be no elected Welsh Assembly. The only Parliament building in Wales remained the one in Machynlleth to which, nearly six hundred years ago, Owain Glyndŵr summoned his Parliament when, for a few brief years, Wales had last been an independent state.

The Devolution Referendum meant that Wales would still have no 'Parliament'. It did not mean that *Plaid Cymru* was dead.

Source 254 *(See opposite column)*

It did not do away with Wales, or Welshness.

Source 255

POLL FINDINGS OF IDENTITY ATTITUDES IN WALES

	(percentages)		
	1968	(June) 1979	(Sept.) 1981
Welsh	69	57	69
British	15	34	20
English	13	8	10
Other	3	1	2

Source: John Osmond, ed., *The National Question Again*, Gomer Press, 1985, p. xxvii.

What then did the whole Devolution debate mean? There can be no final answers to such questions.

Everyone who lives in Wales and who regards himself or herself as Welsh must at some time ask what it means to be Welsh. Even the quarter or so of the population who live in Wales but who are not born here, those who have come into Wales to work or to retire, must ask the

Source 254

GIVE NOW FOR WALES !

Dear Friend,
    This year, St. David's Day marks the tenth anniversary of Plaid Cymru's first-ever general election victories — as well as the fifth anniversary of the referendum fiasco
    Both events show how important Plaid Cymru is for the good of Wales — and how vital it is for Plaid Cymru to be strong.
    During the last decade Plaid Cymru has fought a more determined series of campaigns for Wales than ever before — just look at the list of successes. The occasional disappointment may sometimes lead us to forget how much Plaid Cymru has achieved since 1974. Ask yourself — where would Wales be today without Plaid Cymru?
    In 1979, we learnt how little we could trust other parties to protect the interests of Wales.
    The Labour Party, conservative to the core, seeks nothing but to cling on to local power and patronage in the interests of their establishment. The Liberal-SDP alliance has just dumped its commitment to a Welsh parliament.
    Today only Plaid Cymru fights for Wales' interests — economic, social and national. We are the only party consistent in its commitment to nuclear disarmament, women's rights, civil liberties and the Welsh language and culture.
    Plaid Cymru is at this moment deeply involved in important campaigns:
* Protecting employment — such as jobs in Welsh mines, Plant Breeding Station etc.
* Fairer water charges.
* A new Language Act.
* Defending the health service.
    This year, we are mounting a substantial European election campaign with four excellent candidates — the ablest of any party in Wales. Our aim is to get our message to every home in Wales, and for the first time we will co-operate with parties on the continent who share our vision of a fairer and safer world. We can win at least one seat.
    But to succeed, we must have your practical help. Many of our members give generously of their time and money, and we thank them sincerely. If every member and supporter helped Plaid Cymru as generously, we would have the resources to do a thorough job.
    Not everyone can be in the front line every day, as are our officials, councillors and MPs. But everyone can contribute. I appeal to you once again to dig deeply into your pocket to give Plaid Cymru the resources we need.
    Yours sincerely, DAFYDD WIGLEY

DAFYDD WIGLEY, M.P. for Caernarfon since October 1981 (when he succeeded Gwynfor Evans, who had led Plaid Cymru since 1945). They've given everything for Wales — now Dafydd Wigley asks you to help.

PLAID'S SUCCESS LIST 1974-84
* Setting-up of S4C.
* Dust disease compensation.
* Disabled persons' Act.
* Transfer of responsibilities from London to Welsh Office.
* Establishment of Welsh Development Agency and Rural Development Board.
* Forcing Devolution Bill through Parliament (later sabotaged by Labour treachery).
* Helping the Nuclear-Free Wales declaration.
* Setting-up of Select Committee on Welsh Affairs.
* Trebling number of Plaid local councillors — control of Merthyr and Rhymni Valley District Councils 1976-79.
* Purchase of permanent Plaid Cymru National H.Q. and opening of ten local offices.

WHERE WOULD WALES BE WITHOUT PLAID ?

Source: Reproduced in Pack 3 of the Documents produced in association with H.T.V. Series, The Dragon Has Two Tongues.

question. One gets the impression sometimes that they ask it more often and more seriously than the native Welsh. There are all kinds of ways in which people express their Welshness.

Welshness is about two things. The one, the Welsh language, is a reality. Some Welsh people speak Welsh, others do not. The other, identity, is a concept. Many people who do not speak Welsh have a strong sense of being Welsh. It is obvious that those taking part in *Eisteddfodau* are demonstrating that they are Welsh. It is obvious that those people who shout for Wales at the National Stadium on international day are expressing loyalty to Wales. To people from outside Wales there is still a notion of Wales as a country of coalmines, harp players and male voice choirs. What do you think of as 'Welshness'?

Wales is a country with a history and literature and tradition which go back much further than those of England. Images of Wales, and the self-images of Wales, are many, varied and extremely complex. This is how some recent writers of books about Wales have seen their country.

Source 256

'The Welsh experience . . . induces a sense of humility, of the transistory, deceptive quality of political and economic achievements, of the fragility of a national culture treasured over centuries by the common people . . . Amid the cataract of evidence that illustrates British national decline, the Welsh might reflect that their social culture, still flourishing in its many forms from the hill farms of Gwynedd to the steel works of Gwent, remained a living, distinctive part of the evolution of the British and the European world. That culture had survived and had been triumphantly renewed, against all the odds . . .'

Source: Kenneth O. Morgan, *Rebirth of a Nation Wales 1880-1980*, Cardiff and Oxford, 1981, pp. 420, 421.

Source 257

'Since 1945, as the economy and society of Wales altered yet again, there has been fostered a new, false image, cosy and heart-warming, sentimental and nostalgic about the past. Television adaptations of the golden past, all the more golden for being hardships from which we have apparently moved, are soaked up; Max Boyce is loved as he takes a basically decent, rugby-loving, beer-drinking picture of the Welsh proletariat across the border, bearing the vestiges of that distinctiveness like sporrans and haggis . . . That is the image now. And the reality is uniform housing estates, lego-block cities, sodium lighting that changes the colour of the moon, and steel and glass shop fronts as in Burnley and Leicester and Tooting High Street and the planet X.'
Source: David Smith, *A People and a Proletariat*, London, 1980, p. 237.

Source 258

'What is called for from the non-Welsh-speaking majority . . . is a positive act of imaginative sympathy to try to understand the near-desperation of the minority at the dire prospects for the language and the culture based on it. The Welsh-speaking minority need to recognise more readily than some of them always do that there are a great many of their countrymen who find deeply hurtful the suggestion that those who do not speak the Welsh language are to be regarded as being either not Welsh at all or at best second-class Welsh people. Language is not the only component in nationality and until recent times it has not been regarded as the all-important one . . . There have been other factors besides language which have gone to the making of the sense of Welsh identity . . . They deserve to be more widely known and more fully appreciated. There is a strong case in the twentieth century for emphasising what the Welsh have in common rather than the differences between them . . .'
Source: Glanmor Williams, *Religion, Language and Nationality in Wales*, Cardiff, 1979, p. 33.

Source 259

'I write these words in a blistering summer in one urban corner, congenially cosmopolitan, ringed appropriately by a hospital under threat, a Conservative Club and a funeral parlour . . . I walk to the river, which is my river, here a canal running under the giant Le Corbusier stands of what used to be called Cardiff Arms Park before inflation set in, in this city which I am assured, all appearances to the contrary notwithstanding, is the capital city of my country . . .

One thing I am sure of. Some kind of human society, though God knows what kind, will no doubt go on occupying these two western peninsulas of Britain, but that people, who are my people and no mean people, who have for a millennium and a half lived in them as a Welsh people, are now nothing but a naked people under an acid rain.'
Source: Gwyn A. Williams, *When was Wales?* Penguin, 1985, pp. 304, 305.

Source 260

'Wales will continue, for a while yet, to be a place of argument, of tension, even of conflict. The 'borders' of 'Wales' are mapped out differently in the diversity of the Welsh mind; and yet they still overlap . . . the Wales that is projected to the outside world is not a Wales that most of the Welsh know or recognize as anything of their own . . . We are already a long way down the road which England, our large and defining neighbour, has just begun to contemplate. After all England, too, is a country of the mind'.

Source: Dai Smith, *Wales! Wales?*, London, 1984.

It will be obvious that these historians see Wales in different ways. The important thing is that the judgements they make, although they are different in emphasis, are *informed* judgements based on years of reading and thinking about the history of Wales.

Poets, with their different kinds of insights, also differ dramatically in the way they have seen their country.

Source 261

From Merthyr to Dowlais the tramway climbs,
A slug's slime-trail over the slag heaps.
What's nowadays a desert of cinemas,
Rain over disused tips, this once was Wales.

Knowing neither language nor dialect, Feeling no insult
We gave our masterpiece to history in our country's MPs.
Source: 'The Deluge', 1939—Saunders Lewis (trans. A. Cowan) included in *The Valleys*, J. Davies, M. Jenkins (ed.), Poetry Wales Press, 1984.

Source 262

Now I'm just as Welsh as any other Taffy,
I cheers for Holmesy down at the Arms Park,
I can hum Land of my Fathers with the next man,
And I even know two lines of Sospan Fark.
Source: Frank Hennesey—'A Citizen of Cardiff' from *What Goes on in Cardiff after Daaark.*

Source 263

Marwnad yr Ehedydd

Mi a glywais for yr hedydd*
Wedi marw ar y mynydd
Pe gwyddwn i mai gwir i geirie
Awn a gyrr o wyr ar arfe
I gyrchu corff yr hedydd adre.

Ond chwalu gwae ymysg ei gywion
Mae y bradwyr a'n sibrydion
Mi gymeraf Iw i'r Mawredd
Nad ywn wir ei fod e'n gorwedd
A'i fod yno'n llawn dihunedd.

Mi a wn ei fod ar y mynydd
Ar dan i ledu ei adenydd
A bod ei nyth ef yno weithion
Iddo ddodwy ei freuddwydion
A gwireddu ein gobeithion.

Clywais adlais ei anadlu
Ac ar gynydd mae ei ganu
A dyheu sydd am yr adeg
Pan ddaw'r hedydd eto i hedeg
Ni achwynwn ni ychwaneg.

I have heard the lark
Has died on the mountain
If I knew that word were true
I'd take a troop of men in arms
To bear the lark's body home.

But spreading woe among his chicks
Are the traitors with their rumour
I vow to All Highest
'Tis not true that he is slain
But is up there, very eager.

I know that he is on the mountain
On Fire to spread his wings
And that his nest is there now
Where he may hatch his dreams
And realise our hopes.

I heard the echo of his breathing
And his song is ever rising
And there is such longing for the time
When the skylark flies again
And we will complain no longer.

*Possibly a reference directly to Owain Glyndŵr but more about the 'national spirit'.
Source: Myrddin ap Dafydd. Set to music by Plethyn, 'Blas y Pridd'.

*   *   *

What is important for those of you who read this book, and what has been important to me in writing it, is that we *ask questions* about our history—the history of our community and our country. It is obvious from the last eight sources that study of that history will not provide the same answers for us all. This book has not set out to provide answers. It has tried to ask relevant questions and to provide some information useful for debating those questions. It has also tried to suggest that there are correct methods of going about studying history and that there are particular questions which historians need to ask of their evidence. Your answers, informed by the methods of looking at evidence, will be your own and valid for you. They will also determine the kind of Wales we shall have in the future.

Further work on the evidence

Source 237: This is a newspaper interview with the Secretary of State for Wales. What are its strengths and weaknesses as historical evidence?

Source 238: On the basis of this document alone, what *general* comments could you make about the membership of Plaid Cymru?

Source 240: How reliable is the evidence in this newspaper account? Does the choice of headline tell you anything about attitudes towards *Plaid Cymru*?

Source 245: How far is Mr. Rosser in a good position to know about this subject?

Source 247: What does this editorial tell you about the *Western Mail*'s attitude to devolution?

Sources 250, 251: What do these sources tell you about the sort of support there was for a Welsh Assembly?

Source 253 On the basis of these figures and a map of the counties of Wales, make as many comments as you can about the devolution vote.

Source 254: What kind of document is this? What sort of bias might there be in a document of this sort?

Appendix—Conversion Table

Old Money to Decimals

It was in 1971 that the decimal coinage which we use today was introduced in Britain. Until then the value of our money was expressed in pounds, shillings and old pence (£.s.d.). Therefore most of the amounts of money mentioned in the Sources in this book are expressed in these old money values. To convert them into the decimal values of today you should use the figures below:

Old Pence/shillings/Pounds		New Pence
1 old penny	=	0.41 new pence
12 old pence or 1 shilling	=	5 new pence
240 old pence or 20 shillings or £1	=	100 new pence or £1

Price Equivalence

As we know all too well what our money is worth *today* (that is how much it can buy) will not be what it will be worth in a year's time. This is because of *inflation* which simply means that over a period of time the value of £1 will decrease as prices rise. Over a long period of time, such as the period of about 150 years which we have looked at in this book, there will be a great change therefore, in the value of money. Throughout this book the Sources include references to money, such as how much people earned and how much things cost to buy. To get some idea of what these figures mean we need to try to relate them to the value of our money today. This is not at all an easy thing to do and we have to be very careful with such calculations, therefore. However, one of our major books has tried to do these calculations for the period 1883-1983 and its figures are set out below. They should give you some help in making sense of what the various prices mentioned in the Sources actually mean in terms of our money today.

1883
£1 then	=	3½ today
1 shilling then	=	0.17p today
1 old penny then	=	0.014p today

1913
£1 then	=	3½ today
1 shilling then	=	0.17p today
1 old penny then	=	0.014p today

1923
£1 then	=	6p today
1 shilling then	=	0.3p today
1 old penny then	=	0.025p today

English Translations of Welsh Documents

Source 25

Well, to start with, at that time almost everybody went to chapel, and far more people lived in the villages. Large families of 6, 8 or 10 children were quite common. Can you imagine a father and mother with their children walking behind them in one long single file, other families emerging from their homes and joining them until the road was full of people making their way in one direction or another to their respective chapels?

Source: Tomos, *Llechi Lleu,* p. 78.

Source 35

The Song of the Quarryman's Wife

Happy, happy is my child
In his deep afternoon sleep
He saw his mother's eye as he went to sleep
But he did not see the cloud within it;
And at her breast he did not hear
The sound of the fears and anxieties.

Still, still is the summer's day,
Everything is beautifully calm;
The soft breezes blow gently,
As if afraid to awaken care:
Little do they know of the turmoil
That is in the heart of the quarryman's wife.

You breezes that fly
past my cottage in turn,
Do not carry the sound of shots
Do not murmur about dangers.
You do not have to swell the pounding
that is in the heart of the quarryman's wife.

Why are the men coming home
Before time at the end of the day?
Why are the women in the doorways?
What is all the questioning in corners?
Perhaps there is no terror looming—
It is better to hope than to fear.

Why must I wonder
When I hear the rock shattering?
Why do I see in my dreams
A bier on grey shoulders?
I do not ask for luxury or feasts—
Only for protection for the quarrymen.

Alafon
(t. 48 Cathlau Bore a Nawn)

Source: Printed in Dewi Thomas, *Llechi Lleu,* Caernarfon, 1980, t.79.

Source 45

THE SONG

Oh royal benefactors of dear Wales
Give your help to poor workers
Who are fighting for their liberty
In a situation of cruel fate:

On account of the revenge of the oppressor
We were all 'locked out'
Because we would not bend to place
Our principles under foot.

We endured countless years
Of more and more repression,
By the scourge of violence and oppression
We received frightful blows a hundred times;
Idle was it for us to implore
For justice at work,
All our complaints were ignored—
Our damp cheeks were mocked.

All our rights were trampled on
We were punished without trail or justice
And because we dared stand up
For our rights—the works were locked
Closing the work in the depth of winter—
Casting the workers into shame,
Without any means of earning
Bread for their dear families.

Our homes under the tribulation
Are groaning night and day,
And the firmament of our consolation
Today is in deep darkness;
Desperate poverty advances quickly
Like an old dark general
Leading his armies
To destroy us from all sides.

Oh, it worsens every day
All the time it is darker and heavier
And the streams of adversity flow widely
Further and further into our snug homes;
Sadness paves our roads
Grief stalks through the households
  of the country,
And there is dark, painful famine.

Oh! looking at our family
Who are so poor and grey their countenance
On their knees weeping heavily
To receive a small morsel of food,
That is what defeats our spirits
Until our pure tears
Sink into our hearts,
Like drops of fire.

Can a heart of stone withhold
Without giving way to floods of tears,
Seeing the father sharing out the crust—
The last crust in the house.
At the table through a veil of tears,
The mother looks at her children's
  countenance,
Seeing the crust disposed of
With no more to appease their hunger.

At her breast there is a little baby
Uttering many a cry,
It sucks avidly but Oh! the disappointment
The mothers breast is dry.

The gentle father's heart is torn
By this grim spectacle
Of seeing his children and his dear wife,
Withering away beside him.

Cold dwellings, empty cupboards,
There are sad hearts throughout the
   neighbourhood,
Sounds of singing and every joy
Have all fled,
Groaning and suffering
Fill our dwellings night and day,
Oh! when will our salvation come?
Only heaven knows.

Oh take pity on our suffering,
Give us help now
To deliver our families
Who are today in such dire distress,
Ease our heavy burdens
Still our troubled life
Dear benefactors, Oh! have pity
Today on the poor quarrymen.

Source 64

A WARNING

Penrhyn Quarry will be open on Tuesday, June
11th, to all former employees who have
applied for work and have been accepted.

As was announced last February, the Rules
of Discipline have been changed and a new rule
has been drawn up and agreed to, which will,
in effect, grant a half holiday on the last day of
each month; in all other respects, the Quarry's
Rules remain as they have been (The New
Rules referred to are printed below). During
the next fortnight (i.e. not later than June 4th),
I am prepared to receive further applications
from former employees (except for boys) who
wish to return to work. Every applicant must
give his serial number in the Quarry and the
Gallery, also the full name and address.

Applications from 'boys' to return to the
quarry cannot be considered until at least a
fortnight after the men have re-started work.

In order to carry out the law in relation to
threat or harassment through violence or any
other means (under the Conspiracy and
Defence Act) adequate police protection has
been promised by the Chief Constable,
Colonel Ruck.

E. A. Young

Port Penrhyn, Bangor
May 20th, 1901.

THE NEW RULES

Discipline . . . All censures will be through
'stoppages' or dismissal, for example, if a
worker comes late (other than on account of
ill-health or a sudden matter of great importance), on the first occasion he will be warned;
the second time he will be 'stopped' a quarter
of a day, and for the third offence the stoppage
will be for half a day—but persistent offenders
will be fined more heavily or dismissed.

End of the month . . . On the last Tuesday of
every Quarry month, the workers after
handing over their 'stores' and accounts and
arranging their 'bargains' for the coming
month, are free to leave the quarry for the rest
of the day, if they so choose.

Source: Gwynedd Archives Service.

Source 66

THE BLACKLEG'S POUND

This was a song composed at the time of the
Penrhyn Strike about men who returned to
work in the quarry and had an extra pound in
wages for doing so. It is important to remember
that 'cynffon' means 'tail'. It came to mean
'flatterer' and then, in our terms, 'blackleg'.

Tune: 'The Black Pig'

Did you hear the ugly story—
The story of treason, and the story of
   conspiracy
Worse than the Treason of the long knives
Is the story of the Blackleg's Pound.

Chorus: Oh! how sad are we,
Oh! how sad are we;
We are sick at heart
The Blackleg's pound—what a horror!

It is useless to speak about people
'Tails' are the subject of the tale
If for the troubles of the family of the tail
Enquire of the order of the 'white shirts'.

Chorus: Oh! how sad are we etc.,

To shake a tail a body is necessary
Who is that—the silly body!
It is very strange that there are only tails
All frolicking on the banks!

Chorus: Oh! how sad are we etc.

Oh! how valuable is character
Not all the gold in creation will buy it;
The whole world cannot buy men—
A pound can buy a tail!

Chorus: Oh! how sad, etc.

Oh! Quarryman! be faithful,
Act the man before the master
The eternal ages
Cannot free man of his responsibility.

Chorus: Oh! how sad, etc.

Workers! May you all bear your crosses,
You will receive the blessing of a thousand
   ages
Will 'the tail' be seen on mountains
Splitting the rocks in a thousand years?

Chorus: Oh! how sad, etc.

Oh! how beautiful will be their countenance!
Oh! how beautiful will be their countenance!
Strong men—all faithful,
And every 'blackleg' in his grave.

Source: Gwynedd Archive Service.

Source 68

The Trouble at Bethesda: Henry Jones announced the result of the most recent vote—a majority of 31 in Bethesda in favour of ending the struggle. Little interest has been shown in it by those working from home. Saturday night, November 14th 1903. It was officially decided that the battle was over.

Dated 28 November, 1903. *Source:* Gwynedd Archive Service.

Source 206

It is most fitting that the *Ddraig Goch* (Red Dragon) should record with regret the death of Mr. E. T. John at 73 years of age. Mr. John was a sincere Welsh nationalist. He devoted a long life to battling for the political rights of Wales, introducing a Home Rule Bill for Wales in the House of Commons, publishing many books and pamphlets on the topic, studying exhaustively the economic aspects of the matter and fighting his last Parliamentary election in 1924 as a candidate for "Welsh Labour and Nationalism", and it is well-known that it was because of his insistence on retaining the last two words in its title that Ramsay Macdonald refused to come to Brecon to speak in support of his candidature. In these last years, Mr. John gave generously of his wide knowledge and bold judgement to the Nationalist Party and his presence on some of Plaid's committees was of great benefit to her.

He was an honest and a good man. At one time he was very wealthy. Few know of the vast extent of his private generosity. Formerly, before the coming of the industrial depression and his losing many thousands of pounds, his name did not appear often on the list of remarkable and famous subscribers. This was because he preferred to give in secret, and only a few of us know of his self-sacrifice to those who depended on him.

Some of us were afraid that he was to an extent, wasting his time with his favourite institution, namely, the Celtic Congress, but the last word has yet to be pronounced on that and perhaps when its history comes to be written it will be seen that Mr. John did not labour completely in vain either for it or through it. A good man has gone to his rest, and Wales has lost a son who loved her genuinely and wholeheartedly.

Source: Ddraig Goch, March 1931.

Source 218

Y DDRAIG GOCH (September 1937)

Special Edition on the Release.

Y DDRAIG GOCH (The Red Dragon)
(The organ of the Welsh Nationalist Party)

FROM THE PRISON OF FEAR HE EMERGED FREE

This is a photograph of Wormwood Scrubs taken by Dr. Gwent Jones when he visited Mr. Saunders Lewis in prison. It is a very remarkable photograph. 'The Three' were behind these impenetrable walls and, above them, the malignant birds of Hell—two effective symbols, one of the age-old oppression borne by Wales, the other an indication of disfigurement in our day. A picture of despair, a picture of things which are oppressing Wales, a symbol of the barbarity which has threatened in every generation.

But to the National Party this is a picture of hope, a symbol of victory. Because it is a picture of an enemy which we have foiled and conquered, a monster we have slain. And that enemy and monster is fear. Within these walls something was demonstrated that no-one could have believed before then—that Wales was a country for which one could suffer as well as from which one could benefit, that she was an object of affection as well as a spur to ambition. Within these walls the good name of Wales was safeguarded in the light of the judgement of her own History and in the sight of the world. Above all, within these walls Wales became flesh and blood and turned from being a museum piece and the preserve of the historian to become a living force. As in Homer's Odyssey the spirit of the dead prophet Teiresias could not speak a word to the living until he drank from the sacrificial blood so there were many to whom the spirit could not speak until the sacrifice and suffering of the three poured blood into their feeble veins and enabled their mute tongues to speak.

Source 219

NATIONALISM'S WELCOME TO THE THREE

A national Welcome Meeting to receive back the Three to their own country from the foreign prison of Wormwood Scrubs was held on Saturday, September 11th at 6 o'clock. Caernarfon Pavilion, the largest public hall in Wales, accommodating 12,000, was packed to overflowing and it was believed that there were some 5,000 outside the building. The Llanberis Band played. The congregational singing was led by Mr. Ffowc Williams of Llandudno. Professor J. E. Daniel took the chair. The Three delivered their speeches in the following order: Lewis Valentine, D. J. Williams and Saunders Lewis. Resolutions passed unanimously were (a) of welcome, (b) proclaiming unyielding opposition to the Bombing School and calling on the Government to withdraw it immediately, and (c) condemning the attitude of the Council of the College in Swansea towards Mr. Saunders Lewis. Resolution C was not on the agenda of the meeting—it emerged from the audience's admiration for one of Wales' greatest sons. The collection realised £66, £40 worth of literature was sold and 500 new members joined Plaid (the Welsh Nationalist Party).

Source: Y Ddraig Goch, October 1937.

Source 222

DECIDING THE FATE OF TRYWERYN ON APRIL FOOL'S DAY

The majority of the nation accepts Plaid's Lead

by our Political Correspondent

On the 1st day of April, the Liverpool Corporation Bill for the flooding of the Tryweryn Valley will come before the House of Lords for its Third Reading. And we already know that it will be Wales that will play the part of the fool in the House of Lords that day.

We know that a pretence will be made of giving fair play to both sides in the debate. But the decision will have been taken before hand because the Lords do not have, and never have had, the slightest notion of Welsh national consciousness. Lord Woolton will pronounce the Government's blessing on the scheme. Similarly, the majority of the Welsh Socialist Lords. The brave stand of Lord Ogmore of Gwaunysgor will have been to no avail. Wales will have been cheated for yet another April and the Welsh will go on believing that they can receive justice for their national rights before a congregation of Englishmen.

Before the House of Commons

Then, of course, later on, the Bill (doubtless having been passed) will be presented to the House of Commons. There will only be some 30 Welsh Members there as against some 600 English Members.

We shall then see how much authority (and how much sympathy towards Wales) Mr. Henry Brooke will have. Also how much influence Lady Megan will have had on the Labour Party. I wonder whether that Party will oppose the Bill officially? It now has a sufficient number of fiery Welshmen in its ranks to enable them to win the Party's backing. We shall wait hopefully.

But one indisputable fact confronts anyone who seeks to view the Welsh political situation impartially. And that is that in general, Wales has accepted the lead of Plaid Cymru (The Welsh Nationalist Party) on the Tryweryn issue. The Welsh Members of Parliament, after sitting on the fence for a long time have, in the end, had to acknowledge that lead and appropriate it for themselves.

This has consistently been the story in Wales since the end of the war—in respect to opposition to the War Office, the Forestry Commission etc.,—Plaid leading, and the Members of Parliament following.

Safeguarding Our Heritage

No greater tribute can be paid to the Nationalist movement than that our Members of Parliament have had to wave its slogans and fight its battles. No stronger argument could be advanced for strengthening the movement. This is also further proof that, despite the size of the election vote, the movement is stirring the nation.

May Wales stand united behind her Members of Parliament on the Tryweryn issue, for if they remain united, then not even an all-English Parliament can readily ignore them.

Who leads is not a matter of great importance. What is important is that Wales is being defended and her heritage safeguarded.

Source: Y Ddraig Goch, April, 1956.

Source 244

WITHIN AN ACE OF CAPTURING CAERPHILLY!

Another week would have turned the Scales

In face of the united and determined opposition of the three English political parties, Labour, Liberal and Tory, Plaid Cymru (the Welsh Nationalist Party) came within a hair's breadth of capturing the Caerphilly seat. Labour's majority was reduced by about 20,000 and the 28.9% swing to Plaid Cymru was the biggest in a British by-election for more than twenty years—except for Hamilton.

The other parties fought shabbily and dishonestly. At the last moment the Labour Party distributed a lurid leaflet accusing Plaid Cymru of being Fascist. A few days earlier, the Tories accused us of being 'dam busters'. And the previous Sunday, Mr. Emlyn Hooson sought to spread the baseless rumour that the Welsh and Scottish Parties had received gifts of £37,000 from the U.S.A.

And yet, all this was to no avail. On the day of the by-election, the 3949 votes for Plaid Cymru in the 1966 General Election had increased to 14,274. All the other three parties suffered grievous losses. The Labour majority went down from 21,148 to 1,874, the Tory vote from 5,182 to 3,949. The Liberals got only 1,257. The last two lost their deposits.

Caerphilly demonstrated quite clearly that the swing towards Plaid Cymru persists strongly even in an industrial and non-Welsh constituency. The swing towards Plaid Cymru has grown in strength from 17% in Carmarthen and 26% in the Rhondda to 28.9% in Caerphilly. To win the seat Plaid needed a swing of 31.6%.

After Caerphilly it is evident that Plaid Cymru is a credible and serious challenge to Labour in all the constituencies of the south and no single seat in Wales is safe from our onslaught any longer. It also proves that Wales will not turn either to Toryism or to the Liberals for salvation.

But what is likely to excite the main fears in the ranks of Labour is the fact that young people and people up to the age of 40 in Caerphilly have swung solidly behind Plaid Cymru. It was only the aged, who could not shake off their old loyalty to Labour, who voted for her.

It was obvious that Plaid Cymru would have taken the seat easily if the young people of 18 + had had the vote. And with 2,000 of these young people annually receiving the vote, it is obvious that Plaid Cymru can win the seat in 1970.

Dr. Phil Williams, leading Plaid Cymru's campaign, made a deep impression on the electorate, even on those who continued to vote Labour. The by-election result was a considerable shock to them, in particular.

Night after night, day after day, for three weeks, Plaid Cymru presented to the people of Caerphilly impressive arguments as to why control of the life of Wales should be moved from London to Cardiff; that we had ourselves to take responsibility for working out our own salvation. The example of the small Scandinavian countries was constantly put before the electorate as the ideal. It was emphasised that a Welsh State would be a weak one and that the welfare of the individual and his society would take first and last place.

Indeed, the whole campaign was described by English correspondents as a vast teach-in on nationalism. People from the Rhymney Valley flocked to our meetings asking wise and sensible questions. The hearts and minds of the pensive and young of the valley were captured. Only the weight of tradition together with the deliberately brief campaign, kept the seat for Labour.

I asked Dr. Phil Williams what effect the explosions and such had had on the electorate. He said 'the methods employed against us in this by-election are certain ultimately to destroy our opponents themselves'. It appears that the baseless rumours had very little effect.

But why wasn't the seat won? The chief reason, according to Dr. Phil Williams, was that the campaign had been so short. 'It is obvious why the Labour Party gave us so little time to campaign, for our three canvassers showed the swing increasing every time. And what would have been the outcome of another week of campaigning'?

Plaid Cymru was fortunate in its candidate. Tribute was paid to him from all sides. Not even the Labour Party could smear him. Indeed, on the radio, the day after the election, Michael Foot invited him to join the Labour Party.

The fears of the Labour Party that Caerphilly can be won in 1970, or earlier, by Dr. Phil Williams and his young generation cannot be more heavily underlined. The by-election planted the Welsh flag manacingly firmly right on the edge of the capital, the domain up until now of Callaghan and George Thomas.

The Caerphilly Figures

Fred Evans (Labour)	16,148
Phil Williams (Plaid Cymru)	14,274
Robert Williams (Conservative)	3,687
Peter Sadler (Liberal)	1,257
Labour majority	1,874

General Election 1966

Labour (the late Ness Edwards)	26,330
Tory	5,182
Plaid Cymru (John Howell)	3,949

The Swing Towards Plaid Cymru

In Carmarthen	17%
In the Rhondda	26%
In Caerphilly	28.9%

Source: *Y Ddraig Goch*, August, 1968.

Index